Cave of My Ancestors

Cave of My Ancestors

VISHWAKARMA AND THE ARTISANS OF ELLORA

Kirin Narayan

The University of Chicago Press CHICAGO AND LONDON

The University of Chicago Press, Chicago 60637
The University of Chicago Press, Ltd., London
© 2024 by Kirin Narayan
All rights reserved. No part of this book may be used or reproduced in any
manner whatsoever without written permission, except in the case of brief
quotations in critical articles and reviews. For more information, contact
the University of Chicago Press, 1427 E. 60th St., Chicago, IL 60637.
Published 2024
Printed in the United States of America

33 32 31 30 29 28 27 26 25 24   1 2 3 4 5

ISBN-13: 978-0-226-83527-3 (cloth)
ISBN-13: 978-0-226-83529-7 (paper)
ISBN-13: 978-0-226-83528-0 (e-book)
DOI: https://doi.org/10.7208/chicago/9780226835280.001.0001

Library of Congress Cataloging-in-Publication Data

Names: Narayan, Kirin, author.
Title: Cave of my ancestors : Vishwakarma and the artisans of Ellora /
Kirin Narayan.
Description: Chicago : The University of Chicago Press, 2024. | Includes
bibliographical references and index.
Identifiers: LCCN 2024004753 | ISBN 9780226835273 (cloth) | ISBN 9780226835297
(paperback) | ISBN 9780226835280 (ebook)
Subjects: LCSH: Viśvakarman (Hindu deity) | Ellora Caves (India)
Classification: LCC BL1225.V49 N37 2024 | DDC 294.5/35095479—dc23/
eng/20240205
LC record available at https://lccn.loc.gov/2024004753

♾ This paper meets the requirements of ANSI/NISO Z39.48-1992
(Permanence of Paper).

For "Pa"
Narayan Ramji Contractor (Dahisaria)
who first handed over clues for this story
and
for "Bhai"
Kapred Kumar Dahisaria,
who, a half century later,
shared ways to follow them

Contents

A Few People Who Reappear through This Book ∗ *ix*
A Note on Transcription ∗ *xiii*

Joining Palms at Ellora ∗ 1

Part I. Names and Speculations

1. The Cave, Code and Cord of Vishwakarma ∗ 13
2. The Carpenter's "Hut" ∗ 27
3. Shadows of Makers ∗ 43
4. Surpassing Humane Force ∗ 57

Part II. Communing with Ancestors

5. As Regards the Cultural Migrations of Artisans ∗ 69
6. The Debt to Gods and Ancestors ∗ 83
7. The Pride of the Vishwakarma Lineage ∗ 97
8. Open Sesame! ∗ 109

Part III. The Resident of Ellora

9. Via-Via ∗ 123
10. Ila the Serpent Maiden ∗ 135
11. From Mantras to Tools ∗ 149
12. An Injured Finger and Other Tokens of "Proof" ∗ 165

Part IV. Forms in Flux

13. Vestiges of Worship * 181
14. Transformations through Water * 195
15. Locating the Goddess * 209
16. On the Move * 223

Hands inside Hands * 235

*Acknowledgments * 249*
*Maps * 251*
*Notes * 255*
*Bibliography * 273*
*Index * 281*

A Few People Who Reappear through This Book

BA: my intrepid grandmother, Kamlabai Ramji, 1900–1987. Married to Ramji Seth; mother of my father Narayan (Pa).

BHAI: my first cousins' father-in-law, Kapred Kumar Dahisaria, 1927–2022. Practiced as a building contractor. Bibliophile and mentor for this book.

JAYANTIBHAI GAJJAR: my second cousin Prakash's niece's father-in-law. Carpenter who reskilled as a technician, becoming foreman in a gold refinery. Source of many Vishwakarma stories.

KESHAVJI KHIMJI: my grandfather Ramji's father, died 1899. Carpenter who determined to build a Vishwakarma temple in his village as an alternative to the pilgrimage to Ellora; commissioned a Brahmin scholar in Morbi to compose a book about Vishwakarma.

KHIMJI BHAGAT: my grandfather Ramji's grandfather, died 1890. Father of Keshavji. Carpenter with a passion for devotional song, remembered for his otherworldly ways.

MA: my mother, Didi Contractor (Delia Hildegarde Kinzinger), 1929–2021. Married Narayan (Pa) 1950; moved to India 1951. Painter, interior decorator, designer, adobe solar cooker propagator, vernacular architect.

MAUSHI: my great-aunt, "Nanduba," sister of Ba, 1892(?)–1974. Grandmother of my second cousin Prakash and other cousins in Bantva, Gujarat. Prolific creator of massive embroideries that often featured scenes from the life of Krishna.

PA: my father, Narayan Ramji Contractor, 1927–2002. Son of Ramji Seth and Ba. Studied in the United States, 1947–1950, where he met Didi (Ma); returned to India 1951 and fitfully practiced as a civil engineer.

POPATLAL DASADIA: father of Prakash and son-in-law of Maushi, 1935–2020. Left village, where he made wooden farm implements, for Ahmedabad, where he was employed as a technician in industries and ventures associated with the Sarabhai family.

PRAKASH MISTRY (DASADIA): my second cousin, born 1965. Maushi's grandson and Popatlal's son; married to Sonal. Welder with a love of making and mending things, and the source of many connections for our research.

RAMJI SETH: my grandfather, also known as Dada, Sethji, and Ramji Keshavji, 1865(?)–1959. Son of Keshavji, grandson of Khimji Bhagat. Married to four consecutive wives; Kamlabai (Ba), his fourth wife, was mother to my father Narayan. Leaving his village for Bombay, he worked as a carpenter, municipal contractor, and contractor for private and commercial building projects. Celebrated for charitable deeds. Joined his two brothers in completing the Vishwakarma temple that their father Keshavji had envisioned.

YESHU: my first cousin and dear childhood playmate, born 1960. Daughter of Pa's younger brother Shantilal; daughter-in-law to Bhai. Retired teacher of art.

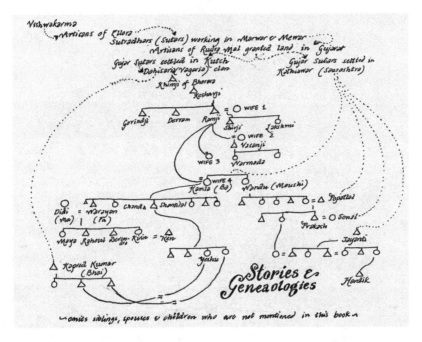

A Note on Transcription

Hoping to make this book welcoming to all readers, I've adopted a dual system for transcribing names and words from Indian languages.

In the main text, recounting my quest, I have limited the use of diacritics. Two such marks seem helpful, though, to let readers know just how a word is pronounced.

A flat diacritic (or macron) above a vowel indicates that its sound is lengthened:

> ā as in *aah*
> ī as in *beet*
> ū as in *pooch*

A dot below a consonant (ṇ, ṭ, ḍ, ḷ) indicates a retroflex against the palate.

I diverge from convention in sticking with *sh* rather than *ś* and *ch* rather than *ć* (for example, *darshan* rather than *darśan*, *chaitya* rather than *ćaitya*). Apart from these constructions, an *h* after a consonant indicates that the consonant is aspirated.

For the scholarship behind this narrative, I've maintained standardly recognizable spellings for names of Indian authors but inserted conventional diacritics, including *ś* and *ć*, in the transcribed titles of Indian-language sources. So, while Vishwakarma appears in the main pages, books on Viśvakarmā will be found in the bibliography and endnote citations.

Joining Palms at Ellora

My father always loved a far-fetched story. He was never beyond some clever plaster and vivid paint to make his version of events more astounding. As I learned to read, he showed me how playing with words could remake the world: spell backward, pun between languages, slide sideways through metaphor. In conversations and in correspondence, he thrived on provoking laughter. Yet throughout my childhood, when Pa mentioned Ellora, he set aside this habitual irreverence.

When I recall Pa speaking of our family's connection to the ancient, rock-cut cave temples at Ellora, I sense sea breezes blowing across the porch of our home in what was then Bombay. I can't picture Pa's face or hear his exact words. What I do remember is the essence of the story and his marveling tone. Our ancestors, Pa said, had made the Ellora caves. At that time, many centuries ago, they still worked with stone. They hadn't yet turned to wood, hadn't yet become Suthar carpenters.

At Ellora, he continued, was a temple to Vishwakarma. "The Architect of the Universe" was how Pa, a University of Colorado–trained civil engineer, described Vishwakarma. As hereditary Suthars, we were Sons of Vishwakarma. No matter where in India our Suthar ancestors later migrated to find work, they came back on pilgrimage to Ellora.

Near this Vishwakarma temple was a sacred pond, the Vishwa Kund. Pa said that when our artisan ancestors bathed in this pond, they gained the right to wear the upper castes' sacred thread.

I hadn't been to Ellora and had no expectation that Pa—rarely an attentive parent—would take me there in any way other than words. Imagining Ellora, I thought not of temples and caves I'd actually visited but of stone monuments at the periphery of my world: pale marble pillars in Greek ruins on picture postcards that our American grandmother Nani sent, along with precious foreign stamps; huge, seated sandstone figures, soon to be submerged by the Aswan Dam, from a slideshow our usually

1. Kirin and Pa, Bombay, 1967. Photograph by Didi Contractor.

aloof British neighbor Stella Snead had invited us children to view; overgrown, disintegrating temples in jungles from photographs in Stella's signed book. I remembered the cliffs of Petra, whose building facades I had carefully colored pink for a social studies assignment at the Bombay International School, and the labyrinthine South American temple where Tintin and Snowy were trapped in one of the comic books passed among my classmates....

I wondered whether other small girls were told of their ancestors' role in making places of ancient grandeur. A long cord of Suthar ancestors seemed to twist backward like an unwinding turban, pleat forward like a wrapping sari, tilting and curving into an enormous question mark with Ellora circled at the base.

✳

I might never have looked more closely into this family story if my husband Ken and I hadn't begun research on how religion and technology combine in the figure of Vishwakarma. As the deity who makes marvelous objects and miraculous places in both Hindu and Buddhist mythologies, Vishwakarma has long been claimed as the ancestor of hereditary artisans in India. With industrialization, workers handling tools and machines also turned to Vishwakarma as an icon of ingenuity and for their protection in the workplace.

When Ken and I began traveling around India in September 2017, we found that for some upper-caste and upper-class people, Vishwakarma was unknown or dimly remembered as a maker for other gods. "But how did you even *think* of such a project?" they would ask. Mention of Vishwakarma could evoke anecdotes about how some worker—a carpenter constructing architectural models, a computer repair specialist, a man summoned to fix a club's swimming pool pump—had inconveniently refused to handle tools on a day of Vishwakarma worship.

In contrast, our interest was immediately understood in artisans' homes and community temples, and when we joined celebrations amid bedecked machines in workshops or factories. Learning of our research, a hereditary carpenter who owned a flour-processing mill declared, "All gods have their moment. Vishwakarma's moment has now come because he is the 'technical *devatā*'—the technology god." As we moved across India, we learned how Vishwakarma has been historically honored in different regions' iconographies, calendars, ritual practices, and stories. It was only to the west that we kept hearing about Vishwakarma's association with "*Ilorgarh*"—that is, Ellora. What I'd grown up thinking of as my own family story turned out to be shared with other families allied with Vishwakarma in the states of Gujarat and Rajasthan.

Today, the rock-hewn caves at Ellora, in the Sahyadri mountain range in the state of Maharashtra, are recognized as a UNESCO World Heritage site, as are the nearby Ajanta caves. Both Ajanta and Ellora draw scores of tourists from all around India and across the world; when I mention working on this book, I often meet a delighted response that conjures the pair as conjoined twins: "I love Ajanta-Ellora!" The two sites are similar but different. At Ajanta, the thirty exquisitely sculptured and delicately painted Buddhist caves extending along the mountain cliffs of a ravine were made between the second century BCE and fifth century CE. At Ellora, thirty-four Buddhist, Hindu, and Jain caves were excavated into the scarp of a mountain between about the sixth and tenth centuries CE. Numbered from the south, the Ellora temples, shrines, and dwellings stretch across a mile and a quarter, transected by two waterways that can become spectacular monsoon waterfalls.

In January 2018, Ken and I flew into Aurangabad, the city nearest the caves. Our driver, who had escorted many scholars, cordially asked what brought us to Ellora. He looked over his shoulder, startled, when we said, "Vishwakarma."

"In thirty-four years of driving a taxi in Aurangabad, you are the first to mention Vishwakarma!" he said.

"Cave 10 is also called the Vishwakarma Cave," I responded.

"Yes, yes," said our driver. "Yes, that used to be the name of the cave... Vishwakarma." He studied me in his rearview mirror. "But how did you think of *this topic*?"

Ken was silent, making space for me to reply. I could have said something about my family, but hesitated. How absurd would it seem for a woman with not-quite Indian looks to step off a plane and announce a local connection spanning fourteen, maybe fifteen, centuries?

Yes, I was born in Bombay to an Indian father. But my mother was American, and ever since scholarships took me to college in New York, I had mostly been based in the United States. And being with Ken—of German and Welsh descent, raised in New Jersey—further emphasized my foreignness. Ken and I had worked as cultural anthropologists in American universities for years, but to complicate identities even more, in 2013 we took up jobs in Australia. This meant that for many people we met through research, we were primarily Australian. Just before our Ellora trip, I had watched the MC at a Vishwakarma-related celebration in Ahmedabad tapping my name into his mobile phone: to my first name, spelled more conventionally with an *a*, he appended the respectful sisterly title *ben*, then added a new place-based surname. I had become "Kiranben Ostrelia."

Sensing that our work as scholars might be dismissed as my diasporic identity quest, I tended to respond to queries about *how* and *why* we chose this topic by summoning larger, more inclusive stakes.

"All these heritage sites were made by actual people," I said. "We don't know much about them or the feelings they had about the places they made. But here at Ellora, artisans have kept coming back to offer worship to Vishwakarma."

Our driver nodded, mulling this over, and our conversation turned to other topics. Leaving Aurangabad, we headed into open fields, with the lava formations of the Deccan plateau like faraway ships on the horizon. We drove onward past the conical hill of the Daulatabad fort, a tall tower rising at its side, onward through dusty villages and occasional stone ruins. The Ellora mountain came into view, its gently curving slopes yellowed by dry grass and speckled with low green shrubs and scattered trees. A thick gray band of basalt cliff ran along the mountain base. Coming closer, we bent toward the car windows on our right to glimpse the doorways of caves receding into darkness.

We drove past the entrance gates to the UNESCO World Heritage site at Ellora, then small shops and roadside vendors offering snacks and souvenirs in the adjoining Verul village. Turning the taxi toward our hotel, the driver mused, "Vishwakarma. . . . Yes, Gujaratis like to come to that new temple about two kilometers away."

Suthars in Gujarat had also told us about the recently built temple. But for the moment, our focus was on Cave 10, completed in the seventh century and long known as "Vishwakarma," "the Carpenter's Hut," and sometimes "the Cave of Kokas the Carpenter."

✳

Ken and I stood in line for a ticket to visit the caves, and then turned right, bypassing Cave 16, the most celebrated of all, to go directly to Cave 10. In the mild January weather, tourists, pilgrims, and school excursion groups surged around us, bringing bright color, calling voices, and a swirl of movement to the composed backdrop of basalt. Friendly people enjoined Ken to stand beside them for selfies. As usual, he tended to oblige, while I walked on ahead.

I was present but also far away, imagining ancestors who, generation after generation, had traveled to this destination. Climbing the steps to Cave 10's pillared porch, moving toward the carved doorway, I grasped a bag with a notebook and held a camera. But those hands within my hands had surely reached down to touch the threshold, then forehead, greeting the sacred space.

Those ancestors' faces had lifted toward the enormous seated stone figure inside the vaulted hall, his face illumined by natural light from the open door and a high window.

Joining palms, looking into the god's eyes, they had communed with Vishwakarma, their ancestor. When they left, departing into the brightness outside, he remained sitting, facing the rectangular doorway. Each year, about a fortnight before the spring equinox, the setting sun drenched his face in gold. Seasons changed, generations came and went.

And yet, this is Buddha.

Yes, Ellora's Cave 10 is a Buddhist *chaitya*, a worship hall housing a domed *stupa*. While the stupa form was originally designed to hold relics of the Buddha, in this last rock-cut *chaitya* excavated in India, the Buddha is seated before the stupa, emerging from it. His hands are poised by his chest as though explaining something dear to his heart. He holds the

6 JOINING PALMS AT ELLORA

2. Cave 10 interior viewed from doorway, Ellora, 2018. Photograph by Kirin Narayan.

teaching pose (*dharmachakra mudrā*), as he sets the wheel (*chakra*) of his teachings (*dharma*) into motion through his address. The two smaller standing figures flanking him are Bodhisattvas, or Buddhas-in-the making. More Buddhas, Bodhisattvas, serpent-beings, chubby cherubs, and other attendants look on and listen in from panels above the pillars.

These days, my Suthar relatives mostly worship Vishwakarma in a very different form. As "Dada," grandfather, he is represented with a long white beard, holding tools and encircled by tools. Sometimes he is depicted with a third eye that imagines creations into being. Usually his dark-haired sons are shown gathered close around him, hands reverently folded. For Vishwakarma is said to have given his boys, our ancestors, the first tools, along with the skills and knowledge to make and repair all things that would be needed for coming times.

3. Vishwakarma and sons in framed poster from 1930s, Bantva, 2018. Photograph by Ken George.

But the young, seated figure in Cave 10 holds no visible tools. Why, amid Ellora's twelve Buddhist caves, was this Buddha seen as the God of Making himself?

✳

Past travelers and scholars writing about Ellora acknowledged that Cave 10 had long been associated with Vishwakarma and with carpenters; occasionally they mentioned locally circulating stories to explain the connection. When the hereditary artisans whom we met in Gujarat, far to Ellora's northwest, celebrated Vishwakarma as "the Resident of Ellora," they shared stories, images, and printed Gujarati texts, and sometimes they tried out hypotheses about why this cave was Vishwakarma's abode. Ken and I were able to follow further leads to Vishwakarma's presence at Ellora in libraries and archives around the world. Poring over rare manuscripts, drawings, and photographs, our questions multiplied. *Why* Vishwakarma in Ellora's Cave 10? turned to *When? How? What did this mean to generations of artisans?*

At the distant times of the caves' making, Ellora lay on key trade routes connecting the subcontinent west to east and south to north. Artisans seeking work, merchants, pilgrims of various faiths and sects, and other travelers all moved along these routes. Following clues to Vishwakarma at Ellora, we met all sorts of other story-caravans richly laden with myths, legends, folktales, anecdotes, travel yarns, and unusual histories; from these, we selected relevant stories. As our own assembled materials grew, we continually turned for help to fellow anthropologists, archaeologists, historians, art historians, Buddhologists, Indologists, Sanskritists. Pulled across time and space, moving through different disciplines, we could see that artisans' perspectives on an ancient archaeological site hold insights of value in many intellectual currencies. But rather than setting up camp to transact theories in any one disciplinary domain, we continued following the stories.

These stories brought clues in four arenas that became the main sections of this book. First, *names and speculations* connected Cave 10 to artisan castes as wondrous Ellora was viewed through time as the work of a supernatural Maker, skilled human makers, or both working together as Vishwakarma and his artisan sons. Second, *ancestral histories* linked artisans' skills, migrations, and claims to a higher status with Vishwakarma at Ellora. Third, *myths* about Vishwakarma and his family's sojourn at Ellora reflected on the wonder and ethics of making; while retold, reread, and reprinted among hereditary artisans in the megacity of Ahmedabad in

Gujarat, these stories are not known beyond caste circles, and I attempt the first English translations. Fourth, *transformations* at the sacred center of Ellora reveal how devotion offered in and around Cave 10 changed in expression from colonial times onward, as archaeologists barred religious decoration while restoring the cave's Buddhist identity.

The Sanskrit word for cave—*guhā*, signifying a space of interiority—is closely linked with "secret." For me, it was uncannily appropriate that a preoccupation with Cave 10 nudged some family secrets into view. As we went about our research, people we met sometimes retold family stories that I'd written about in an earlier book, *My Family and Other Saints*. In these more distant versions, events I thought I'd understood changed form, exposing jagged, unresolved edges. As I learned about my ancestors' lives, I was struck by how the artisans' pilgrimage to Ellora is celebrated as a way of repaying a debt to ancestors and assuring earlier generations of a good "onward journey." I began to wonder: if sons of a patrilineage were seen as primarily responsible for rituals to ancestors (and for producing more sons), as a daughter, could a close attention to family stories also settle debts to ancestors?

Another term used for a rock-cut cave (*layana, lena*) emphasizes a place of residence and refuge. For me, Ellora offered imaginative shelter. I tend to be adrift and overwhelmed without a creative project, and through the course of our research I was often gripped by sorrow. As we moved about India, I was constantly bracing myself as remembered calm, green spaces turned out to have been swallowed by concrete, asphalt, and trash. I tried to rationalize that all adults everywhere today may feel their childhood world has been irrevocably transformed. Yet I remained haunted by the corpses of giant shade-giving trees, deadening limbs lying prone beside the expanding highway connecting Ajanta and Ellora. Even in the Ellora heritage precinct, at the edges of the carved beauty, plastic water bottles bobbed in the rock cisterns and empty snack packets, products of other faraway machines, were snagged in bushes. If Vishwakarma is celebrated as the force behind all human projects of material making, this meant not just ancient marvels like Ellora but also the progressively dire consequences of the extraction, production, and waste involved in making. As I read accounts of Ellora and of Vishwakarma at Ellora, I kept wondering: could these stories carry any wisdom for our planetary crisis?

Ken and I collaborated on these research adventures. As we sorted out how to write about what we learned, we agreed that Ken would take the lead on journal articles and I would work on "the Ellora book." But what sort of book? Each book I've written has taken an entirely different form, as a particular person, a recurring theme, or a vivid metaphor has transfigured my perceptions. With this book, I felt as though I was excavating into darkness, unable to discern the spaces and shapes I might write into being. I began writing as an intrigued anthropologist, suppressing the personal reasons for my interest; then, on what would have been Pa's ninety-second birthday, I started again in the voice of memoir. Through the following months, I composed short segments, not quite chapters but "chunklets" that I arranged and rearranged like jigsaw pieces, trying to discern what fit where. As perplexed friends—in person and via screen—kept asking just *what exactly* I was working on, I tried out various explanations.

Though centered on a mystery and fueled by the thrill of discovering clues, since the narrative had no clear crime or culprit, I couldn't call it a detective story. It was also not quite a family history, memoir, ethnography, place history, study of religious practices, or art historical account of a site. So then what? As I neared a first imperfect but complete draft, I semi-playfully declared my emerging genre as *questography*, the account of a quest. For me, a questography is shaped by the imperative to follow curiosity, unconstrained by intellectual borders, current factions, cresting trends. Steering me beyond this moment of intensified political appropriation of religion, my curiosity has guided me toward more inward, imaginative connections with a deity and a place across time.

These stories leading to Ellora reveal how a community of artisans embraced a widely loved multifaith World Heritage site across many centuries. Focusing on Vishwakarma as an ancestral God of Making, the stories record the satisfactions and the dangers of making things, and the great mystery of ongoing connections with our own departed makers.

PART I
Names and Speculations

4. Gangaram Tambat, "Interior of Vishwakarma"; the earliest depiction of Cave 10, 1790s. Yale Center for British Art, Paul Mellon Collection, B1977.14.22323.

* 1 *

The Cave, Code and Cord of Vishwakarma

When British colonial archaeologists numbered the Ellora caves from south to north, the caves were already known by names. In the first guidebook to the complex, published in 1877, the archaeologist James Burgess noted that Cave 10 "is locally known as the *Sutār's jhopra* [Carpenter's Hut], or Viśvakarma, and is much frequented by carpenters, who come to worship the image of Buddha as Viśvakarma, the patron of their craft."[1]

Reading Burgess, I remembered how Pa had once written a few lines about our own identity as "Sutar," connecting this caste name, associated with carpenters, to Vishwakarma. (The name, pronounced with a short *u* and long *a*, has in recent decades been more commonly spelled "Suthar"; I use that spelling except where the sources from which I quote use "Sutar").

Pa had not been reliably present as I was growing up. Before he and my mother formally separated, he had often lived apart; even under the same roof, he could disappear into his own struggles. He wrestled with an addiction to alcohol, long spells of gloom, paralyzing anxiety over failed business ventures. I was uncertain of his love. And yet, when my older siblings had left home and my mother moved out, taking me with her, I began receiving letters that are lasting tokens of Pa's love and encouragement. The first letter I can find, from when I was fifteen, acknowledges, *I hardly knew you, and you being the youngest, bore the brunt of my chaotic life and erratic, irrational behaviour. In brief I was a sick man. I am trying to recover....* He went on to suggest, *I wish you would get into correspondence with me on any subject. I like to write letters. Someday, if you want me to, I would like to write to you about all I believe. Who are you? Who am I? Why is all this? Why do we die? Why are we unhappy? Etc. Etc. I do not have the answers, but we can certainly ask these questions and maybe solve them or ask even more and more questions, ad infinitum!* (November 1, 1975).

These are big questions to share with a teenager, but I was honored. And Pa turned out to be a surprisingly reliable correspondent. When I took up a scholarship to college in New York, he wrote each week (as I did too, to each of my separated parents). Most of his letters were composed on pale blue aerogrammes threaded into the blue-gray Olivetti typewriter that my American grandmother had brought from Europe. That unusual Olivetti keyboard, with its Z in the top row, led to typos, Pa wrote, that could make him *sound just a little Czech* (April 25, 1977). For as a son in the Vishwakarma lineage and a licensed civil engineer, he understood how tools help translate inner conceptions into outward form. The tools of writing, he emphasized to me, are not unlike the tools of material making.

Sharing key dates from the ritual calendar, Pa wrote: *Today is Dhan Teras, i.e. we worship wealth, gold, if you have any, otherwise your tools of the trade. In your case it would be a pen and I suppose in my case, a measuring scale or a plumb bob or a square* (November 18, 1979). With new technologies, he noted, writing tools would change too: *Now about the Holidays ... the 13th [lunar day] Dhan Teras (worship of instruments of crafts, swords, in your case maybe your pen or typewriter or the computer)* (October 2, 1986). Casting himself, Narayan Ramji Contractor, as a sage, "Narayanswami," he invented a cautionary aphorism about our shared love of fountain pens and their promised flow of inspiration: *"A new Parker pen maketh not a Tolstoy" quote—unquote Narayanswami* (October 10, 1986).

Recognizing me as a writer, Pa urged that I chronicle family stories. Whether written as history or as fiction, he said, they would fill several volumes. I understood without question that he meant his own family's stories, not those my mother told about American (British, Irish, Dutch) and German (Bavarian) ancestors. Pa shared choice materials in his letters and in person; gave me leads on whom to talk to; set aside books, like one published by his father Ramji in 1901. Pa referred to my projected work as *Ramji and Sons* or sometimes *The Ramji Saga*.

Across many years, if we happened to be together when this project was mentioned, it was my habit to reply—sometimes smiling, sometimes bristling—"But what about the *daughters*?" For my grandfather, often known as Ramji "Seth" (pronounced *sate*, and meaning "master" or "prosperous man"), had fathered four daughters in the course of his four consecutive marriages; three of his sons had fathered daughters too. My aunts loved remembering how much Ramji Seth had worried about the welfare of the family's daughters. Just why he had been so apprehensive was never discussed, but they reported that he had done a ritual for our well-being "near Bhavnagar." I now wonder if this might have been the Dadva shrine of Vishwakarma's own goddess daughter, Randal Ma. For this radiant daughter, her unique doubled form encompassing herself and her shadow self, is often approached for boons.

5. Goddess Randal shrine, Dadva near Bhavnagar, 2018. Photograph by Kirin Narayan.

Though Pa was so certain I would become a writer, I was determined to extract myself from the turmoil of his finances and needed a more stable job. In college, courses in anthropology had helped me make sense of my cross-cultural childhood and so I applied to graduate programs in cultural anthropology, hoping (in the spirit of Vishwakarma's doubled daughter) that I could be both a writer *and* an anthropologist. *Anthroapology?* Pa queried. But he adapted to my choice, and through the years

I spent working toward a degree at Berkeley, Pa regularly tried out the writing persona of a bemused Participant-Observer to the cultural practices around him. Filling an entire aerogramme on naming practices across India, he offhandedly spun toward our own identity at the very end: *Oh, we are Sutars. Sutra-dhar = keeper of the Code.* Immediately, he related this title to our divine ancestor: *Vishwakarma has the Code in one hand, the ruler in the other, the plumb [bob in the third], and the fourth hand is in blessing* (June 30, 1986).

※

Ken and I worked together on our first and most complicated collaborative research proposal through the Australian summer holidays of 2015–2016. Christmas and New Year's Eve passed almost unnoticed as I reread Pa's letters, pored through publications that mentioned Vishwakarma, wandered the internet, and took notes. Writing and rewriting, the proposal drafts on my computer screen increasingly became an arena of dull, dutiful despair. Then on New Year's Day of 2016, I woke from a dream in which I had been handed stakes made of rainbow light.

A presence stood behind me.

I couldn't see a face but knew this was Vishwakarma. He was passing me glowing rainbows about the length of a footrule, and I was receiving these over my right shoulder. I understood that these were to map the ground for the research: to stake out plans with times and locations, to set down ideas in appropriate ratios.

Ken, always scrupulous, was concerned that we'd have an unfair advantage in being given these tools of blessed measurement. Though the rainbow stakes had come through my hands, I assured him that he especially deserved this gift.

I wrote down the dream in my Canberra study. Most mornings, prisms in the northeastern window cast rainbows across the room's ceilings, walls, and off-white carpet. Depending on the sun's angle, I may be surrounded by brightly banded buds, shoals of exotic fish, or showers of red-tipped stakes streaming indigo tails. Sometimes as I sit by the window, a plump rainbow colors my hand holding a fountain pen and lingers on the open page. I recognized these rainbows as inspiration for the dream. But I also reflected: while I accepted the glowing stakes from over my shoulder, I hadn't turned to see the face of my benefactor.

Trying to give form to the unseen presence, I brought out a photograph of the Vishwakarma Murti that my grandfather Ramji Seth had worshipped daily in his home altar. A Murti (*mūrti*) is a material personification; later, thinking with this word, rather than "statue," "idol," or "image," helped me focus on the giant seated image in Cave 10 as a manifest presence to whom visitors may attribute different identities.

Ramji Seth's crowned Murti of grandfather Vishwakarma had been crafted from a five-metal alloy by a Karachi-based relative sometime in

6. My grandfather's Murti of Grandfather Vishwakarma, 2013. Photograph by Kirin Narayan.

the 1930s. Vishwakarma sits radiating authority, each of his four hands holding an object associated with projects of making: a book carrying knowledge about building, a plumb bob suspended from a cord to establish vertical lines, a footrule for exact measurement, and a pot of water to purify spaces in preparation for the transformations involved in making.[2] A full-length cloth dhoti is tucked around his waist and draped over his legs, and his chest is bare except for beads looped around his neck and a sacred thread draped from the left shoulder to the right hip. A goose (or swan), his signature vehicle, presses close by his feet.[3]

In this small metal image, the narrow book modeled on a palm-leaf treatise doesn't carry a name, but some statues and paintings of Vishwakarma display a title on the cover, often "Shilpa Shāstra," for an ancient building manual, or "Vishwakarmā Purāna," for a collection of ancient stories. When Pa described Vishwakarma as holding a Code, he meant the codes for making contained in the book.

"Code" is one way to translate the Sanskrit word *sūtra*. As a crystallization of knowledge, a *sūtra* is an aphoristic statement with pared-down, abstruse words that can be unpacked further in commentary (*"A new Parker pen maketh not a Tolstoy"*). A collection of such distilled principles can also be called a Sutra—whether these principles are about yoga, grammar, sex, or any other kind of specialized knowledge. Here is an example of a making-related Sanskrit *sūtra* from an eighteenth-century building text titled the *Vāstusūtra Upanishad*, composed in Orissa, Eastern India:

Who has the knowledge of circle and line is a *sthāpaka* [a builder].

Expanding on this pithy statement, the commentary describes the tools a skilled artisan would use to project such circles and lines into the world and relates how tools and knowledge work together in projects of both outward making and inward transformation: "Holding in hand a measuring rod of *khādirā* [acacia] wood and a cord of *durbha* grass fitted with a ring, that is his outer aspect. This knowledge is the knowledge of Art. From the knowledge of Art arises divine knowledge, and such knowledge leads to liberation."[4]

On the other hand—and for Vishwakarma, *in* another hand—the word *sūtra* can also mean "cord," the simplest of tools. Sometimes this is a short length of cord pulled straight by the weight of a plumb bob, sometimes it is a twisted coil in Vishwakarma's upper right hand, directly above the book. The many uses of this sort of *sūtra* among Suthars is explained in a colonial handbook on caste in western India: "The name Sutar or Suthar appears to be a corruption of the Sanskrit Sutradhar, meaning a holder of string,

CODE AND CORD OF VISHWAKARMA 19

referring to the strings used either in joining planks or in planning and measuring."[5] The handbook also affirms that four groups of Gujarat-based carpenter Suthars—Gujars, Mevadas, Pancholis, and Vaishas—"claim descent from Vishvakarma, the divine architect."[6] (When Pa wrote, "We are Sutars," he could have specified this identity further as Kutchi Gujar Sutar (or Gurjar Suthar), pointing to the Kutch portion of Gujarat and the specific in-marrying caste group.)

Here is a Sanskrit invocation that opens many Suthar community publications, saluting Vishwakarma as the primordial Sutradhar carrying both a cord and a Code.

> Holding a footrule, a cord (*sūtra*),
> a waterpot,
> and a book with the Code (*sūtra*) of knowledge,
>
> He sits on a swan, has three eyes,
> wears an auspicious crown,
> his body expansive and ancient.
>
> He made these three worlds, homes for all the gods,
> palaces for kings,
> mansions for us.
>
> He is the Sutradhar who looks out
> for the welfare of this universe:
> Hail to Vishwakarma!

✳

Vishwa means "all," everything in the universe; *karmā* here is "maker"— Vishwakarma is literally the "All-Maker," though I prefer "The God of Making." In English, the titles used to identify him accord with changing times and sensibilities. As Ken and I assembled the sparse existing scholarship on Vishwakarma, we observed how Vishwakarma shifts from being the "God of Arts and Crafts," to "Divine Engineer," "God of Technology," and even "God of Infrastructure."[7] Pa's preferred translation, "Architect of the Universe" interestingly echoes the Freemasons' conception of their deity as the "Great Architect of the Universe (GAOTU)."[8] Vishwakarma has taken on new informal designations in the Indian diaspora. In Australia, we have heard him referred to as the "God of Tradies" (tradesmen) and in England as "the God of Chippies" (carpenters).

In the Rig Veda, thought to date from between 1400 and 1000 BCE, two major hymns to Visvakarman celebrate him as a sacrificer, a blacksmith, a carpenter, a father, and a deity who can be implored for help with work. Other Rig Veda hymns venerate a related deity, Tvashtar, "Fashioner."[9] Hereditary carpenters sometimes merge these two Vedic craftsmen figures by explaining that "Vishwakarma" is really a title, while "Tvashtri" is his real name. This makes sense, as other gods are sometimes saluted with the epithet "Vishwakarma." Also, brilliant craftsmen in ancient epigraphic records can be honored as "a Vishwakarma," or from "the family of Vishwakarma."

While celebrated in the Vedas for making the universe, as gods were reshuffled and elaborated in the Ramayana and Mahabharata epics and through major Puranas, Vishwakarma was mysteriously demoted to making things for *other* divinities. Brahma became known as the Creator and Vishwakarma was relegated to the role of *devshilpī*, craftsman of the gods, making weapons, ornaments, flying vehicles, forts, palaces, and even entire cities like Lanka, Dwarka, or Hastinapur.[10] Yet in the mythology of different artisan groups across India, Vishwakarma has retained an identity as a primal maker, Parabrahma or Virat ("Vast") Vishwakarma.

For his devotees, Vishwakarma can be envisioned in close association with any of the three great Hindu gods responsible for cycles of universe making and unmaking, whether Brahma the Creator, Vishnu the Preserver, or Shiva the Destroyer. In his grandfatherly form, worshipped in Gujarat and parts of Northern India, Vishwakarma is Brahma-like, with a long white beard, a waterpot, and a goose or swan at his side. Depending on the story, Vishwakarma is sometimes Brahma's son, sometimes a brother, and sometimes a wise elder called in to chastise Brahma for unacceptable behavior. Vishwakarma can also be seen as an epithet or aspect of Vishnu, nurturing the universe through different eras. Just as Vishnu manifests in ten incarnations to rescue the universe at key moments, so Vishwakarma is sometimes said to reappear ten times, with different names and life stories. Then too, represented with five heads and ten arms in regions of South India, Vishwakarma has a Shiva-like form. While Shiva's powerful third eye destroys, Vishwakarma uses this eye—a gift from Shiva, in some stories—to create. Hereditary artisans spoke to us of carrying this eye of Vishwakarma inside themselves as a source of inspiration.

In Eastern India, though, Vishwakarma's form is not unlike that of Indra, king of the gods. A dark-haired young man with a mustache and four arms, his black elephant is a counterpart to Indra's white elephant,

Airavata. When Ken and I shared Vishwakarma images from different regions of India during a lecture in Kolkata, the contrast between the grandfather in the west and the youth in the east was apparently written up in a local newspaper as evidence that the deity became rejuvenated as he moved toward Bengal. Our hunch, though, is that the youthful, Indra-like Vishwakarma emerges from Buddhism, for in Buddhist mythology it is "Vissakamma" who executes the will of Indra or "Sakka" (from Indra's alternate Sanskrit name, "Shakra," which means "the Powerful").

Jataka stories about the Buddha's past lives on the way to enlightenment tell of how, whenever a Buddha-to-be needs something, Sakka's throne heats up. Sensing that some action is required, Sakka summons Vissakamma and issues orders to make whatever is needed, whether an idyllic hermitage tucked away in a forest or high on a mountain, leaf-roofed huts for spiritual practice, promenades for strolls, cloisters for other monks, water sources, or even fruit trees.[11] Vissakamma might be called on to build a grand, seven-story stone palace or to adorn the Buddha-to-be, wrapping him in many cloths.[12]

I was struck by the Jataka tale in which the Buddha astounded a big gathering of people when he took a mango seed and caused it to grow instantly into a tree. To celebrate this miracle, Sakka asked Vissakamma to construct a space for the Buddha to preach in. Vissakamma made an enormous pavilion from precious metals and rare gems, decorated with blue lotus blossoms. There the Buddha gave teachings, then set off for heaven, using mountains as stepping stones, to spend the rainy season teaching deities. When the Buddha was ready to again descend to earth, Vissakamma built him a staircase of gold, silver, and jewels.[13]

Vishwakarma appears so steadily in widely known Hindu and Buddhist tales that it's not surprising that he traveled, through the spread of these tales and with migratory groups of craftsmen. We have attended crafts and vocational school initiations in Thailand honoring "Witsanukam," come across bronzes and tales of "Pisnukar" from Cambodia, seen photographs of a big sculpture of "Bishukatsuma" in Japan's Kyoto Museum. As in India, these other Asian forms show the god holding a tool or tools: plumb bob and measuring stick, set square or axe (Thailand), chisel and hammer (Cambodia), hammer (Japan).

But what about the Buddha in Cave 10, also recognized as Vishwakarma? I was at first puzzled by the absence of a tool in that seated figure's hands. But to jump ahead, we later learned that the worn-away edge of the Murti's robe, draped around his left wrist and falling below his hands, was sometimes interpreted as a dangling cord.

7. Otherworldly Beauty, Ellora, 2018. Photograph by Kirin Narayan.

Holding the cord?
A Sutradhar.
Transmitting codes for making to other figures sculpted around the cave?
Again, a Sutradhar.
In fact, a late nineteenth-century Gujarati book that we located in the British Library names Cave 10 as the shrine of "Vishwakarma Sutradhar, the Artisans' Guru," identifying the Buddhas, Bodhisattvas, and attendants in the panels above the pillars as 360 assembled Sutradhars: "amid this is Vishwakarma's image; this sacred place has an otherworldly beauty."[14]

✳

Suthar is just one of many caste names translated as "carpenter."[15] Though we were focused on Gujarati carpenters' perspectives, we also found mentions of Rajasthani carpenters' attachment to the cave. Rajasthani carpenters didn't identify as Suthar so much as "Khati" (from Sanskrit kāshṭh, wood), even as they also used the title "Sutradhar" to honor great architect leaders. Yet their claim to Ellora ran on parallel lines to the Suthar one. My friend Ann Gold sent me an entry in the 1891 census of Marwar, then a princely state in Rajasthan: "The Khatis trace their descent from Viskarma, and regard his oath as a most solemn adjuration. They declare Eloregurh in the Deccan to have been their original home."[16] A hundred years later, another overview of castes in Marwar district described how Khatis view themselves as Vishwakarma's descendants and stated that Vishwakarma "is said to live in Ellora . . . his famous cave temple is in Ellora. Members of the Khati caste even now go there to do *pūjā* and worship him. Some people also go there in order to do the sacred thread ceremonies."[17] Similarly, while researching the Nathadwara tradition of painting, another friend, art historian Tryna Lyons, found that carpenter-turned-painters also claimed to have originated in Ellora (*Alaurapuri*) and that they too honor Vishwakarma in Cave 10. As Lyons writes, "According to legend, his sons (from whom all craftsmen are descended) worshipped their divine father in this cave temple before excavating the rest of Ellora's monuments."[18]

Many Suthars, including my own grandfather, took on the title "Mistri," and even today this remains a preferred surname for some relatives. Drawn from the colonial Portuguese word *mestre*, for "master craftsman," Mistri (Mistry, Mestri) entered assorted Indian languages, and became adopted by skilled craftsmen regardless of caste and even religious affiliations. Someone named Mistri might identify as Hindu, Parsi, Muslim, or Sikh. (In a similar sort of inclusiveness, Vishwakarma can be viewed as accessible to anyone working with tools and machines, regardless of background. As a hereditary Suthar in England told us, "Vishwakarma does not belong to any religion. He is present wherever people are doing this sort of work.")

When my grandfather Ramji Mistri moved from working as a carpenter to gaining lucrative building contracts, he shed the appellation "Mistri" for the more forceful "Seth." Born in 1927, Pa was a rich Seth's son, raised amid plenty and sent to an English-medium school. This was a Parsi school, and he joined boys with surnames like "Engineer," "Doctor," and "Merchant"; because of his father's reoriented profession, Pa became "Narayan Ramji Contractor."[19] This was the surname I grew up with and later shed.

Even though, to my knowledge, Pa never learned any sort of carpentry, there was no question that as a Suthar son of Vishwakarma Pa would pursue a profession that involved making things. At his father's insistence, he trained, then fitfully practiced, as a civil engineer, never enjoying this work. He could in fact be sardonic about his own alleged caste predilection for building. One of his letters, written at a time of noisy renovations, describes how a fever and stomach cramps had kept him from getting to

8. Master Narayan Ramji Contractor, Bombay or Nasik, 1930s. Photographer unknown.

the office: *So, I just lay down with carpenters making all those hammering, sawing sounds and their electric portables making whining sounds as they drilled holes in the wood, in the wall, which actually sounded like music to me; smell of fresh cement, plaster etc. are perfumes, being a Vishwakarma.*

He went on, as usual, to cast my grandmother Ba as his foil. *Poor Ba was driven mad by these same wonderful sounds, and she had a severe attack of flu too plus High B.P. plus depression* (September 13, 1986).

Reporting on Suthar community functions, Pa portrayed himself more as a bemused observer than enthused participant. When my cousin Yeshu was to be married in an abridged ceremony, he admitted how he was relieved to have shed the customary *five days of festivities which are normal in a family of our kind where relatives from Kutch and Saurashtra descend on Nasik and stay for 4–5 days and we had to acquire the neighbourhood bungalows and sanitariums, etc. In old days, the train fares were also paid to the celebrants, plus of course the sari to the ladies and a turban or its equivalent to the men. There used to be pan-supari-tea-coffee-nasta attendants [serving condiments, caffeine, and snacks] for each group of guests and there were agarbattis [incense] and attars [perfumes] and the atmosphere of jollity, bonhomie etc. prevailed, partly from the free food and transport and partly due to creation of carnival effect* (January 23, 1984).

Pa went on to tell how Ba held her own at such gatherings: *I am just required, as I am just alive, and happen to be the senior male. Ba, of course is the eldest and I am sure loves to be the Eldest in the whole community, and I am sure she has a large audience of white-clad aged ladies, smiling, complaining, approving the new generation with their star-like teeth, which come out, and cursing the daughters-in-law, the wayward sons, not-so-able sons, husbands, etc. etc. I was told by all the guests, mainly our KGS (Kutchi Gujar Sutar) community, that the food was excellent.*

✻

While Pa first taught me that "Sutar" came from "Sutradhar," tools of scholarship remind me that even as *sūtra* has at least two meanings, the figure of the Sutradhar also has a doubled identity.[20] I had been following the Sutradhar in constructing outer spaces, but the Sutradhar can also preside over the unfolding of a story.

In ancient theatrical productions, the Sutradhar was the narrator, stage manager, or producer; his commentary offered a cord of connection between disparate parts of the story. While in Sanskrit plays a Sutradhar as narrator often disappeared after offering audiences an orienting introduction, in folk theater a Sutradhar might periodically return to introduce more scenes and characters, to interject asides, and even to deepen the story through dialogues with characters. The Sutradhar builder directed the transformation of a physical space; the Sutradhar narrator constructed a shared imaginative space.

Though the Sutradhar seemed always to be male, I took inspiration from this double-faceted personage and again remembered Vishwakarma's doubled daughter. The constructing Sutradhar instructed me to measure out the ground, design a form, and assemble sources into mosaics of new juxtapositions; the narrating Sutradhar insisted that many strands could twist into a cord connecting all the moving parts of a story.

Pa didn't ever write to me about this second Sutradhar, but he sometimes shared thoughts on crafting the forward momentum of prose. I must have reported on some Indian American event I had attended as a graduate student in Berkeley, for Pa wrote, *I was thinking about horizontal and vertical movements in prose and how often it is done by masters of this art. By vertical, I would mean bouncy—jumpy, noisy, rebounding, etc. as you have done for the parties and fetes, the glitter of the clothes, the multi-accented conversation, the pandemonium of crosstalk along with reaching of arms to grab salt, the wine or mutton cutlets and no doubt the Filmi Music in the Background. By horizontal I would mean, keen and even but with liberty to move in any direction one chooses, something like straight bat in cricket* (April 22, 1986).

He went on to adapt advice from the enigmatic Seymour Glass of J. D. Salinger's fiction, located near the anthropology paperbacks in my childhood home: *But then remember what Seymour said, "Write only what you want to read again!"*

* 2 *
The Carpenter's "Hut"

Though none of us could have known this in 1984, when Pa described my cousin Yeshu's marriage, this happy event would turn out to carry a great boon for our Vishwakarma research. In 2017, when Ken and I arrived in India, Yeshu's father-in-law, universally known as "Bhai," became our primary mentor. Bhai had been intrigued by Vishwakarma's presence in Cave 10 since he was a boy. Across almost eight decades, he had been reflecting on stories and gathering books that offered clues to the very questions we were just starting to formulate. His lean, bespectacled face glowed with pleasure as he shared these materials and his ideas about them.

The term Suthar, Bhai emphasized, meant more than carpenter. "Suthars have always been doing all sorts of engineering works," he said. "It's not just carpentry; it's mechanical work, architecture, being in charge of construction projects."

He remembered how, in the colonial port city of Karachi, Suthar relatives designed the Manora Point Lighthouse, using a lantern with hundreds of wicks and strategically placed mirrors. He told us how his own maternal grandfather designed the hydraulic system to pump excess brackish water from the Karachi swamps. Later, a paternal relative laid out the first road network for the princely state of Kutch; another established the electric grid. Meanwhile, in Bombay, elders worked on assorted construction projects. Among these Bhai named the Byculla Railway Station, Victoria Terminus, Standard Chartered Bank Building, and Gloria Church. "See, they were all Suthars!" Bhai said. "What mattered was *finding good work and doing good work.*"

Bhai was from the same Dahisaria "branch" (or clan) of the Kutchi Gujar Suthar community as Pa. Our recent ancestors had for a few centuries been settled in Kutch villages around twenty miles apart. Though Bhai was just a year older than Pa, the two had been raised in very different circumstances. While always on cordial terms, they had never been close. Pa had died in 2002, and now, fifteen years later, Bhai's perspectives brought new light to family stories.

Bhai described to us how waves of incredulous relatives had flocked to my grandfather Ramji Seth's Bombay apartment the day after Pa returned from the United States with a foreign bride and a baby girl. Bhai had whisked the three new arrivals away for a sightseeing drive around the then-green city. In subsequent years, as Bhai watched Pa fall under the spell of alcohol, Bhai stuck with what he called "Kutchi beer," or salty buttermilk (*chhās*). Even when Pa and Bhai were living at different ends of the same city, they had rarely seen each other except at community events. But then my childhood playmate Yeshu married Bhai's older son, and a few years later her younger sister married Bhai's younger son, moving into the same joint family household. As Bombay became Mumbai, traffic constantly thickening, my two dear cousins' presence in one place drew me across town during visits to India. Our aunt Chandaphui had been the first to alert me that I could learn a lot from Bhai, and I usually brought along a notebook. But, distracted by other projects, I wasn't ready to give him my full focus.

When Ken and I arrived for formal research, it was sheer luck that Bhai had just relocated to Ahmedabad. We had written grants to explore Vishwakarma traditions across different regions of India, but we needed a base: we chose Ahmedabad as a more manageable megacity than, say, Mumbai. We were drawn by Ahmedabad's architecture and design schools; many small-scale workshops and manufacturing units where Suthars and other hereditary artisans now worked; a few family connections; my best friend from childhood, and another dear friend met in graduate school. This seemed like a good enough base from which to make further connections. But then, a few months before our arrival, Yeshu's eldest son was offered a plum job in Ahmedabad. Having lost her husband and mother-in-law a few years earlier, Yeshu decided to move and keep house for her busy son. While the rest of the family commuted between Mumbai and Ahmedabad as studies and jobs allowed, Bhai came along. And with Bhai came his books.

Bhai stored his books in a carved wall-length triptych cupboard with a mirror at one end, glass doors over shelves, and drawers of many sizes. This beautiful piece of furniture had been crafted in his grandfather's time by workers gathered inside the small apartment where Bhai's uncles, then Bhai himself, had lived, in the Bombay suburb of Matunga. Reassembled in Ahmedabad, the cupboard stretched across an entire wall of Bhai's bedroom.

Like many of his generation, Bhai moved easily between languages: Gujarati, Hindi, Marathi, English, some basic Sanskrit. (Kutchi, the dialect of his childhood, he still understood but didn't speak much.) Bhai's books, though, were mostly in English or Gujarati. He wistfully remembered how, as a college student, he had hoped to study literature. But when his older uncle fell ill, he was redirected to the family construction business. All the same, he maintained his love of reading and of learning. Across many years, on lunch breaks and on weekends, he had visited bookshops, pavement booksellers, and book fairs. He could still name and describe the contents of books he had hesitated to buy because of the cost, then never seen again. For every book that came into Bhai's care, he added an extra protective jacket.

In addition to books, Bhai preserved self-published booklets, pamphlets, and newsletters that circulated within the Suthar community, sometimes with invitations to community events slipped between the pages. He also maintained scrapbooks with newspaper clippings of reviews and articles of interest. With this personal archive at his fingertips, our conversations with Bhai were often punctuated by his withdrawing from the sitting room to consult his library and to bring out materials.

9. Bhai's home library, Ahmedabad, 2017. Photograph by Kirin Narayan.

"All these years, I was collecting books," Bhai once told us, voice breaking with emotion and with laughter. "Only now, I realize it was for you!"

✳

When we arrived and mentioned Ellora, Bhai said, "Just wait."

In his early nineties, he was frail and slightly stooped. He moved with care as he went down the hall, then reappeared carrying a few relevant books. He began with some slender overviews. *A Pictorial Guide to Aurangabad, Daulatabad, Ellora, Ajanta* (in brown paper) set the caves within an interconnected region. *Hyderabad: A Guide to Art and Architecture* (in crackling cellophane) located Ellora within the area that had once been the Nizam of Hyderabad's dominions.[1] *Buddhist Shrines in India* (wrapped in a glossy real estate advertisement) situated the Buddhist caves of Ellora amid a longer tradition of constructing sacred spaces.

As Bhai began sharing his own memories of travels to Ellora, our conversation grew more specific.

"So why do you think Cave 10 is called 'the Carpenter's Hut'?" I asked. Bhai nodded. "Just wait."

He disappeared again into his room, this time returning with a heavy armload of art books. He leafed through pages until he located a photograph of Cave 10 that showed a view of the interior with its vaulted stone ceiling. Tracing a finger along the long central beam with equally spaced rafters curved around it, he looked over at us: "You see how this all looks like it is made of wood?"

Next, he found a photograph of the exterior, where protruding beams and cross-planks had been chiseled into the cave's overhang. The square ends of eight more beams seemed to emerge from just below the upper part of the window. As Bhai explained: enclosed within rock, the cave didn't need such support, yet the artisans had carefully recreated these wooden features.

The earliest Buddhist *chaityas*, Bhai told us, had been large assembly halls made of wood. Later rock-cut *chaityas* at various cave sites at first included wood—for example, the second-century *chaitya* in the Karle caves near Pune. Later yet, wood features were rendered in stone, as with two *chaityas* at the Ajanta caves. As the very last Buddhist *chaitya* excavated from rock in the subcontinent, Cave 10 shares a continuity with these earlier designs.

Cave 10 is a *skeuomorph*, an object made to echo the materials and technology of an earlier form. I grasped how, on viewing the stone sculpted to evoke wood, hereditary carpenters might perceive Cave 10 to honor

10. Exterior of Cave 10 with simulated rafters and planks in stone, Ellora, 2018. Photograph by Kirin Narayan.

the work of carpenters, and so a splendid place to worship their divine ancestor. Yet through further reading I learned that ancient sculptors were also referred to as *shailavardhakī*—literally "stone-carpenters"—acknowledging artisans' shared traditions of making across different materials.

But if the evocation of wood was behind the choice of a *chaitya* as Vishwakarma's residence, what logic lay behind the choice of this *chaitya* at Ellora? After all, there were other *chaityas* at other magnificent rock-cut sites. Was it something about the location or something within the iconography of the cave? Bhai, as we learned, had his own theories.

※

Ellora was at first just a minor strand in our research, and Ken and I were constantly on the move. No sooner had we arrived in Ahmedabad than we flew to Kolkata to record the annual September 17 Vishwakarma celebrations among factory workers and mechanics in that region. Next, we were off to Hyderabad, then Mysuru, to meet scholars who'd written about Vishwakarma traditions among artisans and to observe tool worship at the festival of Dassera. Back in Ahmedabad, we met with academics from architecture and design schools, visited museums and libraries, and began making connections for field research. We stayed in hotels and guesthouses, growing ever more dispirited as we viewed apartments offered to us at vertiginous foreigner rates. Yeshu often invited us over for home-cooked meals and to do our laundry at their home beyond the highway, where fields were giving way to new building complexes. Some days, we came for lunch but got so lost in conversations with Bhai that, at Yeshu's insistence, we ended up staying for early dinner.

It wasn't until November that we moved into a congenial furnished apartment with a makeshift kitchen. At first, Yeshu brought Bhai with her for reciprocal half-day visits. Later, Bhai rode into the city by himself for absorbing Thursday afternoon sessions of discussion, reading, and translation. As Bhai didn't have a phone, Yeshu would see him into a cab, then call us, and we would wait for him to appear at our door. But once we'd been trapped in the building lift, forced to crawl out on all fours between floors, we didn't want to risk Bhai riding seven floors up by himself, so we went to the driveway downstairs to receive him. When a vehicle finally appeared, Bhai's face visible on the passenger's side, he was usually in rapt conversation with a smiling driver. After exchanging a few last words, he opened the door, gripping it for support as he carefully emerged, glowing with anticipation.

Discussing research materials, Bhai always emphasized the limits of what he knew. His presentation of an idea as "See, in my thinking" could give way to "might be"; some of our questions were met with an emphatic "No idea!" For one of Bhai's rules of thumb was "Better not to say anything than to say something incorrect."

If, in our gushing American style, we thanked Bhai for his generosity, his reaction was, "*Arre*, what is the use of any knowledge if it is not shared?"

Or else, "A book must come to help somebody, no? Otherwise, it has no value, it is just paper!"

Yet he cautioned that the appeal of much that we read together lay in lively stories, for which he sometimes used the Gujarati word *vārtā*. He observed, "Everyone loves a good story, according to their imagination. It's only those who read history who might have some idea what *actually* happened."

Following leads from Bhai, we started on literature reviews in local libraries and began wandering the internet with its many resources, like

11. Afternoons with Bhai, Ahmedabad, 2018. Photograph by Kirin Narayan.

the beautiful website *elloracaves.org*. We began to grasp some of the larger frames situating Vishwakarma's presence at Ellora.

First, the area around Ellora is a *tīrtha*—a holy place near water.[2] The mountain and its waterways seem to almost carry a sacred magnetic field, drawing practitioners of different faiths to these slopes, streams, pools, and waterfalls. While the caves now enclosed within the World Heritage precinct are broadly grouped from the south as Buddhist (the first twelve), Hindu (next seventeen), and Jain (final five), a closer look at iconography reveals more fine-grained sectarian distinctions. The twelve Buddhist caves, for example, aren't just "Buddhist" but represent the iconography and ideology of the Vajrayana sect, a Tantric form of Buddhism. Emphasizing the worship of powerful goddesses and spatially unfolding audience with different deities, these caves were organized as sacred *maṇḍalas*.[3] Beyond the World Heritage site and higher on the mountainside, there are dozens more caves made later, some roughly finished, that were once occupied by holy men of different backgrounds.[4] Many sorts of pilgrims were drawn to Ellora, and even those primarily visiting Vishwakarma in the Carpenter's Hut probably also paid their respects to other deities in the vicinity.

Second, the mountain has long been a site of goddess worship. Female deities adorn all the caves, whether they are Buddhist, Hindu, or Jain. Further up the slopes are temples to Girija—Daughter of the Mountains, also known as Parvati. The Velganga or Ila Ganga stream flows west past the most prominent Girija temple on the Mhaismal plateau, twisting and spilling downward through multiple pools, including those adjoining the rock-cut shrine of the goddess Jogeshwari. Reaching the escarpment, the stream plunges downward and makes a spectacular waterfall in the monsoon. The small Cave 28, located just behind this waterfall and depicting an eight-armed seated goddess, was once known as "Dhareshvari," Goddess of the Flowing Water. This helped us understand the importance of female figures in Gujarati myths of Ellora, especially the serpent maiden thought to have invited Vishwakarma to the mountain, and why Vishwakarma's goddess daughter was visited upstream.

Third, the goddess Parvati's consort Shiva is a powerful presence in several Hindu caves at Ellora and in the nearby Verul village. While Cave 16, also celebrated as "Kailash" or "Kailashnath," is a temple complex excavated for Shiva, the Ghrishneshwar Shiva temple, built near the banks of the Velganga in Verul, is considered one of twelve great Shiva *jyotirling* (lingam of fire) shrines spread across the subcontinent. The title "Ghrishneshwar" has several derivations, including a connection to the Sanskrit word "to chisel" (*ghrish*) that would connect directly to the caves.[5] Stories about Shiva and Parvati's presence on the mountain are retold in Sanskrit texts like the Sahyadrikhanda of the Markandeya Purana as well as in Marathi texts, myths, and legends. Both the Kailash complex and the bathing pond close to the Ghrishneshwar temple turned out to be orienting presences in Suthars' attachment to Cave 10.

Fourth, situated near major north-south and east-west trade routes, the Ellora caves continued to draw a range of visitors across the centuries. When Buddhism in the region declined sometime after the eighth century and the presence of Buddhist monks and pilgrims dwindled,

THE CARPENTER'S "HUT" 35

Ajanta, Ellora's sister marvel, receded into overgrown, tiger-filled jungles. But at Ellora, excavations for other faiths continued. Assorted travelers and pilgrims continued to come through Ellora; holy men of different orders camped out; armies were sometimes parked in these spacious quarters; people from the village below may have found shelter during heavy monsoons.[6] Set within shifting sacred geographies, the caves saw times of desolation, abandonment, and even desecration; they saw other times of repurposing and renewed devotion.[7] As archaeologists sought to protect the caves, adornments and offerings were prohibited. The artisans making their pilgrimage adapted, reorienting their devotional practices.

Since the time of the caves' making, Ellora has been known by many names and spelled in various ways, including Verul, Elapur(a), Elaichapuri, Iloura, Elora, and more.[8] In the Suthar community, Ilorgarh (*Ilorgarh*) remains the most popular name, emphasizing the fortress (*garh*)-like appearance of the sacred mountain.

✳

Bhai helped us understand how a wood construction rendered in sculpted stone might appeal to carpenters. But why call the spacious cave a hut? After all, a *jhoprā, jhoprī,* or *jhūmprī* is a small temporary structure made from materials like branches, bark, bamboo, grass thatch—or in later eras, recycled plastics and metal. And since a hut is often made from whatever is at hand, possibly not even requiring tools, how did this name connect to artisans' skills?

Popatlal Dasadiya, elderly father of Prakash, another of my cousins, shared his own theories. Popatlal had gone to Ellora with a fellow Suthar on their way back from a technician training workshop in South India sometime in the 1960s, and one evening he looked through photographs from our own Ellora trip on the iPad. Leaning against the wall behind his bed, cap pulled low across his forehead, he reflected in Gujarati, voice filled with wonder: "If you go all around Ellora, Cave 10 is the *only* cave with an arched ceiling. It is also the only cave that is called a *jhoprī*. This is because of the shape."

A *jhoprī*, Popatlal explained, was often constructed around an arched skeleton of long bent sticks, thatched over with any available materials. Just as reclusive holy men might withdraw to a cave, so too a hut in the forest could provide temporary shelter for spiritual practices. Popatlal recalled how the deities Ram and Sita were said to have lived in a *jhoprī* during their forest exile. "For anyone in the jungle with nowhere to stay, you can make a *jhoprī*," he concluded. "See, during Vishwakarma's time of living in the jungle at Ellora, doing his spiritual practices, this was the *jhoprī* where he stayed."

Following this theme of a makeshift shelter, I wondered about the housing of artisans who had once assembled to work on the caves at Ellora. Each time we drove toward the gated colony where Bhai now lived, I noticed how construction workers set up huts beside the apartment buildings rising higher in what had until recently been fields. Might the artisans working on Ellora have also camped near their worksite in *jhoprīs*, I asked Bhai.

"No idea!" he said. After a moment he added, "Might be . . ."

Bhai recalled his own childhood in a Kutch village, where caste identity determined neighborhood and Suthar homes were clustered along one lane, though they had a separate collective workspace. He recalled that workspace as an extended compound where tools were kept and wood was stacked. Usually, one or two people were present, busy shaping farm implements, simple furniture, or ritual objects. "There might have been some *jhoprīs* there, as sheds to work in," Bhai said.

This gave us yet a different way to think about the *jhoprī* as a "carpenter's shed," or a place of work.[9] Such a connection to a workplace was made again in Suthar stories celebrating Ellora—and implicitly Cave 10—as the location where Vishwakarma gave his sons tools and teachings.

But with a big smile breaking over his face, Bhai added a new possibility.

"To say that this is 'just a *jhoprī*' shows humbleness. But a *funny* sort of humbleness, you know? Like some rich person at his mansion, saying, 'Welcome to my *humble* abode!'"

If this magnificent cave can be so offhandedly referred to as "just a hut," the implied contrast, Bhai reminded us, was to Cave 16. This was the great Kailash or Kailashnath complex, an undisputed wonder in its scale and the ingenious complexity of its extraction: first downward, then inward.[10]

The epithet "Kailashnath" honors Shiva as the Lord of Kailash, the mountain that is his home. For this eighth-century Hindu temple, artisans began at the top, shaping the temple's finial, moving lower to the dome, gradually extracting a cave temple from the surrounding mountainside all the way down to a spacious courtyard flanked by what would become further shrines and sculpture galleries. The artisans' challenge of starting with the finial's tip, no larger than a tiny tamarind leaf, is summarized in a Marathi verse:

> On a tamarind leaf a temple was made;
> First the finial, then the base.[11]

The Kailash complex was extolled as a wonder as early as the ninth century CE in two copper plates unearthed a millennium later, while

12. View from above Kailash complex excavated downward from the finial, Ellora, 2018. Photograph by Kirin Narayan.

workers dug house foundations in Baroda (now Vadodara, in Gujarat). Though made in the year 812–813 CE, the "Baroda copper plates," as they are known, had lightly raised protective edges and were entirely legible. They turned out to record a royal Rashtrakuta land grant to Bhamu, a Brahmin from Lateshwara, as the Gujarat region was then known. The twenty-eight Sanskrit verses include two verses (11 and 12) that mention a wondrous Shiva temple on "the hill of Elapura."

An English translation of this inscription was published in 1839, inspiring much scholarly speculation about just where this "Elapura" might be.[12] In 1883, the great Sanskritist R. G. Bhandarkar sharply corrected earlier hypotheses, pointing to Ellora and identifying the Rashtrakuta king Krishna Raja as the patron who sponsored this temple. Here is Bhandarkar's influential translation of the verses relevant to Ellora:

> (That king), by whom, verily, was caused to be constructed a temple on the hill of Elapura, of a wonderful structure,—on seeing which the best of immortals who move in celestial cars, struck with astonishment, think

much constantly, saying, "This temple of Siva is self-existent; in a thing made by art such beauty is not seen," a temple the architect-builder of which, in consequence of the failure of his energy as regards (the construction of) another such work, was himself suddenly struck with astonishment, saying "Oh, how was it that I built it!"[13]

I was thrilled to see a mention of an "architect-builder"—the Shilpi, which can, very generally, also mean "artisan." But I found the twisting and turning clauses hard to follow. Seeing that the original Sanskrit text was in verse, I turned to friends around the world for help with a new translation. Our kind friend David Shulman sent us these verses from Jerusalem:[14]

> The great gods flying through the sky
> see this miracle of a temple on Elāpura Hill
> and exclaim: "This home for Shiva
> came out of nowhere, born of itself,
> since no clever construction could even approach
> its beauty."

> Not only that: even the architect himself
> wonders how he could have made it
> just like that, as if by chance,
> knowing for certain that he didn't have it in him
> to make another.

Astonishment bursts through both verses. First, the gods roaming the sky in aerial chariots look down over Ellora and, seeing this temple chiseled out of the hill, are struck with wonder. This can't possibly have been made, they reason; it must have emerged of its own accord. Second, the Shilpi charged by his royal patron to accomplish the task, voices his own surprise: "How did I make this?" Even if he tried, he knows, he could never repeat the feat.

Mentioning the astounded Shilpi, the inscription affirms that the marvel didn't arise by itself but through a maker's skill. Or rather, it manifested *through* the Shilpi, mysteriously, without his fully understanding how. This sense of a living force directing insights or action, is familiar, I think, within moments of intense creativity. The celebrated art historian Stella Kramrisch read these lines as expressing Vishwakarma's energy moving through an artisan like a form of spirit possession, arguing that the Indian tradition of art "carries each practitioner straight to the fountain head, the Creative Principle, to Viśvakarmā himself, the Lord of all creative work, who is the spiritual ancestor of every craftsman"; for her, the startled sculptor conveys how, "in amazement, the ego recognizes the creative spirit when Viśvakarmā has finished his work."[15] Similarly, the archaeologist T. V. Pathy identifies the Shilpi *as* Vishwakarma: "Even the master-architect Visva-Karma, is said to have exclaimed, 'Oh! Has this been achieved by me? How could I ever accomplish a thing like that?'"[16]

Even as the Kailash temple brought luster to any artisan—human, superhuman, or divine—associated with its making, it also reflected this luster outward, to the artisans' "hut."

✳

Across our first months together in Ahmedabad, as Bhai shared his knowledge, memories, and library, he ruefully spoke of other relevant books locked away in his village home far to the northwest, in Kutch. These were books he had sent his mother, who also loved to read and who used to read aloud to women neighbors and a blind man who dropped in at the family courtyard. After his mother died, Bhai had maintained the house for occasional visits. But since the massive 2001 Gujarat earthquake, the house had been damaged, becoming inaccessible.

Bhai was apprehensive about traveling to Kutch at his age. As he joked, "mind going fast, legs going back," the gap between his quick mind and recalcitrant body could lead to falls. To reassure Bhai, his younger son, a structural engineer, joined us from Mumbai. In January 2018, we all set out together. We hired a spacious car for the long day's drive between Ahmedabad and Kutch, and made a hotel in Bhuj our base. The next morning we sped along a new highway connecting to Mundra, now the largest private commercial port in India.

I was disoriented. The poetic landscape of villages with millet fields that I had conjured from family stories had become an extraction zone for various mining ventures, including gravel and sand. The desert was crisscrossed with power lines. The road was crowded with trucks. As we neared Bhai's village, four smokestacks of a power plant rose in the distance, and a gray band of pollution lay low across the horizon.

"Do you ever wonder about what your life would have been if you had stayed in the village?" I leaned forward from the back seat to ask Bhai.

"I would have been a nil person," said Bhai, eyes on the road. "There was no education beyond primary."

A nil person: someone insignificant, vulnerable, without prospects. I wondered what fate my grandfather Ramji saw himself as walking away from, tools in hand, when he left for Bombay. I reflected too, with some alarm, who I, his granddaughter, might have become. I doubted that I would be sitting in the back seat of an air-conditioned van beside my fellow professor husband.

We were heading to the house built by Bhai's grandfather. Bhai had told us how, in 1930, when he was just four years old, his father had returned to this home from working in Bombay and soon was very ill. Bhai came to shyly sit beside his father's bed. Peeling open a sweet lime, he had reached out to offer a segment to the prone patient. He remembered his father's smile, his intense stare, and the slow, silent shaking of his head: no. Later that night, his father died, leaving Bhai's twenty-year-old mother a widow.

Bhai's mother had taken her two small sons to her parents in Karachi for a short time. Then she rejoined her widowed mother-in-law in the village, and this was where Bhai started primary school. When he was seven, his father's brothers took him to Bombay to be properly educated; he remembered the half-rupee pressed into his hand as he left, but soon confiscated by an adult, and the long journey as he imagined the tastes of the treats that he might have bought and sampled at every station . Through school and college, Bhai continued to visit his village home on vacations. Later, he brought his wife and three children, and eventually he purchased the house's second wing from a cousin.

As we turned off the main highway toward the part of Moti Khakkar informally known as the "The Suthars' Lane," our driver navigated narrowing, deserted roads. Suthars had been migrating from Kutch villages in search of work for over a century and a half, and most houses were empty, with crumbling facades. The doorways were adorned with carved wood and lively molded, painted sculptures—cherubs, faces peering from foliage, peacocks. The doors bore heavy padlocks, and the low stone troughs to share food scraps with animals were uniformly bare.

Climbing out of the car beside Bhai's home, we encountered a sign reading DANGEROUS HOUSE and looked up to see deep cracks along the walls. After unlocking the outer door, we carefully made our way through the entrance to a vestibule with a large built-in trunk where Bhai remembered his grandmother lying down to rest while chatting with passersby. Dust and cobwebs hung heavy on every surface. The vestibule opened into an inner courtyard overgrown with vines and calf-deep in dried leaves; across the courtyard were two doors, each with a lock.

Both locks were unyielding. What now?

Thanks to a chain of connection that we'd learned to identify as "Via-Via," a friend in Vermont's friend in Toronto had contacted his friend in Ahmedabad, who before our trip had provided us with numbers of lay members of the Swami Narayan sect based in a nearby village who were

THE CARPENTER'S "HUT" 41

willing to help. When we called for assistance, a few men arrived with tools. They took turns banging at the locks; they twisted, they poured water, they infused the locks with WD-40.

Word of our arrival had spread. As we waited, a few people appeared to greet Bhai, some advising him on the high price that the carved wood features of this old house would command if he tore it down. Ken wandered outside to take photographs and I drifted between courtyards, thinking of cosmopolitan decor around the world that incorporates carved fragments of old demolished homes. Peacocks watched as I gathered their iridescent plumes scattered about among the dried leaves.

I had assembled a magically thick bouquet of peacock feathers by the time one lock slid open. As the helping men turned to the second lock, we followed Bhai into the cool interior.

"My grandfather," said Bhai as we passed a portrait of a young man in a maroon turban—the turban color, Bhai said, most often worn in that era by Suthars. In the inner room, Bhai smiled at the neatly arranged altar with Ganesh and other gods, saying, "They are looking after this place."

But the books were in the second set of rooms, and that other lock remained obdurate.

Eventually, two men set off on a motorbike, returning with a metal grinder. As they looked around for a source of power, it became clear that the house's electricity hadn't been hooked up for years. The group went outdoors, consulted, and then one man shimmied up the nearest electric pole to somehow establish a temporary connection to the fuse box.

A meter began ticking. The grinder was plugged in. The man holding the grinder strained backward, grimacing, amid a shower of red sparks. The lock clanged to the ground, the big metal bolt was slid back, and the heavy door creaked open.

Holding a flashlight, Bhai made a beeline for the innermost, cavelike room. He brought out a framed print of Vishwakarma as a young man with four arms, seated atop a flying swan, and an ancient painting of the guru Swami Narayan that a holy man had presented to the family over a century earlier. Then, moving to the outer room, Bhai opened a cupboard set into the wall and pulled out a lined notebook—his handwritten guide to the covered, labeled, and numbered books. Fixing his pool of light on the notebook, he chose a Gujarati book and handed it to me. I recognized a book about Vishwakarma and his descendants that my aunt Chandaphui had once shown me, published by one of her husband's uncles in 1957. A huge tobacco leaf was pressed inside to keep away insects.

"There's more here," Bhai said, finger moving over the lines of his notebook.

It was getting late, and we needed to return to Bhuj. We didn't have time to sort through which materials were related to Vishwakarma or Ellora. But before we left Kutch, we retrieved six heavy blue sacks of books that we carried back to Ahmedabad.

We knew that the trip had exhausted Bhai. Yeshu reported that he was reorganizing his cupboard to welcome the books from Kutch. Over a week passed before we next saw Bhai and showed him our photographs from the trip. Among these was Ken's photograph of the exterior of Bhai's home, painted with an intriguing slogan in indigo-blue Gujarati script. Nobody else had noticed this at the time, and yet the words so uncannily pointed to our mission that Bhai was certain Ken had doctored the photo as a joke.

"Baba, how do you do these things?"

"No, really! Really, Bhai, this was really there."

Bhai shook his head in smiling disbelief. The slogan translates roughly as: *For success in life, books are important.*[17]

* 3 *

Shadows of Makers

As the daughter of two painters and a student of art history, my mother Didi told me that of course she'd been aware of Ellora. When, at the University of Colorado, the Indian student with high cheekbones told her that his ancestors had made the caves at Ellora, she was intrigued: "I mean, wow!" Her own mother Alice Fish's family had made furniture in western Michigan; her father Edmund Kinzinger came from a line of silversmiths manufacturing jewelry and pens in Pfortzheim, Germany. Learning of suave Narayan's background as a son of Vishwakarma enhanced his allure.

Disapproval rained down on every side. She was nineteen, he was twenty-one. Beyond their cultural differences, he was already engaged to be married within the caste. All the same, in January 1950, about four months after they'd met, Didi and Narayan signed a wedding certificate in a Colorado courthouse. When my sister Maya was born later that year, they took on the names that I knew them by, Ma and Pa.[1] After Pa completed his degree in civil engineering, they traveled to India in February 1951. Ma never graduated, and for the rest of her life would stubbornly insist that if she was interested in something, the heck with formal training—she could figure it out! Over the next seventy years, she intrepidly educated herself, practiced, and held forth on a range of fields—eventually as a celebrated vernacular architect.

At first, Ma lived in Nasik with her wary in-laws. Pa worked in Bombay, returning on weekends. It wasn't until early 1952 that they took a vacation to Ellora, accompanied by Pa's childhood friend Pramod Chandra (later to become a distinguished art historian).

"Did Pa say anything about Cave 10 then?" I asked Ma.

"He was showing off, telling stories. Being grand. You know how those two were together. I wandered off to look around on my own."

I knew how Pa and his friend Pramod reveled in droll stories, punning and playing between Indian languages, dialects, and regional accents. I could imagine how Ma would feel excluded, turning away from their laughing banter to instead find company in the sculpture. I guessed that already my parents' marriage was strained.

Ma thought there might be photographs from that trip. I looked through old family albums, but many pages were stuck together. I glanced at a large tray of slides and felt overwhelmed. I turned to a steamer trunk brought by my grandmother Alice when she moved from New Mexico to India in 1959, where Ma had amassed old family photographs. At the very bottom, I found a white envelope containing a set of large, square negatives: all of Cave 10.

When I had these negatives printed, some images were dark, others overexposed. But from what I could discern, the cave was somehow different. The floor was still rough, not yet smoothed with cement. Most strikingly, the face of the image seemed more tentative, with different proportions to the brow, a changed angle to the nose. How could a rock statue be anything but immobile? We had noticed subtly altered features in other older publications, and it took us many months to make sense of this enigma.

Since Ellora was a few hours drive from the family home in Nasik, Ma visited other times as well, sometimes in the company of my grandmother Ba. Once she went with just my older brother Rahoul. She thought that Rahoul had been about eleven, so this would have been 1964. Where the rest of the family was just then, she couldn't remember.

Ma and Rahoul had moved slowly through caves bursting with life: gods, goddesses, Buddhas, flying celestial beings, sages with topknots, squat childlike *gaṇas*, serpent-beings with human torsos, amorous couples, a variety of animals, trees, leaves, blossoms. . . . Emerging from a cave interior, Rahoul stood before a stretch of bare mountain rock. He seemed transfixed.

"What are you doing?" Ma asked. "Don't you want to see more caves?"

"I'm looking at the sculptures that are still in the rock."

"What?"

"Look how they're imprisoned in the rock—still trying to get out."

At age ninety, Ma shared this memory from her home in the Himalayan foothills by Skype, hunching toward my screen, low light blurring her features and white hair. I glimpsed her younger self, still standing tall in a handloom sari, my brother beside her in T-shirt and shorts. Though I could no longer consult Pa, Ba, or Rahoul for their memories, while

13. A different face found in my mother's trunk, Ellora, 1952. Photographer unknown.

we were still in Ahmedabad, I turned to Pa's only surviving sibling, his younger sister Chanda, to see what she could tell me about family outings to Ellora.

My aunt Chandaphui had been confined to her bed by old age. She liked to keep her own old photographs in a big bundle tied up in cloth within reach: just beside her pillow, or under the bed. When I asked Chandaphui about her visits to Ellora, she reached for this treasury of memories. She sorted photos into piles on the bedcover until she located a few small black-and-white snapshots from a trip in 1946.

My Pa, she said, had come home on vacation from college in Bombay, filled the car with siblings and nieces of their age, and driven the group from Nasik for a picnic at the caves. The photos were mostly outdoors. Chandaphui was wearing a pith helmet that made her head seem big on her slender sari-wrapped frame, her face aglow with adventure. I saw no images of Cave 10.

"Did Pa say anything then about Vishwakarma at Ellora?"

"*Bhagavān jāne*, God only knows! After all these years, will I remember?"

✳

Even as I enjoyed these glimpses of my family at Ellora, Ken and I were becoming aware of a long procession of other visitors who left written accounts in many languages. We didn't always find direct mention of Cave 10, but we read closely, alert to how references to the caves' makers or Maker might hold clues to Vishwakarma's presence at Ellora.

Though the Arab historian al Masudi had very generally gestured toward the caves of "Aladra" filled with holy men in cells in 915 CE, the earliest account of visitors moving between the different caves at Ellora dated to the thirteenth century.[2] This was a Marathi text that narrates the movements of Chakradhar Swami, a charismatic holy man.[3] I met this book in the historian P. V. Ranade's charming article about Ellora's appearance in Marathi oral traditions and texts across time.[4] In addition to accessibly retelling some memorable stories, Ranade mentioned the names of caves in Chakradhar Swami's time. He noted, "Cave 10, now known as Viśvakarmā Leṇe was *Kokas Vāḍhyache Leṇe* [Kokas the Carpenter's Cave]."[5]

Chakradhar Swami had come to Ellora or "Elapur" in the year 1268 CE, arriving with a small group of disciples along the mountain path above the Buddhist caves. They descended to the level of the cave entrances and went into a three-story cave rising in an imposing vertical sweep from a courtyard. In those days, as though the memory that this had been a Buddhist monastic residence (*vihāra*) still lingered, the cave was known as the Rājavihāra—"the Royal Vihara." (Later, it gained the name "Teen Tal" or "Three Floors" and later yet, "Cave 12.")

Taking the rock stairs to the uppermost floor, Chakradhar Swami rested on a stone cot in the vestibule to the main hall. He offered worship to his chosen deity, Krishna, and chewed betel leaf. One of the disciples went down to the Elapur village to buy provisions. A close female devotee named Baisa looked around and asked, "Who made these caves?"

"They were made," said Chakradhar Swami, "by Kokas the Carpenter."

Though they settled in Cave 12, Baisa's sleep within a northern cell was disturbed by weird sounds—crying birds, animals, whispers, lullabies. Chakradhar Swami explained that these were the spirits of the place. Three days later, the group moved to a spot in the Elapur village below the caves.

They stayed for ten months in the area, often returning during the day to wander in the caves. Some caves offered further eerie encounters with supernatural beings, and on two other recorded occasions, Chakradhar Swami mentioned the Maker of the Caves.

One day after morning worship, the group followed Chakradhar Swami on his walk. He stepped into a cave and sat down in the *chauk* (variously translated as quadrangle, pillared square, or courtyard). As the disciples watched from above, they saw a figure appearing out of the wall they faced. The man wore a garment patterned with lotuses. Yet when the devotees stepped down, the man had vanished back into the basalt.

The figure appeared; he disappeared.

The puzzled devotees asked Chakradhar Swami what they had just seen.

"That was a Shadow Person," said Chakradhar Swami. "A sign of the Perfected Sages. The One who Made the Caves deposited his shadow here."[6]

Another day, as the group explored Cave 16, Chakradhar Swami stepped through an opening in the rock. The others followed him into darkness. Baisa held the end of Chakradhar Swami's turban, and every other disciple gripped the edge of a garment worn by whoever was directly in front of them. Moving forward, they came to an illumined spot and found men sitting around a pot, their lowered heads covered by cloth. After the group passed this assembly, Baisa asked what they had witnessed. Chakradhar Swami explained that these were "*agamasama*"—Tantric practices, and a sign of the Perfected Sages.

Pressing onward through the dark tunnel, the group eventually emerged into a cave with a balcony. There they rested, admiring the view of the settlement below. "What is that place?" Baisa asked.

"That's Elapur," said Chakradhar Swami.

Baisa was astonished. They had wandered inside the mountain for so long—how could this still be Elapur? Chakradhar Swami explained that tunnels had been excavated throughout the mountain's interior and that no one knew of the entry and the exit except the One who Made the Caves and Chakradhar Swami himself.

I was enthralled by these apparitions within the mountain: the bird, animal, and human spirits of the place still audible within a rock cell, the mysterious group with covered faces assembled for Tantric practices deep underground, the lingering presence and knowledge of the Maker of the Caves as divined by Chakradhar Swami. Who was this Kokas the Carpenter, celebrated as Maker of the Caves? Kokas was not presented as a Suthar but rather a Vadhai, another title for carpenter. If he was associated with Cave 10, could this mean that by the thirteenth century, hereditary carpenters had recognized Cave 10 as a special shrine? How did Kokas relate to Vishwakarma?

✽

Kokas (also Kokasa, Kokāsa, Kukkas, and other variations) appears in various Jain and Hindu stories that may date to as early as the third century CE.[7] He is described as an artisan so extraordinarily ingenious that some of his contraptions fly, enchanting royal families who want joyrides through the skies. As with Vishwakarma, his name was adopted by groups of artisans claiming extraordinary skills. So, from the twelfth through the fifteenth centuries, assorted inscriptions in various regions of India mention Kokas in relation to a family or a guild responsible for different kinds of skilled making. I particularly enjoyed reading a late fifteenth-century inscription from central India that celebrates a multitalented Sutradhar as "The light of the Kokasa family" describing how this "Sutradhara Chitaku (can work) on wood and stone and also on gold with ease. He possesses (knowledge of) the great science, the science of machinery;" and he even turned out to be an astrologer.[8]

The scholar R. C. Dhere has reviewed Marathi legends that name Kokas as the maker of the Kailash temple, suggesting that perhaps a clever artisan—a Shilpi—of the Kokas family had designed it. Drawing on a sixteenth-century Marathi text, the Kathakalpataru, or "Wish-Fulfilling Tree of Stories" (also summarized by Ranade), Dhere recounted Kokas's role in the making of Ellora.[9]

VISHWAKARMA MANIFESTS AS KOKAS TO CARVE A TEMPLE

Because of his terrible misdeeds in a past life, a king named Yelurai suffered a strange split existence. Each night his body became infested with maggots, yet during the day he was fine. When he went on a hunting trip to Mhaismal, further up the mountain above Ellora, his queen accompanied him. While he was hunting, she visited the Ghrishneshwar Shiva shrine. She vowed to Shiva that if her husband was healed, she would sponsor the building of a palatial temple, and that she would not eat anything until she saw its pinnacle.

When King Yelurai bathed in a nearby water source, his sins were washed away and his body was cured.

When the queen told her husband about her vow, he was distraught. Raising a temple from ground to pinnacle could take years! How could the queen

SHADOWS OF MAKERS   49

possibly survive without food that long? All the same, he immediately began looking around for architects and learned of Kokas, who lived in Paithan, a city to the south situated on the Godavari (the river into which all of Ellora's streams eventually flow).

> A sculptor with magical skills named Kokas the Carpenter
>> lived in the sacred town of Paithan.
> Until bathing in the sacred river, he would not eat
>> Or sit to work anywhere.
> So that he could make this Shiva temple
>> Vishwakarma reincarnated in this form.[10]

King Yelurai's chief minister went off to fetch Kokas, who arrived at court along with seven thousand other talented artisans with many sorts of expertise. The king described the temple that needed to be built, and the queen's vow not to eat until it was done. Some assembled men calculated that even if the work continued day and night, it would take at least sixteen months before a temple finial could be raised.

The king sighed heavily. The queen's life was in danger. Kokas, though, assured the king that he could reveal a finial within a week.

> Taking leave of the king
>> Kokas, a manifest portion of Vishwakarma,
> carved the mountain—
>> shaping the topmost part first.
> Before the seven days were over
>> he showed the crowning finial to the queen.
> Only then could the queen
>> so devoted to her husband once again eat.
> He had sculpted in reverse order, from up to down,
>> for the first time in the world.
> This was named Manikeshwar.
>> Then many famous caves were sculpted—
>> let's leave that aside now.
> This is how this very blessed and beautiful place
>> was settled by Yelurai and named Yelur.[11]

....

In these verses, Kokas is first celebrated as an incarnation (*avatār*) of Vishwakarma who has taken this form for the express purpose of extracting the Kailash temple, here called Manikeshwar, "Lord of Rubies." Also, Kokas is hailed as a manifest portion (*amsh*) of Vishwakarma, who ingeniously carves the mountain downward to reveal the temple's finial first and save the queen.

Presenting Cave 16 as the first excavation at Ellora, these Marathi verses linking the name "Yelur" (Ellora) to a legendary king diverge from the historical record; actually, many other Hindu and Buddhist caves had been made earlier. But the primary spot accorded to Cave 16 is another reminder of how, as a bright crown jewel for Ellora, artisans basked in its glory.

✳

Ranade's survey of Ellora in Marathi folklore and literature includes a story of how, one full moon night, gods, goddesses, and celestial beings came to earth to visit the Sahyadri mountain range, where both Ellora and Ajanta are located. Indra, King of the Gods, told them that they had to be back in heaven before sunrise. But these divine beings so reveled in the beauty that after dancing, singing, and playing on the mountain cliffs through the moonlit night, they were still gamboling about when the sun rose. Indra cursed them, turning them to stone, and here they remain, frozen in spirited motion at both sites.[12]

While Ranade identified this as a folktale still told by villagers in the area around Ajanta and Ellora, he didn't mention a live tradition around any of the other stories he summarized. It was sheer chance that on our second visit to Ellora we glimpsed how Chakradhar Swami's visit in 1268 still guided actions in the present.

In August 2018, we had traveled from Ahmedabad with two friends, both of Suthar background, who were seeing these caves for the first time. We wanted to show them the view down into the main hall of Cave 10 from what is thought to be the music gallery. But the screen door leading into this area from the upstairs outer balcony carried a heavy metal lock. At the end of the day, we asked a guard on duty if he could allow us access, and he obligingly unlocked the door. Joining us in this upper niche, closer to the arched ceiling than the floor, he then offered to demonstrate the echo made by the ribbed rafters.

"*Buddham sharaṇam gachhāmi*, I go to the Buddha for refuge . . ." As the guard began reciting the Buddhist prayer, hands poised on either side of his mouth, his words rippled and returned almost as though other voices were joining in the chant. I remembered how, in Ahmedabad, a Suthar who was a musical performer had told us that you could think of Cave 10 as a massive musical instrument, with reverberation built into its structure.

From this upper level, the curved rafters seemed very near. We enjoyed the chance to be almost level with the figures emerging from the waist at the base of each rafter, the panels of further Buddhas and attendants, and a line of chubby cherubs above the pillars. From this vantage, the basalt seemed to carry a different hue within a circle around the forehead, eyes and nose of the Murti, and we wondered if this had resulted from a reconstruction. As we began photographing, we noticed something unusual transpiring in the hall below.

Four men, taking turns, were stepping out from between pillars at the side, prostrating themselves at an angle to the Murti's throne. Two wore what appeared to be a monastic outfit, topped with unusual cloth caps cut low across the forehead and coming down over the ears. One was in white, one in pale pink. We had occasionally noticed visitors to the cave joining their hands, or even pressing their foreheads to the floor directly

14. View from upper level with pilgrim prostrating at one side, Cave 10, Ellora 2018. Photograph by Kirin Narayan.

in front of the large image. But these men were stepping forth obliquely, stretching out at the side. Were they somehow paying obeisance at the feet of the Buddha's standing attendant, the Bodhisattva Padmapani? Or were they obliquely approaching Vishwakarma? Who were these people? None of us had ever seen monks dressed in these sorts of caps. We left the cave, wondering. We'd still be wondering if not for a chance meeting two days later.

We'd been walking on the quiet mountain path through the forest above the Buddhist caves, turning off toward the Naga Jadi rivulet; a pond; areas where exposed agates and other semiprecious stones appeared to have been roughly chiseled from the earth. Then we started retracing our route along the deserted path.

Coming our way was a kind-faced man wearing the same attire as the men whom we had witnessed bowing in Cave 10. He looked to be around sixty, with spectacles and one of those unusual cloth caps that to me seemed some cross between a chef's toque and a bonnet. When we were practically face-to-face, we stopped to exchange greetings and chat.

The man told us that he lived in a Mahanubhav ashram just beside the caves. It was the ashram custom to send one person each day to seek alms in the village of Khuldabad, and it was to Khuldabad he was headed just then. We said we'd seen him the day before, bowing in Cave 10, and asked if he could tell us *who* he was bowing to.

Our new acquaintance looked from face to face, as though trying to recollect having ever set eyes on us before. (Much later, we figured out that it hadn't been him at all, but another monk dressed identically.) He stepped out of his rubber sandals, as though about to say something that demanded utmost respect.

"We offer worship wherever our Chakradhar Swami went," he told us.[13] "Everywhere else that Chakradhar Swami visited in his time has completely changed. But these caves, they are the same."

I imagined all the cities, highways, and dams sprouting across the landscape since the year 1268; the clamor, the shining built surfaces, the smog-filled skies. Somehow, these caves held out a continuity of connection. I took the chance that maybe this man could offer insight on a question I'd been carrying ever since I had read Ranade's article.

"Did the episode about the Shadow of the Maker happen in Cave 10?" I asked. "Why were you bowing in *that* cave?"

Our new acquaintance looked us over again, face inscrutable. "I'll have to talk to my guru," he said. He took my mobile number and told us his name, Datta Das. Then he went on his way for alms.

SHADOWS OF MAKERS 53

Was it that Datta Das wasn't certain of a Cave 10 revelation, or that he wanted permission from his guru to reveal secret knowledge to outsiders? A few weeks later, when we were back in Ahmedabad, we got a call. "Where are you? I'm ready to take you around the caves and tell you more."

But we had too many other travels lined up and couldn't get back to Ellora before leaving for Australia.

✳

Ken and I returned to Ellora the next year, during the monsoons, just after a trip to Thailand, where Vishwakarma is also worshipped. Datta Das was now living at a different ashram in the Mahanubhav network and came by bus to join us at Ellora. One rainy morning, we recognized each other inside the ticketed entrance to the cave complex. He took us along the road within the complex, lifting the latch to an inconspicuous gate located opposite the caves.

Trailing behind him, I had the quickening sense that we'd walked through the looking glass. We had left behind the bustling World Heritage site and were in a small, unpretentious ashram of three low cottages set around a courtyard. One of the cottages had a thatched roof—for me, a poignant glimpse of older architectural styles of my childhood. The others were roofed with corrugated aluminum. A few monks, all with similar attire and caps, were working outdoors on building repairs and nodded greetings as we appeared.

Datta Das led us into the ashram's main cottage to pay our respects at the altar. Rocks of varied sizes, shapes, and textures had been laid out on four stepped levels of the altar. Each rock, Datta Das explained, was from a place where Chakradhar Swami had once wandered. The uppermost rock had been carved into a statue of Krishna, the central deity of the Mahanubhav sect, and adorned with three silver eyes, a silver turban, and a multistranded silver necklace; the other rocks were decorated just with gleaming eyes and beaded necklaces. I was moved both by the beauty of this display, and the unexpected juxtaposition of rocks being venerated so close to the shrines carved into a rock mountain.

When we turned around, we noticed, atop a pile of mats, a copy of the sect's Marathi guidebook to pilgrimage in the caves. Yes, we could look at it; yes, we could scan it. Datta Das joined the others in their work, and we excitedly settled on a mat spread out on the porch to examine the booklet. Turning straight to Cave 10, I read the Marathi entry: "Today's name: Vishwkarma Carpenter Hut (Viśvakarmā Sutār Jhoprī). Ancient name: Kokas the Carpenter's Cave (Kokasvāḍheyāche leṇe)."[14]

We quickly decided that Ken should scan all 111 pages of the booklet, with its entries for many (though not all) of the numbered caves within the World Heritage site, as well as other caves and sites further up the mountain and in the village below. Some caves were sacred because of an associated story, while some had been infused with Chakradhar Swami's presence simply because he had strolled through or sat down for a rest.

I was holding pages flat for the iPad to scan when an elderly monk came out onto the porch and squatted down to stuff a multilayered steel tiffin container into a blue bag. He was about to take this food to Chakradhar Swami at the caves, he said.

Chakradhar Swami had been at the caves in 1268; this was 2018, 750 years later, and lunch was still being sent each day?

"May I come with you?" I impulsively asked.

"Certainly. Why not?"

Ken urged me to go, saying he could use the weight of his phone to hold the pages flat. I grabbed an umbrella and set off behind the monk. Holding a big black umbrella and the blue bag with the steel tiffin container, he walked with purposeful speed, navigating puddles and slippery surfaces. I scurried along, camera in hand, as visitors to the caves paused to stare.

The monk was a small, wiry man in almost threadbare white garments named Kapil Muni. He told me that in old age, he and his wife had both moved into Mahanubhav ashrams, though because of the current repairs, she along with other women of this ashram were temporarily staying elsewhere.

We were heading to Cave 12, the Rajavihara, Kapil Muni explained, as Chakradhar Swami had stayed there on his arrival. "We don't go up the steps, those are sacred," Kapil Muni said, when we reached that grand three-story cave. He nimbly hauled himself from a ledge onto the ground floor. We couldn't walk through the second-floor hallway, either, as Chakradhar Swami had walked there too. Instead, Kapil Muni stepped out onto the wet stone ledge jutting over the courtyard, and I chased along, hoping it would not prove slippery. We emerged from the stairs to the third floor to face a raised stone cot protruding from the wall.

This stone cot was where Chakradhar Swami had sat when the group first arrived, the place where he first told his disciples about Kokas as the Maker of the Caves. To the cot's right was the small cell where Baisa's sleep had been disturbed. A screen door was now installed to that cave, and someone had tied a red and green thread to the screen. In another token of discreet worship, I spotted a single rose blossom in a carved alcove for an oil lamp by this door.

Kapil Muni set down the tiffin and carefully placed a coconut on the raised bed, as though establishing a presence. He garlanded the coconut with marigolds, then prostrated himself on the floor. Then he settled down cross-legged to unpack the tiffin, laying out round steel dishes. Sprinkling purifying water around the food, he closed his eyes, beads in hand, reciting a mantra.

After a while, Kapil Muni prostrated again, then stacked the dishes back into the tiffin. "We're told by guards not to leave any junk around," he said, meticulously clearing away every trace of his presence. Anyone coming by even a minute later would have no idea that this was a sacred space.

With the lunch tiffin back in the ashram as consecrated *prasād*, the small group of monks gathered to wave lights and sing *āratī* beside the altar. One of the ways they saluted their guru was "Hail to the Holy Man of Cave 12!" (*Rājavihāra Bābā kī jai*).

We were invited to join the group for lunch. After we had all washed our own eating implements, Datta Das offered to show us around the caves. He had the sect's booklet firmly in hand and was already poring over relevant entries for each cave.

We walked to the very south. Skipping over Cave 1, Caves 2–8 contained sacred places to be saluted since Chakradhar Swami had wandered in them. In each cave, Datta Das followed prescribed instructions on where and how to bow, and places to avoid because they were too sacred to be stepped on. Codifying an oral tradition of worship in print seemed to have given this booklet overwhelming authority.

At Cave 10, home of Kokas the Carpenter, Datta Das scrambled up into the cave's lower level from a corner of the courtyard, avoiding the steps sacralized by Chakradhar Swami's feet. Since Chakradhar Swami had then roamed around the hall, the booklet advised, "The whole hall of the ground floor of this west-facing cave is to be saluted." It also indicated the areas where the original floor had been covered over, obscuring the spiritual energy left by the imprint of the guru's soles: "Some repairs using cement have been carried out. About eight or nine feet from the right hand of the Murti, there is an area where no cement has been spread and that is part of the original courtyard. This place is sacred. You should salute this hall from between two pillars." In the accompanying diagram, a star marked the sacred area between the fifth and sixth pillars from the left of the entrance.

Another star designated the "Sitting Place: adjoining the image of the Buddha on its right side is a ledge where there is a tradition of salutation." The Mahanubhav devotees we'd seen prostrating from an angle the previous year hadn't been concerned with the Buddha, Vishwakarma, or even the attendant Padmapani. They were saluting the spot where Chakradhar Swami had once sat to rest, the presence of their guru lingering in that rock.

What about the Shadow of the Maker?

For months I'd been imagining the Maker's shadow appearing within this cave linked by name to Kokas, the Maker. I looked around, calculating: if Chakradhar Swami had sat near the foot of the Padmapani statue, and devotees looked toward their guru from the gallery above, what wall would this figure have seemed to appear from? But when I asked about the Shadow's manifestation, Datta Das shook his head, "No, no! Not here!"

Then where? At our request, he skipped over the worship that could be offered in Cave 11 and 12, leading us directly northward toward Cave 14: "Today's name: The Pit of Ravana (Rāvaṇ ki Khāi). Ancient name: Of the Shadow Man, the Cave of Jalandhar [a demon king]."[15]

Coming up the steps through the doorway, we found ourselves looking into a squarish area with pillars, a shrine, many sculptures of deities, and a crudely cut floor with large round holes, as though for pounding grain. Datta Das made his way to the left of the entrance and reverently bowed his head to a ledge in front of a damaged image of the goddess Durga. Here, he said, was where Chakradhar Swami was sitting when the Shadow Person was revealed.

The description of devotees looking on from above, then stepping down, perhaps referred to a descent from the threshold to the floor, with an accompanying shift in perspective and light. I looked around to see if I could spot anything resembling the tall figure with lotus-patterned garments so grandly lodged in my mind's eye. Of course, I couldn't. "We don't have the spiritual strength to see that Shadow Person," the woman leader of the Mahanubhav ashram in Aurangabad commented to us.

If Kokas the Carpenter, a form of Vishwakarma, had "deposited" his shadow within his creation, it struck me that the shadow selves of Ellora's many artisans are also lingering in the caves. We were increasingly meeting other shadows too: in the sensibilities and observations of travelers who, since Chakradhar Swami's time, had passed through the caves.

* 4 *

Surpassing Humane Force

The next set of stories reporting on an extended interaction with the caves doesn't appear until the early nineteenth century with Captain John Seely's travel narrative, *The Wonders of Elora*. This young British soldier had traveled to the caves in October 1810 and, bizarrely, had arranged to *rent* the Kailash temple complex. Though he didn't end up sleeping in the temple, he stayed at the caves for two weeks. It's something of a wonder that by padding the account of his fortnight at Ellora with personal asides, literary quotes, and rambles through related subjects, Seely filled almost six hundred pages! But for all its bombast, the book offers an intriguing record of what resident priests, holy men, and pilgrims once had to say about Cave 10—in Seely's rendition, "The Carpenter's hovel" occupied by "Visvacarma."

Before introducing what Seely learned, I'll introduce two nearby locations, Devagiri/Daulatabad and Roza/Khuldabad, and survey some other historical writings. For in the centuries after Chakradhar Swami's sojourn, the Ellora caves had been mentioned by travelers passing through the area for shorter visits. Like a prism scattering rainbows of many shapes, the stretch of caves became refracted by these visitors' perspectives into many sorts of colorful stories in different languages. Who had made these wondrous caves? Why? How? Again and again, superhuman and divine forces rather than human artisans tended to be given the credit.

The Devagiri ("Gods' Mountain") rock fort, about eight miles from Ellora, was completed on a key trade route in the late twelfth century. Yadava kings then controlling the region had made the fort by both excavating and buttressing a conical hill beside a market town. Seely would memorably describe the caves and fort as twinned "offspring of the chisel . . . one for religious purposes and one for defence."[1] But oral traditions evoked the places' conjoined fates with rumors of a connecting tunnel underground, sometimes ascribing this tunnel to Vishwakarma's labors.

58   Chapter 4

Devagiri became known for fabulous wealth and was raided from the north toward the end of the thirteenth century by Alauddin Khalji of the Delhi Sultanate. When annexed in 1308, Devagiri was renamed Daulatabad, "Abode of Good Fortune." In 1327, another Sultanate ruler, Muhammad bin Tughluq, declared Daulatabad a second capital and decreed that the Muslim elite of Delhi should move. Among those forced to migrate south were saints and practitioners of the Sufi Chishti order. Our friend Carl Ernst's beautiful book *Eternal Garden* describes the arrival and the lasting presence of Sufi teachers who settled in Roza, or Khuldabad, a short walk to the south from the Ellora caves.

Even after the capital shifted back to Delhi in 1334, Khuldabad remained a sacred Sufi site. From the Sufi vantage, Ellora appears to have been an intriguing place for sightseeing and for addressing large groups. Ernst mentions how a nobleman thrilled to have received a hat from his spiritual teacher visited the caves in 1336, and how in 1347, a Sufi saint gave teachings to an army gathered at the caves.[2] Interestingly, an overview of repairs at Ellora notes that a later ruler, Sultan Hasan Gangu (who revolted against the Delhi Sultanate, establishing the Bahmani kingdom), made a weeklong sightseeing visit in 1352, and that this was the first recorded occasion for which caves were cleaned and roads mended.[3]

A short Persian history of Ellora composed in 1512 presents the caves as a wondrous *part* of Daulatabad. As Ernst, who has translated this account, points out, the author Rafi al-Din Shirazi saw Ellora as less a religious center than a political monument sponsored by a legendary emperor of India aspiring to make something that "will be truly permanent, so that it will be spoken of for years afterward, and there should be wonders and rarities in it so that it will endure and remain lasting for long years and uncounted centuries, and its construction will be famed and well known throughout the world."[4] Shirazi perceived the caves as rock-cut recreations of the palaces, court, workshops, attendants, armies, and animals of the ambitious emperor. I wonder if he was partly elaborating the idea of an assembly of Suthars in Cave 10 when he observed, "The attendants of the workshops, their trade, tools and basis of each workshop have been made to the necessary extent, each one being made in the performance of the appropriate action."[5]

While worship by Brahmins, holy men, and pilgrims probably continued in some form at the caves, their presence doesn't surface in writing until the diaries of the French traveler Jean de Thevenot. Arriving at the caves on the morning of March 12, 1666, Thevenot found ash-smeared holy men in residence, and he was taken charge of by an animated Brahmin guide. As Thevenot reports, "The little Bramen led me to all the Pagods, which the small time I had allowed me to see. With a cane he shewed me all the Figures of these Pagods, told me their Names, and by some Indian words which I understood, I perceive very well that he gave me a short account of the Histories of them but seeing that he understood not the *Persian* Tongue, nor I the *Indian*, I could make nothing at all of it."[6] It's too bad for us that Thevenot couldn't follow the stories narrated about "one Temple that was Arched"—clearly Cave 10.[7]

Thevenot had learned about the caves when he arrived in India, and though he was warned of bandits on the road to Ellora, he "chose rather to run some little risk, than to miss an opportunity of seeing those Pagods, which are so renowned all over the Indies."[8] He had ridden in a bullock cart through the night from Aurangabad, and presumably this fear of bandits led him to leave so he could return by daylight; he stayed only two hours, seeing only some of the caves. Back in Aurangabad, Thevenot was told, "The constant Tradition was, that all these Pagods, great and small, with their Works and Ornaments, were made by Giants but that in what time was not known." While Thevenot seemed reluctant to put Ellora's architecture and sculpture on a par with European creations, he acknowledged the making of the caves as a superhuman feat: "If one consider that number of spacious Temples, full of Pillars and Pilasters, and so many thousands of Figures, all cut out of a natural Rock, it may be truly said that they are works surpassing humane force."[9]

By the time of Thevenot's visit, Ellora had become part of the Mughal empire. A Persian chronicle of the Mughal emperor Aurangazeb's reign includes a royal visit to Ellora in 1683. The author Saqi Mustad Khan described Ellora as a desolate space made by people "of magical skill," emphasizing that surely these skilled humans rather than demons (*jinn*) constructed the caves, "although tradition differs on the point."[10] Aurangazeb himself commended Ellora in a letter as "one of the wonders of the work of the true transcendent Artisan"—a counterpoint to later oral traditions that blame Aurangazeb for the disfiguration of some caves.[11]

Almost a century after Thevenot, the French scholar, Abraham Hyacinthe Anquetil-Duperron visited the "Pagodes d'Iloura" in 1758. Noting that Thevenot had summarily described just a few caves, Anquetil-Duperron set about gathering more comprehensive detail and systematic measurement (using scales like "canes" and "the king's foot"). The first cave that Anquetil-Duperron was brought to by two Brahmin guides is clearly Cave

10. He described the cave as resembling the skeleton of an inverted boat and containing a domed "tomb of Vischnou" where the "God is sitting, painted in red, and of a gigantic size. He has two Schupdars, two Guards at his side."[12] Like many of the earlier visitors, Anquetil-Duperron was told that the caves at Ellora were believed to emerge "from very distant times, as the work of Genies."[13]

I suspect that if Pa had met any of these stories, he would have been very amused by the caves repeatedly being seen as the work not of skilled artisans but of superhuman makers, particularly giants, *jinns*, and genies.

✳

The first explicit mention of Vishwakarma that we could find in relation to Cave 10 dates to an article written at the end of the eighteenth century by Sir Charles Malet of the British East India Company. With the company's growing ambitions, Malet had been appointed as a representative to the Peshwa court based in Poona. During this time, Malet was inspired to document and measure the caves. In the heat of May 1794, he traveled to Ellora with horses, an escort, and even a personal clerk provided by the Peshwa ruler.[14] Before Malet could complete his survey, he developed a bad case of malaria, and it wasn't until December that he sent his findings to the Royal Asiatic Society for publication in its journal, *Asiatick Researches*. In his cover letter, Malet waxed eloquent about Ellora: "Whether we consider the design, or contemplate the execution of these extraordinary works, we are lost in wonder at the idea of forming a vast mountain into almost eternal mansions."[15]

At Ellora, Malet was told that the caves' making had been sponsored by a legendary king, referred to as "Eel" or "Elloo" (that is, Yeluraja, Yelurai, Ila, etc., who I have already mentioned in relation to the Marathi Kathakalpataru). A Muslim man drew on oral sources to describe how the king had about nine hundred years earlier built the town of Ellora, excavated the caves, and gone on to make the Daulatabad fort. A Brahmin man referred to a local sacred text, the Shivalaya Mahatmya, to estimate that this king had lived no less than 7,894 years earlier. Summarizing the story of the king's miraculous cure from a skin disease after bathing in a local pool, the Brahmin singled out the stretch of caves from 16 to 10 as emerging after the king's cure: "Looking on the place as holy, he first constructed the temple called Keylmas [Kailash], &c. to the place of Biskurma [Vishwakarma]."[16] In this account, Kailash again was linked to Cave 10, and again took precedence.

"Biskurma" was identified as the artisan "who fabricated the whole of

SURPASSING HUMANE FORCE 61

these wonderful works in a night of six months."[17] Malet reproduced a story then in circulation explaining why, in Cave 10, Vishwakarma took on the Buddha's form.

······························· ψ ·······························

VISHWAKARMA MANIFESTS AS BUDDHA
WHEN HIS WORK IS DISTURBED

The Brahmen who shows the caves has a legend that they were fabricated by BISKURMA, the carpenter of RAMCHUNDER who caused a night of six months, in which he was to connect these excavations with the extraordinary hill and fort of Doutalabad or Deoghire, about four coss distant; but that the cock crowing, his work was left unfinished, and the divine artist took the Outar of BODE [avatar of Buddha].

… and he retired, having wounded his finger, to this his hovel, in which state the figure in front of the entrance of this beautiful excavation is said to be a representation of him holding the wounded finger.[18]

···

Why unfinished work would make Vishwakarma manifest as Buddha is at first not clear; later, this is explained through the Murti's hands arranged in Buddha's teaching pose, yet interpreted as nursing a wounded finger. Malet himself diplomatically disagrees with this interpretation: "But I rather think, with all due respect to the legend, that the figure is in the act of devout meditation, as many figures, with similar positions of the hands, occur."[19] He did, though, recognize the Murti as a divine maker seated in the cave, observing that "from the orbicular ceiling, and the name and attitude of its inhabitant . . . it may be meant to represent the Almighty, meditating on the creation of the world, under the arch or canopy of unlimited space."[20]

Malet's cover letter to *Asiatick Researches* identified enclosed drawings "by a very ingenious native in my service, named GUNGARAM, whom I sent to Ellora for that purpose, previous to going thither myself, when he was unfortunately too indisposed to attend me."[21] This "very ingenious native" was Gangaram Chintaman Tambat, a painter and sculptor from the Tambat coppersmith community based in Poona. While coppersmiths don't appear to have the same connection to Ellora as carpenters, they too view themselves as ingenious sons of Vishwakarma. It seems fitting that the earliest available drawing of Vishwakarma in Cave 10 was made by the talented Tambat.[22] Flip back to page 11 marking part I of this quest, and look again at that drawing.

The arresting ink drawing captures the symmetries of Cave 10 with the Murti at the center, even as the area between the two sets of pillars seems narrower, as if forced to fit a frame. Interestingly, the Murti is depicted as clothed and sporting a mustache. I wondered at first if this had been Tambat's imaginative elaboration, and only gradually understood that this was probably how the Murti appeared in Tambat's time. Though prepared for Malet, Tambat's drawing was submitted only as a placeholder; Malet's cover letter went on to promise that his friend James Wales would be visiting Ellora along with Tambat to "correct his errors of delineation and perspective," and that better drawings would be forthcoming.[23]

James Wales was a Scottish painter who had left London for India in hopes of better artistic prospects. Under Malet's patronage, he traveled to Ellora in February 1795, and his journals of this visit differ markedly in tone from other historical writings on Ellora, perhaps because they were private rather than official musings. Wales was alert to the political instability and suffering of villagers as the East India Company and different kingdoms in the Deccan tried to gain control of the region: after armies attacked, Wales noted, professional plunderers followed. At the caves, he noticed that some had been used as habitations—for example, by a group of weavers. He observed how earth washing down the mountainside had filled many caves with debris, and how, in places, bats, leopards, and porcupines were in residence. Seemingly identifying Vishwakarma as a fellow artist, he translated the name of Cave 10 as "artist Koorma's hovel."[24]

Malet had arranged for three other artists to accompany Wales: Gangaram Tambat, who had already been sketching the caves; Robert Mabon, whom Malet had helped leave the army to pursue art; and Josee from Goa. In his journals, Wales declares Tambat "Chaplain of the company," mentioning Tambat's religious interests, his guru, and close friends in the Mahanubhav sect.[25] En route to the caves, when Tambat wanted to visit a temple but knew he might be robbed, he calmly set forth stark naked! In a list of interesting things that Wales hoped to someday follow up on was Tambat's "book giving an account of when Verool or Ellora Excavations were made."[26] Whatever this book was, we haven't been able to find it.

After Ellora, Wales went onward to document the Buddhist caves at Kanheri. Developing a high fever, he died in May 1795, just three months after his Ellora trip. In a twist worthy of a soap opera, Charles Malet then married Wales's young daughter Susanna and moved back to London with her, taking along his half-Indian children but abandoning his beautiful wife Amber Kaur (who had also been painted by Wales). When Malet's article on Ellora was finally published, the illustrations were provided by neither Tambat nor Wales but a prominent London-based engraver, James Basire, to whom

15. "The Inside View of BISKURMA or VISWAKARMA KA JOMPREE," 1801; first published image of Cave 10 in *Asiatick Researches*, 1801. British Library SV98 pl.1.

William Blake had once been apprenticed. Basire presumably had never been to Ellora, and the engraving that illustrates Malet's article in *Asiatick Researches*, captioned "The Inside View of BISKURMA or VISWAKARMA KA JOMPREE," is decidedly less accurate than Tambat's allegedly imprecise drawing.

This representation follows Tambat's sketch in presenting a lion's face just above the Murti's head, rather than a plant (representing the Bodhi tree of enlightenment). Two Indian figures have been added for scale: one man wields a measuring stick beside a pillar, while another communes with the Murti—could this be a visiting Suthar? The hall is wider than in Tambat's drawing. Tweaked for John Seely's *The Wonders of Elora*, it grew wider still, minus the two men, but still adorned with the nonexistent lion head. It was this image of Cave 10—with Seely's title, "Temple of Visvacarma"—that moved into the purview of a wide English-reading public.[27]

✺

As Captain Seely confided to readers, ever since arriving in India as a young ensign, he had been fascinated by Hindu mythology, undertaking "intensive study, assuming the dress of a native, living on a vegetable diet, with pure water for my beverage . . . almost mythologically mad for upwards of a year."[28] In 1810, when he must have been in his twenties, he acted on this mythological madness to fund his own expedition to the caves. He took along a Brahmin from Poona, a Goan surveyor, and a retinue of guards in case of attacks from Bhil tribal people en route.[29] The enterprising captain then negotiated a contract with local Brahmins and three orders of holy men to rent the great Kailash temple for two or three bags of rice. But finding that he couldn't sleep and that his guard was anxious about spirits, he soon set up his tent just outside the temple complex.[30] Over the next two weeks, he explored the caves, often joined by "a dozen or a score of different orders of the Religieux"[31]—that is, assorted Brahmins and holy men who seemed to be trailing along for the entertainment and to share their interpretations, which Seely then wrote down. Seely estimated that during his stay, around fifty holy men were living at the caves, and about forty Brahmins arrived on pilgrimage from faraway places.[32]

Introducing "Visvacarma" as "the architect who excavated the whole of these works, under the patronage of Vishnu and the Pandoos," Seely cited an unusual local story drawing on characters and themes from the Mahabharata epic.[33] In this version, the five Pandava brothers ("the Pandoos"), born in exile, set about excavating caves to please Krishna (Vishnu) and regain their kingdom.[34] While the story presented Vishwakarma as working *for* Pandava patrons, when standing inside Cave 10, Seely found the chain of command was recast: Vishwakarma was in charge, and the standing figure at the Murti's right was identified as his "chief assistant" Bhima, the Pandava brother known for his strength.[35]

What about the standing figure at the image's left? That, Seely was told, was Sri Ranga, a form of Shiva. Knowing how powerful a god Shiva is, and how pilgrims to the area were often devotees of Shiva, Seely was perplexed: why would Shiva become an attendant to Vishwakarma? The group assured Seely that Shiva "is but an agent or a part of the Deity . . . a small god, who did the biddings of the great *Brahme* in his destroying capacity."[36]

For in this cave, Vishwakarma became supreme. The group assembled around Seely explained Vishwakarma's manifestation as the formless "Brahme" (Parabrahma), encompassing not just Shiva but also the great gods Brahma and Vishnu. As Seely reported:

They said that *He* was the maker of Brahma—the Great God, the first cause, invisible in appearance, and inconceivable in power. He was Sri Bhagvan: he was Narrayn [Vishnu], Sri Narrayn, "of Him whose glory is

SURPASSING HUMANE FORCE   65

so great there is no image." The idea of the Trimurti [three deities] was rejected in this place; and He was the origin of matter—the all-pervading, all-seeing God, Brahme: in fact, he was all in all.[37]

This sounds like the theology of Vishwakarma worshippers who celebrate the Vast Vishwakarma. The group around Seely also seemed familiar with the idea of Vishwakarma manifesting himself in various ways across time. It's too bad that when they offered to tell Seely more, he wasn't interested in recording what he viewed as their "absurd and impenetrable superstition of Avatars or incarnations."[38]

The group also explained to Seely that the figures above the pillars in the caves represented "the favourite servants of Visvacarma, whom he thus honoured by giving them a station from which they might view the place they themselves had assisted in forming."[39] Seeing the teaching pose of the central seated image echoed by the many seated figures in the entablature, Seely observed that these pious servants were imitating "their glorious master the immortal architect, Visvacarma."[40] Here then, as in some other records, the entire hall was seen as a gathering of the Sutradhars who had made the caves, with Vishwakarma as their leader.

Intriguingly, Seely observed that when Brahmins arrived on pilgrimage to Ellora, they first visited Cave 10.[41] It's not clear if these visitors announced themselves as Brahmin, or if Seely was assuming caste status. At the time of Seely's visit, the caves south of Cave 10 were seen as associated with lower castes, and polluting to Brahmins. Possibly, for those descending along the older trail down the mountainside, near Cave 10, this was the first cave deemed appropriate to visit. I wonder if some of the pilgrims Seely observed to first pay their respects at Cave 10 might have been artisans who saw themselves as "Vishwakarma Brahmins" (Vishwabrahmins)—a theme I will get back to when I consider the Vishwa Kund in relation to artisans adopting the sacred thread.

Seely met with an elderly Brahmin from Hyderabad who was doing religious practices in the music gallery of Cave 10.[42] Sending away his own accompanying Brahmin, Seely had a three-hour conversation with this pilgrim. The old man explained that "the temple of Visvacarma was dedicated to the Supreme Being, and on pronouncing the mystical triliteral word AUM in silence he made three low reverences, with a cloth over his mouth."[43] On another visit, he again chanted "Om" and eloquently shared the cosmological significance of the domed stupa within the arched interior. The "circular altar," he told Seely, was "an emblem of eternity without beginning or end; the arched roof, he said, was space; the whole representing the creative power of the Supreme Being, one and alone; Brahma,

Budha [*sic*], and the other deities being only agents and representative of the great Creator's attributes."[44]

Seely must have asked for corroboration about the story he'd been told about the Pandavas making the caves, for the Brahmin devotee said he wasn't sure just what the Pandavas had done, but "it was his firm belief that they had assisted in Visvacarma's labours, and that Vishnu favored them with his mighty power." The man went on to emphasize that the caves were not human creations: "'It is impossible,' he observed, 'that men could make anything of the kind;' these were literally his words; and he further added that he had heard that there were similar works to this in Misr (Egypt)."[45]

Again, the Ellora caves were cast as a marvel beyond human capacity. Like other wonders of the world, their very making invited imaginative elaboration. But what of those who claimed a family connection to the makers of Ellora? I turn now to some ancestors.

PART II
Communing with Ancestors

16. "Seth Ramji Keshavji Khimji Bhagat (Bhorarawala), residing in Bombay and Nasik," portrait reproduced as "Pride of the Vishwakarma Lineage," Bombay, 1930s. Photographer unknown.

✳ 5 ✳

As Regards the Cultural Migrations of Artisans

Today, the Barot came from our Muluk [homeland], Pa wrote in September 1981. *He had the caste books, and he was meeting me after about 26 years! He came by appointment, previously fixed a week ago, and there were great expectations for his arrival. The menu was decided by Ba, the Matunga people . . . were consulted, the cook instructed to make the most delicious food, the shrikhand was bought, the farsan was selected, etc. After all Barots don't come every day and even slight discourtesy or I suppose bad food can be a ruinous act and the family's name would be mud in the annals for ever and ever. Even I had a slight touch of anxiety.*

The Barot was the caste genealogist who preserved and updated a thick, handwritten book. While I'd grown up hearing about the Barot (also known as the Bhat), I had never met him. I had just started graduate school in Berkeley when the Barot visited Pa. Pa had once lived in Berkeley too, studying engineering as an undergraduate. He remembered himself as *a Hick from Nasik* when he arrived in July 1947, a month before India gained independence. He was befriended by a Rita Frazer, a kind older woman from New Zealand, *a British subject, just like me, for the sake of solidarity under the Union Jack and God Save the King.* Rita taught music and treated him to a season ticket at the San Francisco Symphony. Each Friday evening, he would be ready at the Berkeley YMCA—in his suit tailored by Laffans of Bombay—and she would drive them over the bridge.

Rita did change my life, as I started reading all about the composers before going to the concert: life of Wagner, Beethoven, the Russian composers, etc. and soon I picked up quite a bit. Pierre Monteux was the conductor of the SF Symphony and they had the best brass section in the world. I heard Stravinsky conduct his own work, Sacre du Printemps, etc. . . . After the concert, Rita used to take me to all sorts of places, like Top of the Mark, the Papagayo Room, the Wharf and then late in the evening drop me at the Y. Two years later, when he transferred to the University of Colorado, *those western cowboys ate out of my*

17. "A Hick from Nasik" (right) with fellow Indian students, Bay Area, 1947. Photographer unknown.

CULTURAL MIGRATIONS OF ARTISANS 71

hand, and I was __the__ thing culture-wise. I hope you will also have such miraculous luck, which changes one's life and outlook on life, etc. (September 2, 1981).

To receive the Barot, Pa had also invited his elder half-brother's wife and two daughters who lived in the Bombay suburb of Matunga. By birth and through marriage, they were members of Ramji Seth's patrilineage too, and with Pa they waited for the Barot's arrival.

The bell rang.

A young man and an older man entered. Young man in bush shirt and trousers, pleasant face with mustache (drooping) and the other man in dhoti, white full sleeve shirt and black cap.

I said, I am Narayanbhai.

The young man said, I am the Barot.

Welcome, welcome . . .

We sat down in my room. . . . After clearing the throat, my explaining that we have just moved, that everything is to be polished or mended, etc., I said it must have been about 24 years that we met and the older one said no, it has been about 27 years: Rahoul was just entered into their book. Do you want the date?

I said no and they remembered Sethji [Ramji Seth], the Wadi [fields], Shantilal [Pa's younger brother], etc. and then I told him about Devendra and you, and how much you wanted to meet them and get the history of the Vishwakarma Sutars etc. and some day I would bring you to Dholka where they live, and get all the details for days, and he said most welcome and they were at our service.

Pa was already setting up research contacts for *Ramji and Sons,* and even a possible shared adventure to Dholka, west of Ahmedabad. But then, rather than acceding to the Barot's authority on family history, Pa tried on a scholarly persona for the visitors.

. . . and then I told them of the importance of their books from the historical point of view and also as regards the cultural migration of artisans in old days, etc. From Ellora to Mahabalipuram, from Tanjore to Kambuja (Cambodia), the hotch-potch at Badami, similarities between Konarak and Khajuraho, etc. I hope that they were sufficiently interested.

How did Pa come up with this chain of migrations and connections to famed monuments? Remembering the range of different temples that, in my childhood, different relatives (including my own mother) had casually described as having been made by "our ancestors," I wonder now about Pa's expansive "we" in this trail of glorious monuments. Did he mean actual blood ancestors, or all Indian or India-inspired artisans as fellow Sons of Vishwakarma? Yet there is Ellora at the beginning, as rock architecture stretches to India's south, India's east, and further afield to Cambodia.

Pa went on to broach the more delicate topic of his shocking intercaste marriage, the result of his own cultural migration. At the time, relatives had written, threatening that his name would be erased from the Barot's book if he went ahead with marrying "the American girl." But Pa found that the Barot wasn't judgmental at all, at least when Pa was patron, and in fact said that, historically, marrying brides of other castes wasn't uncommon. Even though my parents had long since separated, Pa felt vindicated: *Bit surprised but happy.*

Pa used the aerogramme's remaining space to summarize a story central to the history of Gujar Suthars: the legend of an astounding temple known as the Rudra Mal (or Mahal, as Pa wrote it), built for King Siddhraj Jaisingh. This temple, completed in the twelfth century, was often cited as the reason our ancestors had migrated from Rajasthan to Gujarat, and why their primary livelihood shifted from stone to wood.

One Gangadhar who had divine powers, was commissioned by Siddharaj to create the Rudra Mahal at Patan, so Mr. G. called his whole clan to Gujarat from Marwar . . . and the Rudra Mahal was completed. The palace was fit to be lived in by the gods from the Svarga [Heaven]. It had one lakh [one hundred thousand] bells of different sizes operable by one string, and when rung, made one sound of a gigantic bell and then also a wheel which fed one grain of rice on top of one lakh Shiva lingams automatically, etc. All the architectural marvels were there, and the King thought verily this is the abode of the gods, and what if this Sutar goes to some other king for money and makes one better than mine? Why not chop off all the Sutars' heads? Long story. More later. Anyway, you are now in the book. Hurray!! Lots of love. (September 20, 1981).

✳

While Pa jubilantly assured me of my entry in the Barot's genealogical register, it wasn't until almost a decade later that I saw "the book." In January 1991, Pa and I were visiting Chandaphui in Ahmedabad, where the Barot lived too, and a plan was made to invite him. A propitious date was found, a meal was planned, and midmorning, two young men arrived on a motorcycle. The Barot, I now realized, was actually a role occupied by different men of the same family. That day, the reciter of our genealogy was Narendra Singh Rathod, dressed in ceremonial white with a pen for updates in his kurta pocket; his companion was dressed more casually, in a shirt and pants.

Chandaphui had spread out a carpet, offering a low, covered stool to greet the book: the *Chopro*. Before the book was opened, it was honored with offerings of cash, flowers, and incense. Then the Barot flipped the long pages downward onto his lap. He started with a page adorned with a red trident and lines of red dots: the trident signified the goddess whose praises are sung as recitations start, and each dot marked an occasion when the book had been opened for a patron. Using a finger, the Barot added another dot with wet red *kumkum* that Chandaphui had brought out in a little steel bowl.

This book, the Barot told us, was about three hundred years old. It was written in the Moṛi script used by Barots. This wasn't Devanagari or Gujarati: a magistrate couldn't read it, a lawyer couldn't read it, a clerk couldn't

18. Caste genealogist Barot Narendra Singh Rathod with "the book," Ahmedabad, 1991. Photograph by Kirin Narayan.

read it either. Pointing to the many folded additions and emendations bristling from the book's sides in various yellowing shades, he said that soon they would again copy out the whole book.

The Barot observed that Vishwakarma had three forms: first, he was present in his images (*mūrti*); second, in his lineage through his descendants (*vamsh*); and third, in the three primordial qualities (*guṇa*)—luminous clarity, active energy, and dense heaviness—that perpetually recombine in projects of making. Reminding us that "Suthar" derived from Sutradhar, the Barot said that the "cord" of the Sutradhar referred to the sacred thread; in other words, validating Suthar claims to Brahminhood.

The Barot only mentioned Ellora in passing. Vishwakarma, he told us, had once been asked by the gods to kill the part-Brahmin demon Lavanasura, and then for the sin of killing a Brahmin, he had retreated to Ellora to perform penance. In the looping handwriting of my younger self, my notes carry these enigmatic words:

Ellora—Buddha also Vishwakarma.
In all yugas he resembles whatever the Murtis he's making.

Just as Pa became cheerful when writing amusing letters, it made sense to me that Vishwakarma might be transformed by his own projects of making across cosmic eras. I could also see why Vishwakarma's offspring might visualize their forefather in terms of the divine images they were preoccupied with making for diverse patrons at different times.

※

During our months in Ahmedabad, Ken and I periodically tried out different routes and intermediaries to connect with someone from the Barot family. One Barot whose number we were given didn't possess the right clan genealogies; another brusquely announced by phone that he would charge 10,000 rupees simply to open the book, which we declined; yet another agreed to meet us but had to cancel after a death in his family. And so the months passed, and we never had a chance to consult any Barot for more details on Vishwakarma or Ellora, even as Bhai teased: with all this interest in caste history, was I not trying to become a Barot?[1]

Yet many of the Barot's stories are widely remembered and retold within Suthar families and reprinted in community publications. Of these by far the most popular story is that of the Rudra Mal, retold in many versions, with different details, flourishes, and connections to other stories. Looking through the Suthar author Bachubhai Vadgama's retelling

CULTURAL MIGRATIONS OF ARTISANS 75

of the Vishwakarma Purana with Bhai one hot afternoon in 2018, I discovered how some versions established a direct link between Ellora and the Rudra Mal.[2]

.... ✿ ....

VISHWAKARMA MAKES RUDRA MALS AT ELLORA

Vishwakarma made two small Rudra Mals at Elorgarh. He presented one Rudra Mal to the serpent Shesh Nag in the underworld. Shesh Nag was impressed and rewarded Vishwakarma with the gem from his own forehead. Vishwakarma brought this radiant gem to earth, and it became known as the Lamp in Carpenters' Homes.

Vishwakarma presented the second Rudra Mal to Indra, King of the Gods. Indra was pleased and gave Vishwakarma barley grains filled with the power of prosperity, wrapped in cloth.

A long time later, King Mul Raj went from Patan on pilgrimage to Ellora. At the caves, he saw a Rudra Mal. This was such a uniquely marvelous creation that he lost consciousness. To bring the king to his senses, a craftsman named Gangadhar had to make a Rudra Mal on the banks of the Saraswati River.

....

Bhai beamed in recognition. He explained that "the lamp in the carpenter's home" (*Sutharnā gharnī dīyo*) was a Gujarati saying that acknowledged how hard Suthars worked: "In a village, at night, everywhere else would be dark, but the Suthar would still be working by lamplight." Reading about King Mul Raj glimpsing the Rudra Mal at Ellora, Bhai closed his eyes, fluttering his hands: "He could not come out of this trance—only muttering '*adbhut adbhut adbhut*, wondrous, wondrous, wondrous. No, yes, no, no . . .' He couldn't see anything, he couldn't talk about anything . . ."

It was getting to be dusk and time for Bhai to return home. As we waited for his cab, Bhai cautioned that people often mixed up the two kings involved in the Rudra Mal's making: Mul Raj, the patron who started the project, and Siddhraj Jaisingh, the patron who completed it. Mul Raj, Bhai said, had murdered his drunken maternal uncle, claiming the Chavda throne to inaugurate the Solanki (or Chaulukya) dynasty in the tenth century. Haunted by this murder, Mul Raj had gone south from his capital at Patan on pilgrimage to Ellora, hoping to bring peace to his uncle's soul. There he became obsessed with constructing the Rudra Mal beyond Patan, near a riverbank site for ancestral ceremonies honoring the souls of mothers. Later, Mul Raj's descendant, Siddhraj, worked closely with the

Suthar Gangadhar (in Pa's retelling, "Mr. G.") to complete the monument, and so the area took on his name, becoming Siddhpur.[3]

"That is just a summary," Bhai said. "There is much more to the story!"

Bhai kept promising to tell us more about the Rudra Mal. "Let me properly recollect," he would say. He too had heard the story from the Barot and from relatives, but the version that especially enthralled him was one he had read as a boy in a Gujarati "book with a blue cover." This book went into the history of the Solanki dynasty and was apparently among those we had brought back from Bhai's village home. Bhai said he knew that the book must be somewhere in his room. But where?

As we were preparing to return to Australia in December 2018, Bhai sent a message through Yeshu that he had found the book tucked under a corner of his mattress. The evening before we were to fly out—bags packed, kitchen dismantled—we came over for an evening meal. As scents of food rose from the kitchen, Bhai launched into an expansive retelling of the Rudra Mal story. For me, the many episodes in Bhai's version (which I can't reproduce here) seemed like a folding screen, each section connecting in poetic ways to themes from our stretch of research. Here I reproduce only the parts relevant to Ellora, migrations, and the peaceful onward journey of ancestors.

⚘

THE KING LOSES HIS MIND AT ELLORA

See, the Rudra Mal is based on what Mul Raj saw at Ellora, buried inside the hill. What happened is that first the servant went in, and he saw dripping water. Then the minister went, and he came back saying there is something there, beyond a pool.

Who knew there was something inside that hill? Then Mul Raj went to see for himself, and when they had partly entered, he saw the Rudra Mal inside. But as they were looking at it, a big flood came and they were swept out. The opening closed. Mul Raj fell unconscious.

After Mul Raj had seen that Rudra Mal, all he could say was "Rudra Rudra Rudra…" They came back to Patan and Mul Raj was continuing to say, "Rudra Rudra Rudra." He was crazed. But no one knew what a Rudra Mal was to make him one.

Like all the other wondrous things said to have been glimpsed inside the mountain, whatever the king beheld on pilgrimage is now accessible only

CULTURAL MIGRATIONS OF ARTISANS   77

through stories. An entrancing structure within the mountain's watery interior suggests that this was the Rudra Mal presented by Vishwakarma to Shesh Nag, the serpent king (that fits well with what we learned about the importance of Ila, Shesh Nag's daughter, in Vishwakarma mythology at Ellora). Yet the perception of a construction hidden within the rock is also a reminder of how all the caves were first imagined, then extracted from basalt. Could the Rudra Mal prototype at Ellora be a nod to the Kailash temple, also dedicated to Shiva? Yet a retelling from the history of the Bakrania clan of Gujar Suthars (a single-page scan sent to us by WhatsApp) focused on Cave 10: the intensity of beholding Vishwakarma within the cave is what strikes the king—in this case Siddhraj—unconscious. Afterward, he can only babble, "*Oh Rudra!*"[4]

In most accounts, the king makes direct contact with skilled Gangadhar, who in some versions, has learned about the King's condition while on pilgrimage with his father's last remains. For Bhai, Gangadhar's father, who he refers to as Prandhar, was first summoned from Champaner to the southeast of Patan (and close to Pavagadh hill, which will reappear in a later chapter).

.... ✽ ....

THE SUTRADHAR CURE

A merchant, who was a friend of the Diwan [prime minister] came to visit Patan. He asked, "What is happening? I don't see anything going on here these days."

The Diwan said, "After seeing Ellora and the Rudra Mal, Mul Raj has lost his mind. He wants to make a Rudra Mal."

The merchant said, "I know someone whose ancestors have made a Rudra Mal. He is in Champaner. His name is Prandhar."

The Diwan said, "Go back to Champaner! Bring him here immediately."

Prandhar came. The Diwan asked him if he could make a Rudra Mal and cure the king.

"Give me six months," Prandhar said. "The only remedy I know is this: I need one room or a hall in which I can paint."

For six months Prandhar worked on painting the walls. He drew the plans.

Then the king was brought there. He saw the drawings and had a flashback to what he had seen in the cave. He immediately came to his senses. "Start building this!" he said.

"We will need to prepare first," said Prandhar.

Prandhar had a son, Gangadhar. He was brought to Patan, and he went to a library there. He began reading and studying all the books of architecture and astrology. After some months, Mul Raj was pleased with him. "What blessings can I give you?"

"You can give me these certain books."

Everyone wanted to start building, but Gangadhar looked at his books and said, "If we start now, something will go wrong."

Then Prandhar died and Mul Raj died—at the same time. Gangadhar still wanted to build the Rudra Mal. He lived until a king was willing to take this up again. He lived for many more years and was an old man, nearly 150 years old! Finally, Mul Raj's descendant, Siddhraj Solanki, was ready to start building the Rudra Mal.

....

For the king obsessed with reproducing a prize monument, the Sutradhar's cure involved a representation and a promise that replication was possible. Knowing Bhai, I was also moved by how, in his retelling, Gangadhar immersed himself in the royal library, and that the main reward he sought was books.

While the King was keen to proceed immediately, the builders first wanted to ensure the project's success by divining a propitious starting moment with astrological calculations from the Shilpa Shastras, and locating an appropriate place for breaking the ground with the help of a guru. For Bhai, Gangadhar's commitment to the project kept him alive to a more than venerable old age.

THE SERPENT MOVES

Gangadhar had a guru, Markand Joshi, from Malwa State, Rajasthan. He called him there. Markand Joshi found the right place to build. They prepared to do the puja in the northeast corner. Markand Joshi put a small peg into the ground for the groundbreaking ceremony (*vāstu pūjā*) in the northeast corner of the plot. This was to peg the head of the serpent [thought in building manuals to be moving around the plot site, so some moments are more propitious].

People surrounding Siddhraj said, "He must be bluffing. How can a serpent who is seven underworlds below, be pegged with something that's just over a hand width?"

Siddhraj tried to remove the peg to see, but his hand was held back. The spirits of Mul Raj and Prandhar were not allowing him. When he finally removed the peg, a spray of blood came out. He put it in again, but the time had changed and now it landed on the tail of the serpent. This would no longer be a stable construction. Everyone knew that this could not last forever, but still Siddhraj wanted to build the great monument.

Gangadhar was almost 150 years old. He said, "Let's not delay. Let's build as fast as we can." All the Gujar Suthars were brought for the construction.

....

Here is where our own family history comes in. Gangadhar is said to have assembled a thousand Gujar Suthar families from Marwar and Mewar to work beside him. Together they constructed the three-story, intricately carved and sculpted Rudra Mal.

Eerily, the ancestors who at an earlier time had begun work on the monument, then tried to hold Gangadhar's hand back from derailing progress by removing a peg, now hovered in the area. They watched the work proceed, eager for their souls' release with the completion of the project.

.... ꕤ ....

THE IMAGINATION OF ALL THESE PEOPLE TOGETHER

As the artisans constructed and sculpted the temple, they became aware that some shadowy presences were also moving around. Siddhraj went at night to investigate. He saw the spirits of Mul Raj and Prandhar at the site. He heard them saying, "Siddhraj is doing this for his own fame, not because of our wish. But we will not be released until the Rudra Mal is finished."

When Siddhraj heard this, he said, "The work must go even faster."

As the project was concluding, the astrologer Markand Joshi advised Gangadhar on how to phrase the inscription. He shouldn't credit the monument only to the royal patron Siddhraj but also to important ancestors, astrologers, and artisans.

"First write Mul Raj's name," said Markand Joshi. "And also write the names of your own ancestors who hold your hand as you carve. Don't forget Markand Joshi and a short description of all the people who gave advice and did the labor in preparing the Rudra Mal. We should know it is the imagination of all of these people together."

Siddhraj was annoyed by the long list. But Gangadhar pacified him, saying, "Let us do what we have to do."

When the temple was complete, the next morning, Gangadhar went to the Saraswati riverbank to make offerings for the souls of Mul Raj and Prandhar.

Gangadhar said, "My time is over now. What I have wanted to do I have achieved."

....

This version ends with a sense of happy repletion: the magnificent monument is complete; ancestors' wishes have been fulfilled, granting their souls' release as they receive offerings; an artisan's life mission is accomplished. Listening to this story on our last evening in Ahmedabad was for me a powerful reminder of how our research was also a construction emerging from the imagination of many people.

Most other versions of the Rudra Mal story, though, emphasize a conflict between the royal patron and the skilled artisans, drawing on a common theme in Indian folklore that sticks to various monuments: the king fears that the artisans who have made him something unparalleled might make another patron something better, and tries to curtail their work by killing them, maiming them, or extracting binding promises. In some accounts of the Rudra Mal, the paranoid Siddhraj threatens to cut off the artisans' heads or right hands. In others, he makes them swear on their clan goddesses that they will never again work with stone. In yet others, Gangadhar learns of the king's plans and himself throws down his chisel, as then, in a chain reaction, do the thousand other artisans. No matter how it comes to pass, in all of these tellings, the Suthars vow to abandon work with stone.

According to the Barot, Siddhraj then offered each of the thousand Suthar families "5–10–15 *bīghās* of land" in villages scattered across Gujarat. A *bīghā* is roughly a quarter acre, so this was just enough land for housing and some farming to supplement livelihoods as craftsmen in wood. Whichever village a family settled in became the source of its clan name. The Barot's records related that our family settled in Vagad, a village west of Ahmedabad, in 1157 CE, taking on the clan name "Vagadia." With Bhai, we pored over the map, located Vagad, and briefly contemplated a day's outing before Bhai reminded us: after all these centuries, what traces could we possibly find?

From Vagad, the ancestors, at some unspecified time, moved west to the village of Dahisara, near Morbi, adopting a new name, "Dahisaria." Bhai told us that he had once visited "Dahisara Nana" and found a shrine within one home to the caste goddess, Chamunda Mata, with the protective warrior Vachda Dada worshipped outside. It was at Dahisara that two young, exiled Kutchi princes were recognized by a Gujar Suthar daughter-in-law named Rupalbai and given hospitality, cooked supplies of white millet gruel, and gifted a black horse to continue to Ahmedabad and seek help. Some years later, when the princes regained the kingdom of Kutch, the Suthar family was invited to become royal craftmen. These Dahisarias then migrated to Kutch around the year 1548 CE. They built temples; worked with wood, ivory inlay, stained glass (in a technique brought back from Europe by a Kutchi sailor); helped found a Bhuj school for crafts training in 1762 CE; made powerful cannons and delicate jewelry; became painters; crafted Murtis from wood and stone; and also became photographers.[5] Bhai's ancestors eventually settled in the village of Moti Khakkar, while Pa's ancestors took up residence in the nearby village of Bhorara.

What of the Rudra Mal that the Suthars completed, then left behind? According to the Barot, this spectacular monument withstood 360 cannonballs blasted by Allauddin Khilji before crumbling (in the early fourteenth century); it was reported to have been further dismantled by Ahmed Shah (in the fifteenth century). The massive earthquakes that periodically shake Gujarat, like a giant serpent moving underground, brought more damage. Houses were built around the ruins; some panels were repurposed in a small mosque.[6] Yet the onetime grandeur of the monument continued to be celebrated. In the nineteenth century, Colonel James Tod recorded sung praises of the Rudra Mal from "Sankla the chronologist," a different caste's Barot.[7] A few decades later, when James Burgess visited Siddhpur, this same Sankla was still alive, yet now it was his nephew who sang of the Rudra Mal's many columns (16,000!) and images (18,000!), shining like the "Kailash of Shiva."[8]

If Cave 10 was the last rock-cut chaitya excavated in India, the Rudra Mal is memorialized as the last stone temple built and sculpted by Gujar Suthars. Like the ingenious single cord that tugged at many bells in Pa's retelling, stories of the Rudra Mal stretch from Ellora through numerous locations, chiming out the migrations of ancestors.

❋ 6 ❋

The Debt to Gods and Ancestors

Sometime in the 1990s, Pa gave me a little book with a fading red cloth cover for safekeeping. This was a book that his Bhorara-based grandfather had commissioned and that his father and uncles printed in 1901. Composed in Sanskrit verses with Gujarati commentary, the book turned out to carry some key clues to my immediate ancestors' relationship with Ellora.

To us, this was known as "Dada's book." Where this had been kept in my childhood, I'm not sure, for though I was always prowling around bookshelves, I don't remember ever encountering this book on my own. In my memory, a group is always gathered as Pa or some other close relative lays the fragile book on the "piano top table" (a unique recycled design by my mother). They flip through yellowing pages looking for the illustrations. The book is always opened to the same page, then immediately turned sideways. A forefinger hovers at the lower right corner.

"Look, there's Dada!"

My Dada, or grandfather Ramji, observes us from a round inset. He and his brothers Govindji and Devram occupy like circles, all men with splendid black mustaches dressed up in dark turbans and collared coats. Sitting above them are two white-bearded grandfathers dressed entirely in white, the varied twists to their turbans perhaps linked to changing styles across generations. Pa's Dada, "Sutar Keshavji," is on the left, and my Dada Ramji's Dada, "Bhagat Khimji Sutar," is on the right. They flank a round inset of "Bavaji Vallabhdasji," a holy man from a nearby village.

The book's opening pages also carry two very different prints of Vishwakarma. One displays the familiar bearded, four-armed Vishwakarma Dada seated with one foot down, the other angled to the side, amid saluting sons. The other shows a smooth-faced young man with two arms, sitting with both feet touching the ground and knees pointing outward,

19. Three generations of our male ancestors in "Dada's book," Bhorara, 1901.

almost as though he is about to break into dance. In the frame around him, naked cherubs hug columns; above him, a male and a female figure emerge from roiling foliage to hold what appears to be an enormous crown over his already crowned head.

This "Shree Vishwakarmaji" looks straight ahead, hands held together by his chest. His bare chest is adorned with a necklace, a flower garland, and a sacred thread, and he wears a pleated dhoti below the waist. On his forehead is a narrow, U-shaped Vaishnava mark. Smooth-cheeked and charming, he looks very much like the god Krishna.

But wait! Once I knew more about Ellora, I wondered: isn't this young Vishwakarma, hands joined in the teaching pose, a reference to Cave 10?

✺

Pa had never communicated with his half-American children in Gujarati, and though I could more or less follow what relatives had to say, I didn't have the confidence to speak or the ability to read. As our research took shape, we employed a research assistant and translator, Hardik Siddhpura. Different friends, relatives, and translators helped bring por-

20. Shri Vishwakarmaji in "Dada's book," Bhorara, 1901.

tions of Dada's mysterious book, and then other books, booklets, and pamphlets, from Gujarati into English. Bhai meticulously wrote out an alphabet for me, and for his first lesson we read through the introduction to Dada's book together.

Dada's book was entitled "Document on the Vishwakarma Way of Life" (*Vishwakarmā Dharm Patrikā*). Its publication marked the culmination of a hugely ambitious project that my great-grandfather Keshavji had dreamed into being. For at some point in the 1880s, Keshavji, a village-based carpenter, had resolved to offer Vishwakarma a new temple in his Kutch village as an alternative destination to Ellora.

Keshavji's aspirations were recorded by the Brahmin scholar Lakshmishankar Pranshankar, a man of religious learning who carried the title "Acharya," and who was based in the town of Morbi. Keshavji had commissioned the Acharya to write the book, and the introduction describes their association.

"I'm not a rich person," Keshavji had told the Acharya. "It's only by the grace of my revered forefathers and my chosen deity Vishwakarmaji that I'm making a comfortable living for my family. Still, it's become my desire that my caste brothers—who have forgotten our chosen god, lost their knowledge, and wander about in total worldly delusion—should gain salvation."[1]

While worried that Suthars had foundered in their relations with Vishwakarma, Keshavji was hopeful that much good would emerge when they reconnected: better behavior informed by a sense of religious duty, improved livelihood so they could better care for their families, peaceful unity, and access to a tranquility that could lead to salvation in their last moments. But how could this be accomplished? Keshavji told the Acharya, "The only path that comes to mind is that a temple be built in the center of Bhorara village and that an image of Vishwakarma be installed." In all of India, Keshavji said, "the only temple of Vishwakarmaji is in Ellora [*Ilolgaṛh*] near Nasik. Since my caste brothers can't get there, they're unable to have audience [*darshan*] even once in their lives."[2]

Not getting to Ellora, Keshavji thought, was the source of the community's problems. "Since we're not going there, we haven't fulfilled our duty: to have audience with and show devotion to our god, and to gain the right to wear a sacred thread. We have wronged our Lord and can't free ourselves from the sin of this debt to gods and ancestors [*devpitrirn*]."[3]

The Acharya too had apparently worried about the spiritual condition of Suthars around him (though why exactly this mattered to him isn't something he explained to the assumed Suthar reader). He also thought that Vishwakarma's sons had forgotten their divine forefather as the source of their knowledge and skills. His diagnosis was that, since they no longer saw themselves as Brahmins but as low-caste Shudras, they couldn't advance. The Acharya acknowledged that he had been hoping to meet a

THE DEBT TO GODS AND ANCESTORS   87

well-established person of the Gujar Suthar or allied castes who shared his wish to bring the knowledge of their religious duties back to the Suthars.

The Acharya had heard of the saintly carpenter Khimji Bhagat of Bhorara village. When he met Khimji Bhagat's son, Keshavji, he found a kindred spirit to engage with. "Now and then, he would come to me, and we would look for solutions and a revival," recalled the Acharya.[4]

A revival? What larger forces had made Keshavji and the Acharya so worried that Suthars were losing touch with Vishwakarma?

Environmental and economic hardships in the nineteenth-century princely State of Cutch (later Kutch/Kachchh) had led many Suthars to migrate in search of work. A steamer service connected the port of Mandvi with two port cities in Bombay Presidency: Bombay to the south and Karachi to the northwest. In both these growing cities, Kutchi Suthars interacted with new machines, technologies, skills, and livelihoods. In Bombay, they mostly worked for massive building projects, sometimes as skilled labor, sometimes as contractors. In Karachi, they specialized more in complicated machinery; their projects included keeping the seawater swamps pumped, projecting films, and making ice for refrigeration ventures. Mastering new technologies and making more money, these Suthars found opportunities to rethink their identities and allegiances. Both in the cities of their employment and in their village homes, to which remittances were sent, carpenters became closely associated with religious sects and movements, especially the Vishnu-oriented Uddhav (Ramanandi) sect, and the Swami Narayan sect, whose first guru had been so popular among Suthars that he was also known as "the Suthars' Holy Man [*Suthārno Bābā*]." (As Bhai told us, the first image of Swami Narayan, in profile, had been made by one of our Dahisaria clan members, Narayan Suthar.) Other Suthars were drawn to the Pushti Marg sect, devoted to Krishna, a form of Vishnu. Some, in cities like Karachi, turned to the reformist Arya Samaj. I wonder if, as Suthars joined other devotional communities, these new associations were seen as competing with their relationship to Vishwakarma.

Through the nineteenth century and into the first half of the twentieth, many artisan communities across India were using caste associations, caste publications, and formal legal petitions to assert that they were Brahmins. A British Gazetteer report on Kutch, published in 1880, before the first conversations between Keshavji and the Acharya, also mentions the Gujar Suthar claim of descent from the "divine world-builder" Vishwakarma in relation to a lost Brahmin-like identity. This report mentions a book that we haven't yet located: "A book on their caste, called Vishvakarma, says that about 3000 years ago when their caste was formed, their ancestors washed regularly, repeated the most sacred text, *gāyatri mantra*, and performed other ceremonies like Brahmins."[5] (I will return to this theme of claiming Brahmin identity in chapter 14, when I introduce the Vishwa Kund, the pond near Cave 10 where Suthar men once bathed before putting on the sacred thread).

It is arresting to see Keshavji's hopes for a revival identify Ellora as the site of the *only* Vishwakarma temple on the subcontinent, near Nasik. Nasik (now Nashik), where my grandfather Ramji Seth later settled, is a pilgrimage town on the banks of the Godavari River in the Deccan plateau of what is now Maharashtra. In Keshavji's time, Bhorara was in the princely State of Cutch, Nasik was in the Bombay Presidency, and Ellora was part of the Nizam of Hyderabad's dominions. Even with new forms of transport like steamships and railways, Nasik was far from Bhorara, and Ellora was even further. Burgess's 1877 travel guide to Ellora, for example, cautioned that despite a recent railway line extending from Nasik to Nandgaon, a visitor would need to travel another forty-four miles to the caves—about six or eight hours by horse carriage, and by bullock cart even slower.[6] A pilgrimage to Ellora, then, would have been arduous for Keshavji's village-based contemporaries, demanding not just days but weeks away from daily earnings. It's no wonder that many didn't undertake this pilgrimage even once in their lives.

The small village of Bhorara in Mundra district, southeast of the city of Bhuj, wouldn't exactly appear more accessible than Ellora. But from the perspective of Kutchi Suthars, Bhorara was near the Mandvi port, where boats went out to meet the steamers connecting Bombay and Karachi; the route inland to Bhuj passed near Bhorara. This meant that the village was easily accessible to those returning from work in cities to their village homes.

With three sons working in Bombay, I think Keshavji would have felt confident donating a portion of the family farmland in Bhorara to offer Vishwakarma a new home. "If we build a temple here, we can be freed from our debt to gods and ancestors," Keshavji told the Acharya. "For caste brothers to gain the benefits of pilgrimage, a temple should be as close as a courtyard is to a house."[7]

✳

Keshavji's mustache and beard might already have been as white as his cotton clothes, but for a project as extravagant as a temple, he needed his elderly father's permission. He confessed to the Acharya that he was nervous that his father might not agree.

In family stories and in the Acharya's book, my great-great-grandfather Khimji Bhagat, "Khimji the Devotee," exudes spiritual otherworldliness and unconventionality. He is celebrated as being so compassionate that he let hungry cows graze away the family fields and occasionally gave away clothes off his own back. His guru was of the Ramanandi order, and Khimji expressed his devotion by singing with a group of musicians and singers who included Keshavji.

The only existing photograph of these two forefathers shows them amid their singing group in the Bhorara family courtyard. Keshavji is a tall, lean man with a close-cropped white beard and a rosewood complexion, holding the four-stringed *tambūrā* he will strum, providing a background drone. Ancient and hunched, Khimji Bhagat clasps a one-stringed *ektārā*, which will add a one-note, twanging accompaniment. We don't know who the other musicians are: neither the man with the joined brass cymbals, nor the man resting his hands on the skins of the *tablās*, set to beat out rhythms with fingers and palms, nor the two sitting empty-handed, whose voices will presumably join in the swell of song. Looking closely at this photograph and the woodcut portraits

21. Our ancestors Keshavji and Khimji with devotional musicians, Bhorara, late nineteenth century. Photographer unknown.

in Dada's book, it's clear that the book's images of Khimji and Keshavji are extracted from this ensemble.

When Keshavji broached his idea for a Vishwakarma temple, his father turned out to be supportive. "Son, for religious work, don't hesitate at all," he said. "This idea has come to you through the blessings of Narayan. I give you my consent. We're not rich, so we'll face difficulties in getting this accomplished. The work might even remain incomplete. But I'm sure that the same Vishwakarmaji who produced the thought will also accomplish the task."[8]

Khimji Bhagat's celebration of an idea coming from both Narayan (Vishnu) and from Vishwakarma made me wonder what connection he might have seen between the two gods. As I've mentioned, at that time in Kutch and Kathiawar, many Suthars were devotees of Vishnu-oriented sects. Since Vishnu sustains the universe and Vishwakarma makes things for the universe as part of this sustenance, some Vishwakarma descendants have argued that he is another form of Vishnu.[9] Khimji Bhagat may have seen Vishnu and Vishwakarma as manifestations of the same cosmic entity. Or he might have embraced Vishnu as his chosen deity for devotion, while honoring Vishwakarma as his ancestor. Also, as the god of building, Vishwakarma would be key to building a freestanding temple alternative to the existing cave shrine at Ellora.

The Acharya's book records that a foundation stone was laid in 1889, and that Khimji Bhagat died in 1890. After a mourning period, building resumed. The temple structure was completed in 1897. Now the deities needed to be installed with appropriate rituals, and for this, the Acharya reports, an appropriate time couldn't be found. Was the delay related to a series of droughts and famines afflicting India at the tail end of the nineteenth century? Bubonic plague, which broke out in 1897 in Kutch, would have held a massive celebration at bay.[10] Possibly there were other deaths in the family. I wonder if the first of my grandfather's wives, mother of a son, Shivji (born in 1896), and a daughter, Lakshmibai, had died during this time.

Whatever the reasons, during this stretch of waiting, Keshavji expressed his wish: "that we print and publish a book of the stories, the knowledge, and the traditions given to us by Shree Vishwakarmaji and that you might know from reading the scriptures."[11] This is how the Acharya came to compose the little book expounding on all aspects of "Vishwakarma Dharma"—as religious practice, dutiful behavior, and ethical ways of living for men and women who are Vishwakarma's descendants. I am told that the Acharya's Sanskrit verses heading most pages are credible but not particularly literary or poetic; his Gujarati translation is long-winded,

THE DEBT TO GODS AND ANCESTORS 91

with unusual spellings and sentences that can fill up entire paragraphs. Interestingly, the Acharya, whose task is writing, starts with a Sanskrit verse of his own composition to thank Vishwakarma for help with the making of the book:

> Having bowed to glorious Vishwakarma
>> whose name brings good fortune to all,
> I am granted the ability to write
>> through his abundant compassion.[12]

Just as various Sanskrit building manuals, the Shilpa Shastras, were framed as dialogues between Vishwakarma and particular sons, the Acharya presented this book as a conversation between Vishwakarma and his descendants. In this retelling, a group of sons approaches their leader and ancestor, the Shilpacharya or "Preceptor of the Sculptors," to ask for guidance on how to worship and to live. The Shilpacharya meditates on Vishwakarma. Vishwakarma then manifests. After he is offered a seat and worshipped, he begins his teachings. He starts by tracing his own connection to his audience, recounting how the god Vishnu urged him to create offspring, and so, with the goddess Kriti, he had a son—the Shilpacharya. The Shilpacharya then had four sons, named Jay, May, Siddharth, and Aparajit (each of whom is connected to a particular Shilpa Shastra). In turn, those sons became the fathers of the gathered Shilpis.

"The right activity for you is creating new things and making drawings," Vishwakarma tells his descendants. "This will make you happy. You should construct different types of palatial buildings, make carvings, become skilled in assorted arts, and make many kinds of divine images. In this way, your fame will grow and you'll gain wealth." He goes on to instruct his descendants to pursue a curious mix of past and present projects of making, mentioning rock-cut caves in passing. "Use your intelligence to make different kinds of machines [*yantra*], invent technologies [*tantra*], construct palaces that will protect kings, build strong forts, learn to create caves, and design tools that are self-powered, machines that set ships moving on water, useful weapons for times of war, projectiles to destroy the forts of enemy armies . . ."[13]

Vishwakarma assures the group that though he also assumes the forms of other gods, his sons have a special right to worship him as Vishwakarma. From here the book takes off into moral injunctions for every stage of life, emphasizing purity, piety, and orthodoxy. After all, the carpenters' claim to Brahminhood emphasized "Sanskritization," or emulating a higher caste's values through strict injunctions about purity, daily rituals, controlling the senses, and the need for restrictions on women.[14] The book offers some general teachings; it advises, for example, compassion, always wishing others well, caring for other creatures, and following the stricture "Nonviolence is the supreme way of life" (*ahimsā paramo dharma*).[15] It includes practical advice, such as straining drinking water, not urinating in streams, and never joking around when sitting at the rim of a well. Prescribing appropriate conduct for women, it issues dire warnings about the dangers of independence and insists that women tirelessly serve others except when isolated during menstruation, that a wife cheerfully defer to her husband at all times, and that widows maintain silence and never again touch a man.

Oh dear! How did my foremothers deal with this? Were these prescriptions dutifully followed? Encountering these passages, I remembered my cousin Narmadaben observing, "Dada had all the rules for the caste written down. And then *our family only* broke most of them."

Above all, the book advised solidarity among caste members:

> Always support a poor person who belongs to your caste: employ him in work, help him in his bad days, and always think well of him from deep in your heart. If there is a poor person among your relations or in the community, do not charge interest on a loan. Live in the same locality as your caste brothers, for that locality is considered holy, like a place of pilgrimage. Never act in a way to harm your community brothers, but always think of respecting them.[16]

"There are three sorts of debt," Vishwakarma tells his sons, "debt to the gods, to the ancestors, and to other humans." He suggests ways that this burden of debt can be discharged: by listening to scriptures, through pious activities like going on pilgrimage to holy places and making offerings to ancestors (*pitri shrāddh*), and by repaying monetary loans. If at death such obligations were left unfulfilled, a person would be reborn and continue with the repayments.[17]

Building this temple, my great-grandfather Keshavji saw a way for himself and for community members to discharge their debt to gods and to ancestors. Vishwakarma, after all, was both a god and an ancestor.

✳

The Acharya recorded that when the manuscript was complete and Keshavji heard it, he was pleased. *Heard,* not read. I don't know if Keshavji was literate, or if his eyesight was dimmed with age, or if it was most appropriate that a religious book he had commissioned be recited aloud to him by the Brahmin compiler.

The temple structure was ready; the book was composed. The deities still needed to be installed. But in the winter of 1898, Keshavji fell ill on a visit to Bombay. When his three sons assembled around him, he asked them to complete the temple inauguration. He wanted three shrines: to Vishwakarma, to Lakshminarayan (a form of Vishnu with his wife Lakshmi beside him), and to Shiva as Kesheshwar Mahadev—"the Great God, Lord of Keshavji." He also asked his sons to arrange that the Acharya's book be published and distributed to all curious community members. Keshavji died on January 11, 1899, on a moonless *amās* day sacred to Vishwakarma.

Two years later, on January 16, 1901, a sacred eleventh day of the lunar fortnight, the three sons opened the temple, named Khīmjī Duvāro, "the Doors of Khimji." Located near a big stand of old trees at Bhorara, the temple compound included a space for pilgrims to stay. Community members assembled for a three-day celebration, and all were supplied with copies of the freshly published red book.

22. The Doors of Khimji temple, Bhorara, early twentieth century. Photographer unknown.

The book also contained a transcript of the stone inscription at the temple:

> In the just reign of the Ruler of Kutch State, King Khengarji,[18] in memory of Gujar Sutar Khimji Bhagat, son of Gangji Kanji, his own son Keshavji had this temple built.
>
> Though Keshavji passed away, his three sons Sutar Govindji, Devram, and Ramji installed the deities Lakshminarayan, Vishwakarma, and Kesheshwar Mahadev inside the temple in Samvat 1957, which is Shaka 1822, on the eleventh day of the dark half of Posh, on a Wednesday.
>
> Our guru Bavaji Vallabhdas took the permission of his own guru Atmaram to offer this Doors of Khimji temple to Shree Krishna.
>
> Samvat 1957, the eleventh day of the dark half of Posh, Wednesday.
>
> May there be prosperity, may there be good fortune, may auspiciousness prevail.

I noted how the temple was offered to Krishna by the guru whose face appeared amid the book's portraits of three generations of male ancestors. Could this partially explain why this Vishwakarma looks so much like a young Krishna, even as he holds the pose of the Murti in Cave 10?

In 1999, when my aunt Chandaphui accompanied me to Bhorara, the temple was still standing. Built in the regional architectural style of its era, it had a low roof of red tile. The exterior was decorated with fanciful, painted plaster figures: miniature cross-legged holy men with bare torsos at even intervals along the roof, a face peering from behind foliage just above the large arched doorway with turquoise doors.

Local men wrapped in rough shawls were sitting chatting under a stand of trees in front of the temple. They watched as I followed Chandaphui through a smaller door set into the larger one. In the outer hall were small marble Murtis of Keshavji and his father Khimji, about a foot and a half tall and familiar to me, as Ba had always kept steel-framed photographs of these statues—modeled from the photograph of their singing group—in her altar. Within one of the three niches for worship was a carved teak altar containing a white marble Vishwakarma, perhaps two or three feet tall. The day we visited, this Vishwakarma had been dressed in red, with a crown and tinsel garlands. With wide painted eyes, his expression seemed amused and alert, and I recognized him as the model for the young Vishwakarma image in Dada's red book though I didn't yet know about the earlier model in Ellora. It was hard to discern, but he seemed to hold something in his hands—could it be a footrule and cord?

23. Vishwakarma shrine in the Doors of Khimji temple, Bhorara 1999. Photograph by Kirin Narayan.

Those were still the days of 35-millimeter film, and it was getting to be dusk. I took a few photographs, thinking that someday I'd return and pay closer attention. But on January 26, 2001, immediately after the Gujar Suthar community of Kutch had celebrated the temple's centenary, a major earthquake devastated Gujarat. The epicenter was in nearby Bhuj, and with a magnitude of 7.7 on the Richter scale, the earthquake leveled buildings as far away as Ahmedabad. In Kutch, tens of thousands of people were killed, more were injured, and scores of buildings came down. Keshavji's temple was among those that crumbled.

Some years later, the Kutchi Gujar Suthar community replaced the ruined structure with a contemporary-style marble temple with high peaks. On our 2018 trip to Kutch with Bhai, we stopped in at Bhorara. While the new temple bears no outward resemblance to the earlier one, we found that it houses all the deities rescued from the rubble. Marble Vishwakarma's clean-shaven face is now painted white, with dimples, and he looks even more like a boyish Krishna. In the new courtyard, Khimji Bhagat and Keshavji, also painted a startling blue-tinged white, sit side by side, still holding their musical instruments.

* 7 *

The Pride of the Vishwakarma Lineage

In 1985, Pa wrote that he was collecting ideas for colorful short stories I might write, all quite unrelated to my dissertation research. BUT *your trilogy or quatrology will be Ramji and his forefathers and his sons and grandsons . . . so be it,* he wrote.

So be it! This sounds like the Sanskrit blessing *Tathāstu*—"may it be so"—as Pa imagined these books coming into material form.

If Pa had said this in person, I would immediately have amended his vision by insisting on including daughters, but since this was a letter, he could continue undisturbed. I wish I had sometime asked Pa: why three or even four volumes? Was each to record the possibilities opening to a different generation, with Ramji Seth's success the fulcrum of social mobility? Would this be a story of a fortune—unimaginable in one generation, amassed in the next, squandered in the third, recounted with wonder by a fourth?

Through his life, my grandfather went by various names. Leaving the village, as his father's son, he was Ramji Keshavji. When he earned his first title as master craftsman, heading work teams, he became Ramji Mistri. Becoming a contractor who oversaw big projects, gathering wealth and property, he was Ramji Seth, a man of substance, or simply Sethji. Portraits of him looked out from the walls of various rooms in the Ramji Mistri Bungalow in Nasik, built in the 1920s, and in his older son's apartment in Bombay. He always wore a maroon turban that seemed to press down the tops of his large ears—ears that Pa said were multiply pierced, as was the custom for Kutchi men of his time. In different portraits, the mustache obscuring the corners of his mouth turned from black to gray.

He had died the year I was born. I never met him, and yet through my childhood, he was recollected so often that it seemed he might still come downstairs from the tower room he had built for himself in the bungalow's northeast corner. People shared stray memories. I knew of the Vicks balm he smeared under his nostrils before sleep, his pleasure in the bland softness of green squash, his habit of keeping fingers circling along beads, praying for family members, even while calling out financial queries to his "Mehtaji" accountant who hovered nearby. But if anyone really got talking about Dada, the stories invariably turned to his ability to make money—and to give it away. Was his wealth thanks to the blessing of his saintly forebears (my grandmother Ba's theory)? Or to Ba's luck-granting presence at his side (again her theory)? Or was this the lucky historical conjuncture of a smart and skilled village man meeting the energies of an expanding colonial port city?

Pa went on to offer me tidbits for what that day he was calling *The Ramji Saga*, and the names of relatives who might help with stories: *By the way Ramji came to Bombay 100 years ago! 1885 and he was about 30? First he stayed in Kamatipura, which is now the Red Light district, in the Sutar Chawl Galli [Carpenters' Residential Lane] near Mumbadevi [city Goddess temple]* (April 6, 1985).

More often, Ramji was said to have been still in his teens when he followed his two older brothers to the city. At first, he worked in a carpentry workshop, planing wood beside his brother Devram. Soon the brothers branched into new arenas. The eldest, Govindji, began crafting, assembling, and transporting deep wooden arenas for "Well of Death" performances, structures within which he and his sons zoomed round and round on motorcycles at fairs. Pa suggested that I meet *one Ratilal, the Circus branch of the family, who can fill in lots of details of motorcycle jumps, ring of fire, the "death-well" performances, etc.* (April 6, 1985). The middle brother, Devram, pursued municipal building contracts, then moved on to mechanized wooden merry-go-rounds that could be packed up and taken wherever there was to be a big gathering: outside a movie theater like the Aurora Cinema, or at a fair. Ramji chose a more staid path. He followed Devram, taking on municipal contracts for the city docks, and then struck out on his own. He was the contractor who laid the cast-iron pipes that after 1892 would bring drinking water to the city from the Tansa dam. This was when he bought his first vehicle, a two-horse Victoria carriage.

Though Ramji moved from working by hand to overseeing others' work, he prided himself on his carpentry skills. A few objects that he crafted still survive: a plain box with a hinged lid, a stationery sorter, a teak trunk. My mother described how, in his nineties, he had berated a hired carpenter at work on a project in the Ramji Mistri Bungalow for ignoring the direction of the wood grain. "What are you, a barber?" he had mocked. Taking the wood plane in his large, gnarled hands, he made a perfect sweep of shavings.

Ma also told a story she had overheard when her father-in-law was talking with a manager from one of Bombay's textile mills. For the first of the mill's buildings, Ramji Seth had been a carpenter's apprentice. When its second building was planned, he subcontracted labor for the doors and windows. For the third building, he was awarded the entire building contract.

By the early twentieth century, Ramji Seth was buying real estate. As he gained more wealth, he became an ever more generous benefactor. My aunt Chandaphui explained, "He acknowledged his wealth was God-given, and he kept giving to others." He funded meals for the poor and in leper colonies, and he distributed hundreds of brass vessels at the time of his birthday on Kali Chaudas, just before the Divali New Year. In memory of his older brother Devram, he installed a drinking water tap in a Bombay public park. In addition, he was a patron for assorted community and religious projects.

The Bhorara temple had been inaugurated in 1901. In 1920, Ramji Seth joined his brothers in presenting a dome to a larger Vishwakarma temple in the industrial city of Rajkot. Finding our way through the narrow streets of the Rajkot old city to this temple in 2018, we read the Gujarati inscription on a marble plaque, "This big dome is constructed and offered with boundless devotional feeling to Lord Vishwakarma by Govindji, Devram, and Ramji, the sons of Sutar Bhagat Keshavji Khimji of Bhorara, Kutch." In 1926, he turned his charitable hand to Bhorara again, installing a grander arched gateway to the temple, along with a resthouse for pilgrims. In 1932, he funded the building of the Shree Kutchi Gurjar Sutar Ramji Keshavji School for Children's Education, an institution that would educate both boys and girls, located next to the Vishwakarma temple in Ramaswami Gadi Khata, the area of Karachi where the community lived. A newspaper report on the school's inauguration, headlined "The Awakening of the Sutar Community," described a big gathering with speeches; Ramji Seth was presented with a letter of appreciation printed on silk and offered on a silver tray, and strands of jasmine were distributed to all as little girls sang.[1]

Along with sponsoring these Vishwakarma-related undertakings, Ramji Seth was celebrated for supporting the Swami Narayan sect in various ways. He provided a well, a dormitory for monks, a clock tower, and more. He had become a disciple of a Swami Narayan guru, Shastriji Maharaj, through the influence of a wife before Ba, though no one was sure which one.

Amid the outward success and largesse, Ramji Seth's personal life was marked by tragedy. His first marriage brought a son and a daughter, and then his wife died. His second marriage brought another son, and again, his wife died. His third wife had no children and perished in a tragic fire, leaving him heartbroken and unwell. Then his guru Shastriji Maharaj told him to go northeast and start a new life. He was about sixty years old when he found land to Bombay's northeast, in Nasik, and once more he began looking for a wife.

There came the pretty, haughty Kathiawari Gujar Suthar village girl, decades younger than him—my grandmother Ba. "After three wives died, I'm here to live!" relatives later recalled her saying. His horoscope might show that the placement of his Mars was not propitious for spouses, but Ba claimed that her Mars was *even more powerful* than his! What's more, lines on her soles could be read as an auspicious lotus, and so *her* presence would bring *him* money! He was apparently much amused by her forceful spirit and addressed her as "Mad Girl" (*Gāṇḍi*). After a baby died at birth, she bore six children, with my father the eldest.

✳

"The Pride of the Vishwakarma Lineage" is Ramji Seth's title in a sheaf of identical colored posters, lightly nibbled by silverfish, that once emerged from Ba's cupboard.[2] My guess is that these posters, celebrating "Sheth Ramji Keshavji Khimji Bhagat (Bhorarawala), residing in Bombay and Nasik," are from the 1930s. Why so many copies? Were these the leftovers after others had been given away? Were they intended to be presented along with his charitable contributions, so he could preside over the spaces he brought into being? I wish I'd asked more when I took away one poster to frame.

Ba's steel cupboard also contained a stack of old photographs mounted on disintegrated cardboard. These included images of some of the grandest Victorian mansions Ramji Seth had built or bought, and also the original black-and-white portrait on which the colored poster is based. On one side of the cardboard, instructions for adding color are penciled in in longhand: "Med. Brown eye, maroon red turban, D. brown coat, white shirt, white pants, gold ring, grey mustache." I have drawn on this forceful photograph to start part II of this book.

Ramji Seth seems about to stand up and peer sternly closer. His broad hands are planted on the armrests of a wooden chair with parts carved like heavy twisted cord. Three tomes are stacked on the table beside him. Only the middle book carries a visible title: *The Standard Illustrated Encyclopedia and World Atlas* (published in London in 1932). When Ken and I later came across other portraits of men of substance from artisan communities, they were always posed beside caste-related books with titles like *Vishwakarma*, *Vishwakarma Purana*, or *Rajvallabh* (a building manual). With this English-language encyclopedia and atlas, Ramji Seth seems to assert his claim to cosmopolitan knowledge. Certainly, that's what his class ascent and emphasis on education made possible for his descendants.

For Pa, educated in an English-medium Parsi school, the village was already receding: a site for occasional pilgrimages to the family temple and nearby clan deities. More education brought more migration, a sense of displacement, and uncertain allegiances. In the early 1980s, Pa wrote that though his parents had settled in Nasik, he himself felt no attachment to this relatively recent family home: *I do not have roots in Nasik. I never had. Parsi School [Nasik] till 1944, Elphinstone College [Bombay] till '47. US till '51. '51–'58 Nasik-Poona-Bombay, '59 till today Bombay. The old thing is not there. It's finished and I'm not sorry. . . . Nasik belongs to Ba and Sethji* (April 2, 1983).

It was with an outsider's eye that Pa mused on the village left behind. In college, I'd written to Pa about the anthropology seminar that introduced Victor Turner's celebration of "communitas," the intoxicating fellow-feeling that can melt away social divisions and hierarchies.[3] Writing back, Pa performed an anthropological persona to discourse on the communitas around him. His letter began by describing the Varkari pilgrims of many caste backgrounds who walked barefoot together through Nasik on their annual visit to their deity, singing with drums and cymbals. He ended with the modern-day communitas in Bombay of the early 1980s: the Sunday feature film on the single Doordarshan channel, drawing together neighbors of all backgrounds, ages, and opinions around his new television.

In the course of this extended riff, Pa touched on how most people in a city like Bombay had migrated from some other "native place" and on our own true village roots: *We are from Kutch, even if I was born in Nasik; you are a Kutchi, even if you were born in Bombay and mother in Milwaukee* [actually Minneapolis] *or some such place. So basically we all have rural bias and we are alienated in any urban situation. Rural social intercourse comprised of caste-community-religious activities and restricted to say a street, a block, or an area of the village and many a time around the shrine of the village deity or a riverbank or a water body like a lake. The bond here was communal partaking of prasad, tirtha, dancing, etc. and for those moments at least the differences of caste and wealth were forgotten.*

As a counterpoint to such communal belonging, Pa also pointed to exclusions: *To be not invited by the Panchayat* [community leaders] *or barred in joining any of these celebrations was castigation, and people in the old days committed suicide if such a thing happened to the family and it was this fear that enforced the so-called moral code* (April 20, 1980).

He made no mention of how this might have mattered to our family. When relatives sometimes let slip how my grandfather had for a time been an outcaste, nobody dwelled on the circumstances; rather, they jumped directly to the steep fine he had paid for reinclusion: "Five thousand rupees in those times!" Now, when I look at my framed print of Ramji Seth, "Pride of the Vishwakarma Lineage," I see an emphatic countermove, a retort to those who had outcasted him: not only did he belong, but his achievements brought them luster.

✳

My mother visited Ramji Seth's deathbed for a final farewell in early 1959. He was in his nineties, with a cancerous tumor in his throat. He had by then accepted her, the foreign daughter-in-law who provided him with his first grandsons. When the tumor festered, she was not squeamish about changing bandages. As she tended him, he called out to her as "Mother."

Morphine had left him unable to speak, but he gripped her hands and gazed deeply into her face. She said that he seemed to be imploring: he wanted a new form.

She too had wordlessly responded: yes, she could offer him a new form.

And she had a condition: she wanted a girl.

Ramji Seth died soon after, and the family became absorbed in the long ceremonies that transform a soul into an ancestor. After that mourning period, Ma said, I was conceived. I was the first baby born into the extended family after he died, and for over a year I was bald, just as he had been in extreme old age, though all my siblings had been born with hair. Through my childhood, I was always hearing how much I resembled my grandfather. Ba would point to *his* eyes, *his* ears, *his* chin—on *my* face. (And yes, some relatives clearly thought it hilarious to imagine that the patriarch who took such pride in living to see grandsons, might come back . . . *as a girl!*)

As I was writing about spiritual quests framing my childhood in *My Family and Other Saints,* Ma often sent me extensive written comments—so many, in fact, that at one point I thought of alternating my chapters with her commentaries. In one undated email, she shared her sense of offering a bridge between Ramji Seth and me.

I believe that qualities, capacities, inclinations extend past death to be passed on, ALONG *with the quirks these have acquired from the departing individual,* Ma wrote. *I felt that I was offering a new physical "home" for the wonderful expansive adventurous intensities I had come to respect in Sethji. He was, incidentally, also a great storyteller with a sense of mischief and irony and a great booming laugh that had been worn into a cackle by age and use.* She'd ended the note observing that like many men of his Victorian generation, he'd been a chauvinist; asserting her staunch feminist will, she'd inwardly insisted she would cultivate her father-in-law's best qualities in a *daughter.*

I wonder now if this repeated reference to a person set in times spilling over the horizon of my own conscious life sparked my interest in family history. Could it have been my bewildered curiosity that inspired others to remember my grandfather's ways for me? Or were others mesmerized by my role as diligent scribe? For ever since learning to write, I had sensed that stories told by and about my family were just as interesting as the adventures of the brave fairies and princesses who usually filled my pages. My rapt attention made some relatives expansive, and as I scribbled, they shared family stories, regional histories, folktales, home remedies, even vulgar proverbs . . . (*Arre Baba, she is writing it!*) Others, like my outspoken cousin Narmadaben, were less than amused. Once, when I telephoned her to check on a detail of family history, she had shrewdly responded, "If I tell you, you will only go and write it!" Another time, she followed up a heartbreaking disclosure with a threat: "If you go and write this, I will kill you *without a knife!*"

My undated notes in a repurposed red 1975 account book record reminiscences from Chandaphui in the company of Narmadaben, her niece but agemate. They discussed Ramji Seth's quirks—his Wolseley car and Sinhalese driver William, his habitual attire of a waistcoat with white pants, the rare flowering trees he planted in the Nasik garden, his teasing jokes, and his love of songs, every kind of song, even wedding songs. They remembered how he had once asked the young Narmadaben to sing for him, and as the other kids stifled their giggles, her own laughter exploded and she ran to Ba's room, where she rolled around laughing on the floor.

Chandaphui and Narmadaben emphasized how concerned Ramji Seth was for daughters of the family, fearing they would have difficult nonstandard lives and that, though he might try, he couldn't fully protect them with his wealth. "He went and performed prayers for girls of the family, near Bhavnagar," read my notes. Chandaphui recalled how, on his deathbed, he was worried about her relationship with her in-laws, jeopardized by my parents' marriage. "What if they don't call you back?" he had fretted. As she said, "Even in his last hours he was thinking of the girls."

Whenever Chandaphui and I set off on an adventure, whether by bus, train, or car, she filled the time by sharing family stories. As the miles fell away, she moved toward stories that were half-forgotten and rarely mentioned. It was from her that I learned that, though we all knew of Ramji Seth's sons from his earlier marriages, there had been a daughter too. Sometimes Chandaphui couldn't remember her half-sister's name; sometimes she spoke of this older half-sister as Lakshmibai.

Lakshmibai had lost her mother when she was very small. She had been married away young, as was the custom, then was calamitously "sent back" by her in-laws. Just why, no one remembered. No one remembered, either, whether she was close to her brother, Shivjibhai, a talented painter who fell in with the Bombay underworld. (A short *Times of India* entry from 1916 describes him as "an indiscreet youth," aged twenty, drawn into questionable business deals that his father refused to back, and reports that he stubbornly borrowed—and lost—10,000 rupees in his father's name.[4])

My grandfather had built himself an apartment in Byculla, at that time a fine suburb of Bombay. Lakshmibai came to live in the apartment's tower room.

"And then what happened?" I asked Chandaphui.

"Then she died," said Chandaphui. "What else?"

By the time Ba entered the picture, Lakshmibai—who would probably have been older that Ba—was no longer alive. No family photographs of her existed. The detail of the tower room haunted me—was this a case of my family's own despairing woman with a nonstandard life, tucked away in an attic?

Chandaphui's voice grew indignant as she remembered her elderly father growing even older. Bitterly telling me how for decades she was shamed by her mother-in-law for not producing a child, she spoke of her father pressing her to come home for long visits and medical treatments. In her bed in Ahmedabad, she brought out the last letter he had ever written to her in a dashed Gujarati script, then seemed to change her mind about rereading it in my company. From her evident emotion as she slipped the letter back into her satchel of photographs, I sensed how she had felt her father's care like the canopy of a large, shade-granting tree. Decades later, she still could feel bereft to have lost his shelter.

During her father's funeral ceremonies, as the Garuda Purana was being recited, Chandaphui said she had momentarily fallen asleep and seen him being escorted out of the house by a group of Swami Narayan sadhus. She was assured by this vision that he had gone onward spiritually protected, surrounded by blessings.

Chandaphui herself never spoke of the possibility of his reincarnating close by. But through the years, I've been alert to friends from different regions of India telling me about a departed person "coming back" to the same family. Premonitions and dreams, physical resemblances, and uncannily similar behavior have served as proof of this return. For example, a Bengali friend in graduate school had as a toddler peremptorily addressed his grandmother as "wife," and the inappropriate use of this kinship term was taken as indisputable evidence that he was none other than his grandfather in a new form. But how, I wondered, was this returning of ancestors supposed to work?

✳

The relationship with ancestors, I knew from watching my grandmother Ba, is cultivated through ritual offerings that usually involve feeding other beings, whether humans, especially Brahmins, or other creatures, with a focus on crows and cows. Such ancestral remembrances are concentrated in the dark fortnight of the lunar month Bhadrapad, culminating in the new moon known as Mahalaya (September/October), and ancestors may be remembered every new moon, a day also sacred to Vishwakarma, as I will later explain.[5] Pilgrimage sites beside rivers and other bodies of water are especially effective sites for ancestral rituals. Ellora ("Elapura") is named in the Matsya Purana—composed before the caves were carved—as an appropriate place to perform ceremonies for the souls of departed relatives.[6]

Looking through a book on Gujarati folklore from Ramji Seth's times for any references to Vishwakarma, I unexpectedly encountered a cache of materials about family bonds across lifetimes. This book had been assembled through correspondence with schoolteachers across Gujarat in the first decade of the twentieth century.[7] Recurring themes emerge in these schoolteachers' remarks on the role of *pitriyas,* or ancestors, in the lives of descendants. The schoolmaster of Dhank explicates the movement between lives through the concept of *vāsanā,* mental impressions left by past actions, concluding that, "if at the moment of death, a man's mind is fixed on the strong attachment he feels for his children, he is born as a descendant of his offspring." The schoolmaster of Kotda Sangani asserts that *pitriyas* who died with unfulfilled desires "reappear as descendants of their children to have these desires satisfied." The schoolmaster of Dadvi shifts focus from desires to debts: "persons dying with debts unpaid with the consciousness that they must be paid, are reborn in this world for the discharge of obligations." The schoolmaster of Charadia elaborates that "feelings, habits and ideas of previous births" stand behind family groups, binding family members to each other as "debtors and creditors" and causing them to be reborn "again in the same family for the proper discharge of debts."

Here, then, are explications of reincarnation within a family as part of a cross-generational system of debts. Yet theories of the afterlife are nebulous, as Pa reminded me in a letter describing a gathering that brought together members of the Dahisaria clan and other relatives at the Ramji Mistri Bungalow. This was a weeklong recitation of the Bhagavat Purana by a professional storyteller, organized by his nephews to bring peace to the souls of his father and younger brother.

I wonder where their Souls are! Do they want such a Puja? What in case they are already incarnate—reborn? Are they in some sort of Bardo? ... I asked Ba and she said, "Don't eat my head, THIS *to be done and* WE *are* DOING IT. *If they are reborn they will be happier than ever before, etc."* (December 4, 1982)

I've studied the photograph of my musical village forefathers uncountable times since I was a child. A print that my sister Maya made for me has been framed in my study for years. Then too, a photograph of a painted portrait of Khimji Bhagat, extracted from this group and long kept in worship by the family, adorned the US edition of *My Family and Other Saints*. While drafting this chapter, I looked more closely at the fading print in my study

24. The girl in the shadows, Bhorara, late nineteenth century. Photographer unknown.

and saw a figure I hadn't noticed before. I don't have a copy of the original photograph, so I asked my brother Devendra to send a clearer image, focusing on the upper left corner.

Behind the seated group, a girl with a covered head stands in the shadows, just inside the open door. She holds the doorframe, bracelet glinting above the metal lock, a small child in white looking up toward her. At first I thought a second woman, perhaps an invalid, was stretched out on the steps, but looking more closely, this is a pile of tarpaulin.

Who is this girl? My grandfather's sister? His first wife? A cousin? A sister-in-law? And who is the child? We were researching Vishwakarma in Cave 10, and yet hidden family stories began emerging around the edges of the research. Just as this girl remains partly obscured, identity forgotten, many of these stories can't be drawn fully into the light. But becoming aware of the stories' presence, shrouded in silence, alerted me to how the outward-facing stories of sunny pride and success I'd grown up with might also hold shadowed interiors.

✳ 8 ✳

Open Sesame!

"My first visit to Ellora was in the year 1938, in January, when I was around eleven years old. I didn't know anything about the caves or what they were. But after seeing them"—Bhai swept out a hand, marking a wide expanse— "my imagination was *totally* transformed. I hadn't known that such beautiful things could be made! I didn't know anything about craftsmanship. Still, at that time, on its own, an interest grew in me."

Bhai's hands gestured upward and outward, like a tree growing from a seed as he continued. "I wanted to see more things like this: to look, look, and look. And then I found books and studied them. Many people said to me, 'What kind of conversations can you have with these lifeless sculptures?' But the sculptures were showing me *their* imagination." Bhai extended his right hand forward, planting an authoritative staff. "They had some sort of freshness and originality that we're not familiar with these days, and we don't often have the chance to see."

Bhai was the only Dahisaria elder I knew who remembered having offered worship in Cave 10. After many conversations across a year, we were videotaping him. He usually chatted with us in English, but this time, for a more formal record, he spoke Gujarati as his younger son helped steer questions and our research assistant balanced a video camera. Bhai leaned back into one of the deep, oversize armchairs of our rented apartment, thoroughly relaxed before the lens. "At this age I am not getting any handsomer," Bhai liked to say. Yet immaculately turned out in white khadi and aglow with enthusiasm, he was resplendent.

On this October afternoon, we had pulled back the apartment curtains for more light. Pigeons nesting atop the building's air conditioners and ledges wheeled about, cooing against the gray sky. Traffic beeping-honking-tooting-tinkling rose in the usual cacophony from the street below. Across the street, dusty trees rose between the tiled roofs and terraces of upscale villas, and then the trees disappeared entirely among buildings of assorted heights and dimensions extending across the smog-smudged horizon. This backdrop for Bhai's memories made Ellora seem not just distant but an altogether different world.

Bhai explained how the 1938 trip to Ellora came about.

"You see, at that time, the railways used to sell zonal tickets. They marked certain zones, and if you bought a ticket you could travel ten to twelve days within that zone. My uncle thought, 'Now that there are these new zonal tickets, let's organize a tour!' His friends were visiting him from Karachi, and they were also interested."

Bhai had yearned to go along. Though he was on vacation, his uncle said there was no room in the traveling group. But his aunt intervened. She persuaded her husband to include the boy. She wasn't planning to go herself, but she privately instructed Bhai on the protocol for greeting Vishwakarma at Cave 10 (*dasvā* number *guphā*).

The group set out by train to Jalgaon, rested at a ginning factory that belonged to fellow Kutchis, and then took a bus to Ajanta. Bhai was wonderstruck by the thirty Ajanta Buddhist caves. He listened, agog, as a guide from the Nizam of Hyderabad's archaeology department wept with emotion when describing the difficulties of preserving the ancient frescoes from bats, animals, and visitors tempted to sign their names. Bhai had wandered off to explore the ravine below the caves, but when local people shouted out warnings about tigers, he ran headlong back to the adults: "*Chooooo . . . !*"

From Ajanta, the group traveled southwest by bus along the road to Ellora, a few hours away. "My aunt had told me: 'Go to Cave 10, the cave of our Vishwakarma.' She also reminded me, 'If you get a chance, mark the forehead of the Murti in the cave.'"

A mark made on another's forehead (*chāndlo*, *tilak*, or *ṭīkā*) is a way to honor and to bless. People most often do this by extending the right hand with the thumb, ring finger, or index finger dipped in red *kumkum* powder. In a temple, a priest would take over such an intimate aspect of worship. But when Suthars arrived at Cave 10, they approached the Murti without any priestly intermediary.

"When I tried to do this worship, the guard wouldn't allow me at first," Bhai remembered. "'Look, if I could only do a little . . . ,' I said. I slipped a rupee into the guard's hand, and he was happy. I got it from the adults—I didn't have a single rupee or a single paisa. Then I made the mark and within seconds, the guard wiped it away.

"Everyone said that this is Vishwakarma in the cave. I wasn't sharp enough to think it through. We went mostly to look around, not to study the cave. In Verul village there is the [Vishwa] Kund and the Shiva temple: we went and saw all that. We offered worship to Vishwakarma and to Shiva.

"At that time, I didn't know anything about Vishwakarma—who is Vishwakarma, what is Vishwakarma. All I knew is that Vishwakarma is our grandfather, and that we should visit him and worship him. Even after that first visit, I couldn't make sense of what was distinctive about the cave. We went to see Vishwakarma; we said, 'This is Vishwakarma'; and we came out."

✳

Bhai was the first person to tell us about this custom of marking Vishwakarma's forehead when visiting the cave. Many months later, as we were sleuthing about in the British Library collections, we came across a startling illustration that corroborated his description. Among the rare books we had requested from the stacks was a treatise on building composed in Sanskrit by Sutradhar Mandana in the fifteenth century and translated into Gujarati in 1878.[1] When we opened the fragile yellowed text in the bright reading room, our whispered exclamations of surprise drew annoyed looks from the woman sitting opposite us with her own piles of books.

The frontispiece inviting a reader into the book resembles a carved wooden doorway.[2] Elephant-headed Ganesh, Remover of Obstacles, presides in the upper panel, attended by his two wives and his mouse, as the sun and moon appear simultaneously behind him. Just below, as though viewed through an arched doorframe, a seated figure labeled "Vishwakarma" faces a smaller standing figure labeled "Sutradhar." Vishwakarma's hands are arranged in the teaching pose, right thumb and forefinger holding the little finger of the left hand beside his chest. Holding a small bowl in his left hand, the Sutradhar lifts his right thumb toward Vishwakarma, as though reaching to mark the deity's forehead.

With black hair visible under a closely fitted cap, this clean-shaven Vishwakarma wears no upper garment; his folded dhoti is tucked at his waist, falling to his calves. He is splendidly adorned with earrings, necklaces, armlets, and bracelets, and his forehead displays a vertical two-line mark associated with the worship of Vishnu. The smaller Sutradhar stands barefoot before Vishwakarma, reaching only to his shoulder, much as a worshipper in Cave 10 is dwarfed beside the Murti. This Sutradhar has a spectacular black mustache, and his black hair is visible under his ornately twisted turban. He wears a pleated dhoti of the same patterned cloth as Vishwakarma's, as though emphasizing their kinship. His upper body is partly draped in striped cloth, and he sports the jewelry once customary for men of Western India: earrings, necklace with a pendant, armlets, bracelets, and even baubles dangling from his turban.

25. Vishwakarma Honored by Sutradhar, woodblock print in building manual, Ahmedabad, 1878. British Library 14053 cc. 50.

Directly above Vishwakarma's name hangs a glass oil lamp, as though emphasizing the light conveyed by his presence. Two other round hanging objects appear to be decorative globes appropriate to a royal chamber.[3] While this evocation of regal grandeur bypassed the setting of a cave, Vishwakarma's pose and the Sutradhar's action point toward Cave 10.

We could find no other references to Ellora in this book, but another discovery in the British Library stacks helped us understand why the image evoked Cave 10. This was a compendium of "Vishwakarma knowledge" composed by K. B. Gajjar, his surname indicating that the author was a Suthar.[4] While missing its original cover and full publishing information, the book's preface revealed it had been published in Ahmedabad in 1898. The book offers a Gujarati compendium of lists of Shilpa Shastras, or treatises on building; retellings of mythological stories; and Sanskrit mantras associated with Vishwakarma. One section is devoted to a description of Ellora (*Ilorgaṛh*).

According to Gajjar, in the great cycles of time, as this final, degenerate Kali Yuga began, Vishwakarma descended from heaven and made Sutradhars from his own body. He taught them all essential knowledge of making and, "in accordance with the times, they first made Ilorgaṛh."[5] The caves, Gajjar writes, were "made according to the Shilpa Shastras, by hand, using tools, and beautified by Sutradhars and others." He marvels at the terraces, domes, pillars, doors, latticework, flat floors, and creatures carved so realistically that they seem to be speaking to the viewer.

After celebrating the Kailash complex (Cave 16) in some detail, Gajjar refers in passing to the deities giving audience in the other caves, and mentions the sages and holy men in residence. Arriving at Cave 10, Gajjar describes the shrine of "Vishwakarma Sutradhar, the Artisans' Guru," enumerating the dimensions of the hall, the carved roof with seventy beams, and the lines of pillars. Above the pillars, he writes, are niches holding 360 Sutradhars, all of them painted, and in their midst an image of Vishwakarma.[6]

For Suthar pilgrims, Vishwakarma as Sutradhar was sitting in state amid scores of Sutradhars gathered within the ancestral temple. Holding the teaching pose, he acted as the Artisans' Guru, communicating the principles of making to his descendants, the pilgrims' forefathers. No wonder the frontispiece of a building treatise would draw on this scene of transmission.

✳

After his first transformative visit, Bhai next returned to Ellora in 1949. He was then a young man of twenty-three, and a construction project had brought him to Jalgaon, a few hours from the caves. By this point he was known by a unique nom de plume, "Kapred," comprising the initial syllables of his personal name, father's name, and clan name (*Kantilal Premji Dahisaria*). After publishing a Gujarati poem in his school magazine as "Kapred Kumar" as a teenager, Bhai had formally changed his name from Kantilal. Among his relatives, though, he remained known by existing nicknames: "Babu" (a match to his paternal cousin, nicknamed "Gabu") and "Bhai," because he was wedged between this same older cousin, also known as "Big Brother" (Mota Bhai), and his own "Little Brother" (Nana Bhai).

On this second trip to Ellora, Bhai was already wearing handspun khadi attire. He had come face-to-face with Mahatma Gandhi at a prayer meeting in Bombay in the 1930s—as he liked to say, pointing right forefinger and middle finger to his face, "I have seen him with *these* eyes!" In 1942, when Gandhi gave his "Quit India" speech and was imprisoned by the British government, Bhai and a group of Bombay student friends joined the widespread protests. Until then, the teenage boys hadn't followed Gandhi in wearing khadi, but now they together vowed to do so. Bhai had kept his word; even as we recorded him, some seven decades later, he was dressed head to toe in textured cotton.

On the way to Ellora, stopping at Ajanta, Bhai was relieved to see more guards on duty ensuring that paintings were not defaced. He started to show other family members around, but a picnic proved more enticing: "after seeing two, three caves they sat down. All they were interested in was the food, nothing else!"

Reaching Cave 10 at Ellora, he pondered the Murti afresh.

"That second time I went, I looked more closely, and I saw that here Vishwakarma doesn't have a beard, he doesn't have long hair. Why was this? Someone said, 'This is a Murti of Buddha.' I was a little confused: is he Buddha or Vishwakarma? But I couldn't find a certain answer."

In 1965, a different construction project brought Bhai to Aurangabad, the city nearest to Ellora, and he made a point of often visiting the caves. By then, a whole industry had emerged around this archaeological site: in addition to hiring guides, one could buy guidebooks, postcards, peanuts, snacks, and samples of various semiprecious rocks from the mountainside and surrounding area. For Bhai, during this time, "A new interest was awakened: to collect rocks."

Bhai had always loved gathering treasures: stamps, coins, inspiring clippings, books. With rocks, he was drawn to patterns that suggested images, for example, the trunk of Ganesh or a woman with a lowered veil. He cherished fossils with their impressions of previous life-forms. From that trip onward, whenever Bhai visited quarries and construction sites, he asked workers to save unusual rocks for him. And as he learned about the qualities of different sorts of rock, he pondered just how the caves had been sculpted within the basalt mountain. In his building experience, when a basalt boulder had to be removed from a construction site, people usually made holes with crowbars, plugged in dynamite, then blew the rock apart. But that wouldn't work for caves: "For making such wonderful things, you can't blast the rock and destroy it!"

How then did they proceed?

Bhai imagined: "Those craftsmen must have used such sharp instruments. Maybe cutters, maybe large chisels along with hammers; maybe cutting chisels. What were these instruments? They would have needed very strong instruments so they could carve and carve and carve. If the rock breaks while carving, you can't do anything. It's not as though if something breaks off you can replace it and put it together again!"

Beyond reimagining the challenges of making art through subtraction, Bhai also speculated about aspects of designing into rock. "Were they first sketching something and then cutting? Or did they imagine this in their minds and start to cut? Nowadays, you mostly draw first and then carve, but this stone is such that even if you first draw on it, there's still the question of just how you'd carve."

Bhai shared other questions that he'd puzzled over across the years. How had teams of craftsmen coordinated their activities as they moved inward through the rock, then downward, making different levels? What had happened to all those thousands of kilos of rock that were extracted from the cave courtyards and interiors yet are nowhere visible on the site today? Had some been transported elsewhere for other constructions?

"I feel like they were such *great* craftsmen," Bhai said about those distant artisans working at Ellora. "Yet now we boast of our skills!"

✳

The Ellora caves are lodged amid vast horizontal layers of dark, gray flood basalt from a volcanic cataclysm sixty-six million years ago that was possibly among the planetary events leading to the extinction of dinosaurs.[7] Stretching over hundreds of thousands of square miles in the Deccan region of central and southern India and more than a mile deep, these layers of flood basalt slowly eroded into the steplike hills whose striking shape is behind the name of India's Western Ghats (steps) and of the geologic region, the "Deccan Traps" (from the Swedish *trappa*, for "staircase"). A fascinating study of how unfinished rock-cut monuments across India reveal the processes undertaken by stone artisans suggests that the basalt of the Deccan Traps is comparatively easier to carve than other igneous stone (like granite), offering an appealing material for rock-cut excavations.[8]

Artisans had been working in basalt for centuries, fashioning structures of many kinds in ancient Egypt, in the empires of the Persians, Greeks, and Romans, and in India. By the time work on Cave 10 began, Indian "stone-carpenters" had for almost nine hundred years been excavating and sculpting Buddhist shrines (*chaitya*) and monastic residential caves (*vihāra*) in what is today identified as Bihar and Orissa in the east, and Gujarat and Maharashtra in the west.[9] Arriving at Ellora, artisans were already familiar with the properties of basalt and had worked out the tools and technology needed to skillfully shape it.

From at least the sixth century onward, stone-carpenters gathered on the Charanadri mountain of the Sahyadri range overlooking the village of Verul. With the steady clink of many hundreds of craftsmen's chisels, close to a hundred caves were excavated in the two thick basalt flows that compose the face of the mountain. The thirty-four numbered caves in the World Heritage site at Ellora sit in the lower of the two basalt layers.[10] Working into the hillside scarp of layered basalt meant that the artisans needed to remain alert to fissures, splits, faults, and fracture patterns in the stone; its hydrology and degree of permeability; and its susceptibility to weathering. As workmen discovered weaknesses in the rock, they needed to adjust the vertical and horizontal placement of caves, and even to abandon some aspects of planned projects.[11] While the main activity went on from the sixth to tenth centuries, smaller caves continued to be excavated on the mountain for a few hundred more years. The mountain's name, Charanadri, linking the site to "sages who levitate" (*chāraṇ*), is in fact traced to a thirteenth-century Jain inscription for residential caves in the year 1234–1235.[12]

The work of art historians suggests that the makers of Ellora weren't ever a *single* set of artisans.[13] More likely, groups came together from various regions, bringing their own techniques, iconographies, and stylistic influences, which link Ellora to other sites across India, even as at Ellora, motifs were transmitted between caves and faiths.[14] The scale and diverse tasks needed to excavate and shape a rock-hewn cave demanded coordinated teamwork. For the construction of *chaityas*, a master architect most likely worked with a foreman to oversee the design, measurement, and stages of excavation and carving. The labor was accomplished by three teams of workers—a team of stone-carpenters and two teams of specialized carvers (for "finishing" architectural features and sculpted figures).[15] Carpenters, haulers, plasterers, and painters would join the stoneworkers in completing a shrine. Work was sometimes undertaken in stages, with additions carved into the rock.

Fascinatingly, Buddhist monks (*bhikkus*) could be active in the design and supervision of monastic building projects. There was even a formal monastic role for the artisan-monk who oversaw new constructions: the Navakami (*navakarmika*), denoting the "Monk-in-Charge-of-New Construction."[16] These Navakamis were expert in monastic codes; as architectural designers and planners, they would ensure that shrines, stupas, and residential halls were made according to rules set down by texts. In addition to monastic codes and consecrations, Navakamis dealt with innumerable practical tasks: lining up and managing donors; seeking loans; buying building materials; appointing assistants who worked for religious merit; recruiting teams of carpenters, masons, sculptors, smiths, and toolmakers; hiring laborers and allocating their wages; holding the cord for measuring out residential monastic projects (*vihārasūtra*); and determining the placement of halls, entrances, cells, chambers, and shrines.[17] The Navakamis might also be lead donors to monastic construction, recruiting wealthy, hereditary master craftsmen from the laity to serve as Avesinis tasked with overseeing excavation or construction.[18] These Avesinis have been likened to the Mistris of later centuries, as master artisans, building contractors, and foremen.[19] Thanks to their prosperity and social status, the Avesinis—like the Navakamis—often made donations to monastic sites. Both the monastic Navakamis and the lay Avesinis might have been regarded as Sutradhars. While other Buddhist sites carry inscriptions naming donors, or may be signed by makers, the Buddhist caves at Ellora remain silent about who sponsored and undertook their making.

Artisans have historically worked for patrons of different faiths, and there's no way to be certain of the religious allegiances of those who made the caves. My own ancestors, who are said to have worked on the caves, may possibly, at that time, have identified as Buddhist and may even have worshipped Vishwakarma from a Buddhist perspective. No matter who all these gathered artisans were or which religious patrons they worked for, the enormity of Ellora as a multifaith undertaking spanning several centuries would have become a matter of pride for those who worked in stone: affirming their identities as skilled makers and possibly enhancing devotion to a divine Maker like Vishwakarma.

※

"Then I met with you and studied this, and understood it a little better, seeing photographs," Bhai said, generously gathering us up into his narrative.

"After that it's occurred to me that in order to establish a place for Vishwakarma and to remember their grandfather, the artisans have given his name to the cave. Because of the immense size, the craftsmanship, this is very distinct from the other caves: it's been given a music gallery; it's been given an arched roof. It's a wonderful thing. Thinking of this in terms of engineering—there are arches, there are pillars. If someone were to do a study of temples, of designing or of engineering, this entire structure is of such fine caliber. It was offered in memory of Vishwakarma by his sons." Bhai raised his right hand, palm outward in emphasis. "That is my impression."

Other people have also reflected on Ellora's artisans wanting a place to honor Vishwakarma. As the colonial arts administrator E. B. Havell reasoned, "If the local tradition preserves its original dedication, [Cave 10] may have been the chapel of the guild of masons who were working at Ellora, and some of the adjoining monastic halls may have been their residences."[20] In his logic, any undertaking on the scale of Ellora would have needed skilled artisans in residence, and they would have established their own place to worship, regardless of the religious identity of their patrons.

My cousin Prakash's father, Popatlal Dasadia, also hypothesized about daily worship by artisans in residence. Reasoning from his own experience in fabrication workshops where Vishwakarma was saluted each morning, he said, "See, while excavating the caves, artisans would have needed to start each day's work by offering their respects to Vishwakarma. Whichever cave they were working on, they would have first gathered in front of their grandfather in Cave 10, in order to gain his blessings."

The artisans' claim to their own sacred space, even as they worked to the will of patrons, was often repeated to us, as though to emphasize the workers' spiritual autonomy despite an economic dependence. People also emphasized their human ancestors' skills on display at Ellora, even as they expressed an allegiance to a divine ancestor. For example, when Ken and I were discussing texts we had discovered in the British library with our friend Vhalabhai, a Gujar Suthar in Ahmedabad, he suddenly burst out, as though worried that we were getting carried away by mythological accounts of the caves' making, "Look, Ellora was hardly made by Vishwakarma blowing on rock and muttering some mantras! The whole place was made by the hard work and the skills of artisan Shilpis! They made everything there and they also wanted a place to honor their own father, Vishwakarma."

If the original artisans had used this as a gathering space for worship, what relation might they have seen between the Buddha and Vishwakarma? Bhai had thought about that too. Another time, as we sat with him looking through historical images of Cave 10 on a laptop, Bhai shared a hypothesis that the two identities might have coexisted from the start. "In my thinking," Bhai said, "those craftsmen wanted a place to worship Vishwakarma, and it was their work to make Buddhas. So they made this Vishwakarma in the form of a Buddha out of fear: they would know how to recognize him, and others wouldn't know it. I cannot say for certain, but this is my imagination."

The question remained open and unresolved; we knew that at some point Vishwakarma was recognized in the cave yet couldn't be sure when this happened. Later, when Bhai had a chance to read a version of this chapter, he discarded his earlier hypothesis. "See, now I'm thinking this was first just the Buddha in Cave 10. Only later, when Buddhists had left India and their caves were empty, then only did people go there to worship Vishwakarma."

The afternoon that we were recording, Bhai mused more on the interplay of human skill and divine inspiration among those original artisans. "Sometimes I wonder about these people. Bhagavan must have come and given them blessings: 'Come on, just start!' It's almost something like *Khul jā sim sim*—'Open sesame.'"

Bhai was referring to the *Thousand and One Nights* story in which Ali Baba learns the magical password pronounced by a band of thieves to access a cavern within mountain rock. This story had inspired at least five Hindi film versions since his childhood. Just as uttering those words caused the rock in the story to slide open, revealing hidden treasures, the certainty of Vishwakarma's blessing empowered artisans to discover sculpted treasures within the basalt.

"Today, it is something to be proud of that we had such great craftsmen," Bhai concluded. "And they were Vishwakarma's descendants— like us!"

Beaming from the armchair, he pointed to his own heart, then outward around the room.

PART III
The Resident of Ellora

26. "Honored Guru Maharaj Vishwakarma, Honored Abode Mountain of Ellora [Irour]." Frontispiece to Vishwakarma Purana, 1911. British Library Guj D 1123.

* 9 *

Via-Via

I wonder if my grandmother Ba ever paused near the entrance of Cave 16 to admire the beautiful Gaja Lakshmi, Goddess of Good Fortune, surrounded by elephants. In this enormous stone panel, Lakshmi sits crosslegged on a lotus throne in a pond filled with lotus pads. On both sides, a small elephant dips a vessel to lift water toward an upper elephant whose trunk is raised to pour a stream of tribute over the goddess's head.

I imagine Ba's chin lifted to face Lakshmi. A fine white cotton sari covers Ba's head and frames her bespectacled face. Her joined palms reveal symmetrical lines of tattooed blue dots along the backs of her veined hands. From her elbow dangles a little khaki bag holding rolls of rupee notes in several denominations and an assortment of clinking coins. Ba always advised worship of a comfortably cross-legged Lakshmi of the sort this panel portrays; a standing Lakshmi, Ba said, might wander off. For Ba's name was Kamlabai—from Kamala, or "Lotus," one of Lakshmi's many names—and Ba felt a special affinity with this goddess.

Ba hadn't always been Kamlabai. She was raised as Kadviben, "Bitter Sister," in Junagarh—one among the many small princely states of the Kathiawar peninsula to the southeast of Kutch. Her father made plows, shaped wooden wheels for bullock carts, and constructed wooden machines to press sugarcane. Her mother, Ba said, was a "softy" (*naram*) who often took to her bed and wept in darkness. In the winter of 1900, a catastrophic famine had been joined by an outbreak of plague. Everyone evacuated the village for the jungle, and Ba's mother went into labor. Ba was born feetfirst, just as the sun rose on Christmas day, *Nātāl*. In the hope that the baby would survive, she was named "Bitter"; just as the word *karvī* could make a mouth grimace with distaste, the name would deflect ill fortune.

A few hours away from Ba's village was the city of Rajkot. Later the city became associated with the manufacture of machine tools and diesel engines, but in those days Rajkot was a hub for the British presence in the region and Suthars found work on assorted colonial building projects. Around World War I, the Suthar community in Rajkot began planning a Vishwakarma temple. In 1920, Ramji Seth and his brothers sponsored the construction of the temple dome. This was how my grandfather made the Rajkot connections that eventually led him to Ba. It wasn't unusual for Gujar Suthar men from Kutch to marry Gujar Suthar women from Kathiawar (though not the other way around). I grew up hearing that "she was sixteen and he was sixty," and many decades passed before I considered how the numbers didn't quite add up, and longer yet to understand how the missing years tucked a painful story out of sight.

Marrying Ramji Seth took Ba from the village, and as astrologers sometimes prescribed, she received a new wifely name: Kamlabai. "Were you scared when you married him?" I once asked, foolishly imagining she might expound on her feelings. "Your Dada was good, he was fine," she responded, pointing toward the wall of her sitting room, where, on the other side of the blue wooden clock that chimed out hours, a large formal oval portrait of him was paired with an oval portrait of her. Gray mustached and visibly older than his other portrait downstairs, he looked on sternly from under his maroon turban. Her black hair was framed by her sari's gold brocade border, and her face was vacant. Yes, he was around sixty, but handsome, fit, and rich. Never one to be outshone, Ba later claimed that really, the lines marking lotuses on *her* soles brought *him* prosperity; he might have made money before, but he made even more because of her!

Ellora is a few hours' drive from the riverside pilgrimage town of Nasik/ Nashik and the Ramji Mistri Bungalow where Ba gave birth to seven children, with four surviving to adulthood. Family members tell me that now and then Ba commandeered the car and driver for a day trip. Arriving at Ellora, she hired a Brahmin to perform various rituals. Moving through the caves, the Ghrishneshwar Shiva temple in the village, and the Vishwa Kund pond, she directed and argued with the Brahmin. No one who tagged along can remember anything more than a busy sweep of ritual activity, so I have no details on just what Ba did in which place, or why.

All the same, Ba became an important figure in our quest because of the connections cascading through her. So far, I've described ancestors through Ramji Seth, all Kutchi Gujar Suthars. But when we arrived in the dusty, sprawling industrial city of Ahmedabad, the hereditary carpenters around us turned out to have mostly migrated from Ba's region of Kathiawar. While the Kutchis had been heading to Bombay and Karachi since the late nineteenth century, many of these Kathiawari Gujar Suthar carpenters had flocked to Ahmedabad: to construct buildings and

27. My grandmother Kamlabai Ramji and her younger self, Ramji Mistri Bungalow, Nasik, 1983. Photograph by Kirin Narayan.

furniture, craft bobbins for textile mills, become technicians for various industries, and increasingly engage with every form of fabrication in small workshops. The descendants of Ba's sister, Nandu Ba, whom we knew as "Maushi" (mother's sister) were among these city migrants.

Maushi had been about a decade older than Ba, her composed sweetness a companionable foil for Ba's feisty energy. (There had been three brothers too, dismissed by Ba as "all rascals" and not worth keeping up relations with.) While Maushi had been married to a carpenter in the nearby village of Bantva, Ba's marriage to Ramji Seth took her to the faraway city of Bombay, then Nasik, and a life of relative luxury. Yet the sisters' closeness endured. And so, Maushi was the relative from Ba's side who, as children, we knew best.

Maushi often stayed in the Ramji Mistri Bungalow, keeping Ba company for months at a time. Freed by daughters-in-law from the grind of village housework, she took up residence in the mattress storage room in Ba's wing of the house. Here she spent her days sitting atop a gigantic built-in trunk by the light of an open window, making huge embroideries. She was known for her inventiveness and her ability to draw exact proportions and circles without any tools or measuring devices. I watched, mesmerized, as she started her compositions by spreading out a stretch of cloth and dipping a matchstick into a steel bowl of ink to portray scenes, most often from the life of her adored deity, Krishna. Then she filled in the scenes with bright cotton yarn, making wall hangings, ceremonial canopies, and smaller devotional pieces: all ways of keeping close to Krishna. I wonder now if she also invoked Vishwakarma. The ways she thought up designs and her skill in embroidering with cotton yarn—called *sūtra*—seem an extension of Vishwakarma's *sūtra* as both code and cord.

Maushi was part of our lives. But apart from her eldest son, who worked as a carpenter in Bombay, we didn't really know her other descendants. My aunt Chandaphui, who lived in Ahmedabad, knew these cousins better. When, having been married for twenty-four years, Chandaphui surprised everyone with the birth of her first child, a son, we in the existing circle of cousin playmates were all older. But Maushi's youngest grandchild Prakash was around the same age and also based in Ahmedabad. And so, Prakash was co-opted to live for extended periods in my aunt's home and to join the family on trips.

I remembered Prakash as a little boy with thick black hair, usually in the background of family gatherings but always helping out. He was known for his ingenuity. From matchsticks, he made a tiny birdcage; from old tin cans, he shaped boats and trucks; from a length of wire, he twisted a perfect little bicycle. Chandaphui put the most astonishing of these creations on display in her glass-fronted showcase in the living room of her bungalow. She would point these out with pride: "See what Prakash has made?"

Ken and I arrived in Ahmedabad to find Prakash a barrel-chested man in his forties with the same thick black hair and a great sense of fun. He still loved the challenge of making things, and he worked as a freelance welder, assembling office cabins, portable lavatories, sentry boxes, gates, grills, and metal frames for advertising.

Prakash always moved fast, as though propelled by urgent curiosity. When he spoke, his Gujarati poured out with such animated excitement that I had to beg him to slow down. But when Prakash wanted to figure out how something functioned, he became very still. He looked from different angles, slowly probing, often listening. Through our months in Ahmedabad, Prakash would appear in our rented apartment to fix leaking taps, recalcitrant flushes, uneven closet doors, broken rice cookers, blinking lamps, and more. We were lucky that he also seemed to view our research as a complex machine to ponder in all its moving parts.

From Prakash, we learned the concept of *Via-Via* (the "Via" pronounced like "Maya").

"How do you get your welding jobs? Do you advertise somewhere?"

"It's all Via-Via. Someone you know talks about you to another person; they recommend you; you get connected."

Prakash's father, Popatlal, was one of seven brothers, of whom six had migrated to Ahmedabad and found employment through a chain of Via-Via. They had worked in various capacities. A few had been employed by the influential Sarabhai family. Popatlal had worked for the Sarabhais, putting up a copper geodesic dome designed by Buckminster Fuller over their Calico Mills shop, making frames for exhibiting textiles, assembling grass cutters and, later, photographic enlargers. One of Prakash's elderly uncles had been a technician at the Indian Space Research Organization (ISRO), founded by a Sarabhai, and had figured out a way to cheaply manufacture a key satellite part. Another uncle owned his own workshop for making adjustable office chairs and had given Prakash his start in welding. Only the youngest of the uncles had remained a carpenter. Now in his seventies and retired, he carved miniature objects for pleasure: tiny tools, inlaid pens, and doll-size shrines, including one with newspaper cutouts that honored the architect B. V. Doshi, for whom he had once worked.

Through Prakash and his family, the Via-Via of kinship began opening around our research; I often found myself drawing on my anthropological training to sketch quick kinship charts to follow just how everyone was connected. From Prakash's father's friend's son, we received the first among many Vishwakarma booklets that celebrated Ellora as the place where Vishwakarma manifested in this world. Through Prakash's wife's brother's participation in a collective ceremony honoring 108 resplendent goddesses in a community hall, we were reminded of how Vishwakarma's daughter's marriage at Ellora to Surya, the sun god, led to her doubled form. Meeting Prakash's sister's daughter's husband's father, Jayantibhai, we heard our first stories of Vishwakarma and his sons' activities at Ellora. Jayantibhai's older daughter-in-law's sister's son was a young architect in his early twenties, Hardik Siddhpura. Hardik's mother was Suthar, while his father was Luhar (hereditary blacksmith)—two groups that considered themselves sons of Vishwakarma, long collaborating across India and sometimes intermarrying. Hardik became our research assistant and translator, joining us on many adventures, including a trip with Jayantibhai to Ellora.

Some of the connections Prakash established for us didn't involve these convoluted chains of kinship. For example, remembering a neighbor's connection to a professional storyteller, Prakash arranged for our invitation to a seven-day Vishwakarma storytelling event under a big pink and white tent, where a regular refrain, sung in Gujarati, was *"Welcome, Resident of Ellora!"* As we took a break from these stories over strong tea served in small paper cups, an intense white-haired man, wearing white, approached us to advise that if we really wanted to research "Grandfather," we needed to go to Ellora. Immediately, this unexpected benefactor pulled out his phone to give us names and numbers for contacts at the new Vishwakarma temple in Verul village: Via-Via.

As pieces of the puzzle around Cave 10 gradually fell into place, we could usually trace our knowledge back to a Via-Via sequence set in motion by Prakash.

And beyond Prakash, to Ba.

✳

Pa could write with sardonic amusement about any experience, and as he neared sixty his assorted personas included *macho-Kutchi-Narayan-Dahisaria of Bhorara (with falling teeth, graying, sagging jowls and an impending stoop)* (October 10, 1986). If we had been based in Mumbai, Bhuj, or some other place filled with Kutchi Gujar Suthars, my Dahisaria of Bhorara patrilineage would have been paramount. Yes, the Kathiawari Gujar Suthars who we were surrounded by knew all about their Kutchi counterparts, and sometimes they intermarried too. But growing up, I had the sense that "Ba's relatives" were always viewed as at a slight distance. No doubt thanks to Ba, who was always larger than life, her relatives were usually assumed to be sources for colorful stories.

In one of Pa's letters from the early 1980s, I found an amused account of Ba's distant cousin Nathalal's connection to a psychic, addressed as

"Bapu." This Bapu apparently carried the blessings of a lineage of wonder-working gurus, and for divination he used a saucer that Pa labeled a *saucerscope*. Ba had long believed there was buried treasure in the fields near the Ramji Mistri Bungalow, and Nathalal, who lived in Bombay, came to convince Pa that Bapu was the right man to find it: *He told me about the misfortune which was haunting his clan, and how Bapu got the ancestor, whose soul was troubled, called, to tell them what should be done to solve it, etc. and what Bapu said about the family elders, for over a century, was true to the best of their knowledge, and soon they are gathering the surviving members of the clan for the prescribed Pooja at some Shiva temple at a place near Morbi.*

This psychic Bapu didn't have anything to say about our own clan ancestors, or how anyone's souls might need pacification. But he affirmed that Ba's recurring dreams about a buried pot brimming with multicolored gems were true. Pa was persuaded to pay for Bapu's first-class train travel—and unexpectedly, the tickets of three attendants—for further consultation in Bombay. When Pa himself went to Nathalal's apartment, *The whole room was filled with Kathiawari people. The Kathiawari types* of the early 1980s—or at least, the men—were, according to Pa, characterized by a *mus[ta]che, ill-fitting Bombay textile pants, and ill-fitting bush shirts with big flower patterns, etc.* He also took note of an ingenious device attached to their television: *The television was on. They had put on a rotating color something in front of the white screen, and it gave an illusion of colour TV. Indira [Gandhi] became blue, green, yellow, orange etc. in slow motion as she was extolling the nation for something or the other. Fantastic device that! After some talk with the people around, I was called inside by Ba.*

Unfortunately, the detailed unfolding ends there, as Pa was derailed by a backache that kept him away from the typewriter. Some weeks later, he resumed the letter, promising eventually to send a full account of what had happened, but this never came to pass. He did mention, though, that despite much *séance-ish talk*, negotiations with spirits, and further expenses, no treasure was located. As he wrote, *When I started this letter, it was all so fresh and could have been called "an experience" but now sort of a story* (February 25, 1983).

Rereading Pa's letters and his assumed distance from Ba's relatives, I wondered what Pa would have made of my bypassing the patrilineage to claim Ba's clan name.

On Divali day of 2018, we visited an Ahmedabad Vishwakarma temple crowded with Kathiawari Suthar families, all dressed up for a New

Year's visit with Grandfather. This bearded Vishwakarma was flanked by the clan goddess and his daughter, and a small sea of food offerings in round bowls had been laid out before the shrine. In the larger hall outside, a table had been set up for donations to help students with the costs of education. Ken and I stood in line. Pen poised, the elderly man behind the desk asked for my clan identification. I produced the name of Ba's Kathiawari-affiliated clan, which I thought gave me a claim to being there: Bakodia.

The man wrote this down without comment and handed over a receipt.

But even if I had brought out Pa's Kutchi clan affiliation of Dahisaria, my donation would have been accepted, for clans were recognized across regions. A few months later, on a sweltering April evening, we visited Prakash's niece's father-in-law Jayantibhai, who called over his friend Kantibhai to join us. (Unbeknownst to me and Kantibhai at the time, we were also related, as he had married Maushi's older granddaughter.) Kantibhai, who was active in community associations, brought along his own friend, Bipinbhai: Via-Via. As we made introductions, they inquired about my "real surname." I understood they were asking my paternal clan name and answered "Dahisaria."

Bipinbhai smiled meaningfully: "*Ohhhh.*"

Why the smile? I later asked my cousins through Pa's side, and they laughed. Hadn't I ever heard the saying "Dahisaria daughters are hot-headed and impatient" (*Dahisariā ḍīkrī ākḷī*)? Pa's oldest niece, raised in Bombay, was used as the example. In the 1940s, she had been married to someone selected by her maternal grandfather in Karachi and gone to her new home in Kutch. The next day she informed her in-laws that the indoor *toilet* in her parents' house was cleaner than their kitchen! Having leveled this magnificently unforgivable insult, she walked out, never to return, and became a successful professional woman.

Though assured that I was at least a semi-insider, Bipinbhai wanted to know just why foreign governments would sponsor our research. When Ken told him that not just Australian and American but also Indian funding bodies were involved, Bipinbhai offered his own theory of why we had received grants. "All gods have their moment," he said. "Vishwakarma's moment has now come because he is the 'technical *devatā*'—the technology god."

He went on to emphasize how much Vishwakarma's blessings were needed for these times, and also told me that I was benefiting from the good works (*puṇya*) of my ancestors. "It's all from the ancestors," he said. "Their blessings are making you do this research."

I assumed he was referring to my paternal forefathers who built the

Bhorara temple. I smiled, imagining Via-Via at work in circles expanding not only in the present but across time, encompassing also ancestral oversight of our quest.

✳

"Whenever I sit to make a new thing, when I can't figure out what to do, then I just sit for two minutes and think of Vishwakarma," Prakash told us. "Then by itself, from within, the energy arrives and gives me the 'idea.' I get inspired, and the solution comes to me. Yes. I've experienced this myself, many times."

His father, Popatlal, recalled how in the era when men wore turbans, if they needed Vishwakarma's help, they would sit down, respectfully place their turban by their knee, and think of Vishwakarma. Others spoke of how, when tools were taken in hand, the inner "eye of Vishwakarma" opened inside them—a belief connected to a story set at Ellora that I introduce in the next chapter.

Prakash told us how someone was boring a tube well, and the drill became detached deep underground. Prakash happened to be present. He thought of Vishwakarma, and a solution came into his mind: he then and there manufactured a small device to retrieve the drill. The man wanted to pay him, but Prakash refused. It was inappropriate to charge for a gift of grace, he said.

"I had a sort of disciple," Prakash remembered. "That is, he thought of me as his guru—he worked under me and was my 'helper.' Now he lives in a village; he went back to the village and then, one time, he was working on something. He was stuck and he had to get it done. He remembered me and thought, 'How does Prakashbhai do this?' Then the work was accomplished, and afterward he phoned me. He told me, 'I couldn't understand a thing about how this should be done, but I contemplated you in this way, and this energy spontaneously arose. When I did this like you, it was done.'"

Vishwakarma's grace, Prakash thought, could be accessed by anyone introduced to the god in a sort of spiritual Via-Via: that young Bihari worker with no preexisting connection had felt the same inspiration. While hereditary artisans often emphasized to us that the power of Vishwakarma was transmitted "in the blood," Prakash was emphatic that Vishwakarma could manifest within any skilled person.

"A person who knows the work, who is skilled in making, is a small portion [*amsh*], of Vishwakarma," Prakash told us. "Vishwakarma isn't in everyone. For those who are part of his family, yes, it's in the DNA.

But others carry Vishwakarma too. When we say that holy men carry god inside them, maybe 90 percent are fake, but a small number genuinely carry a small part of god, and they are the real saints. In the same way, there are people who aren't sons of Vishwakarma, but they also carry a small portion of Vishwakarma within them."

Prakash was also certain that even if women hadn't usually taken up the tools of caste-based professions, Vishwakarma inspired whatever creations they set their minds to—whether embroidering like his grandmother, or crocheting, stitching, making beaded objects, even composing elaborate henna patterns for the hands. (There was disagreement on this point among women themselves: as daughters in the lineage, their observations ranged from "We've never heard of daughters getting the blessings; no, women don't say they're inspired by Vishwakarma," to "Whatever blessings Vishwakarma Dada has given sons, *of course* daughters have those same blessings.")

It was on a trip with Prakash to visit Maushi's other grandsons, who still lived in the village, that we first encountered a framed poster of

28. Prakash with a celebratory canopy embroidered in the 1960s by his grandmother, my great-aunt Maushi, Ahmedabad, 2009. Photograph by Kirin Narayan.

Vishwakarma titled "The Resident of Ellora [*Ilorgaṛh Nivāsi*], Four-armed Vishwakarma." This Vishwakarma had once watched over the carpentry workshop of Maushi's husband and was now on the kitchen wall of our hospitable relatives—Prakash's first cousins and my second cousins. "I

29. "Resident of Ellora, Four-Armed Vishwakarma," decorated and framed poster from 1932, Bantva, 2018. Photograph by Ken George.

keep this as a memento of my grandfather," said our host, who maintained the family profession of carpenter. My cousin's wife had at some point expressed her own devotion and artistry, adorning the poster, and Vishwakarma's name, with varicolored spangles. At mealtimes, when we all sat on the floor in a circle, Vishwakarma looked on, twinkling and shimmering.

Signed by an artist, L. A. Joshi, the poster had been printed in Dakor, a pilgrimage town with a famed Krishna temple; since the 1920s, Dakor had also hosted a Vishwakarma temple. The poster carried the familiar Sanskrit invocation praising Vishwakarma's crowned, three-eyed grandfatherly form, shown holding a footrule, cord, waterpot, and book and accompanied by his goose/swan. With his four arms, one leg tucked up onto his seat and the other resting on his swan's soft white feathers, this Resident of Ellora didn't seem to resemble the Murti in Cave 10 in any way.

In this village where Maushi had once lived, we were paraded around to visit neighbors, and people dropped in to meet us too. A few houses away, we encountered a 108-year-old woman, shrunken as a little doll, who had been Ba's friend. She sat with legs outstretched, head covered, no glasses, reaching out to embrace the descendant of her glamorous city-dwelling friend. Generations of daughters-in-law gathered around the bed, recollecting how Ba sometimes arrived in a car to sweep her friends off on pilgrimage. Ba, they said, had especially enjoyed taking everyone to nearby Mt. Girnar to visit rock-cut caves, temples, and holy people.

Through the warm Via-Via of neighbors, a tall woman with thick white hair shared some songs to help our project. Savitaben was Rajput herself, but living beside a community of carpenters, of course she knew Vishwakarma. When she joined other women in gatherings for devotional singing, Vishwakarma and his daughter Randal were among the deities they praised. One of these songs was set to a melody so catchy that Savitaben's powerful voice made the very words dance. After twelve verses extolling various aspects of Vishwakarma, the final lines proclaimed:

tame Ilorṇā chho vāsī	You're the Resident of Ellora
o rāj	oh Lord,
jyān joun	Yet wherever I look—
tyān Viśvakarmā	there's Vishwakarma!

❋ 10 ❋

Ila the Serpent Maiden

"What about your food?"

"So, if you're not doing anything else on Sunday, what about lunch?"

"If your plane arrives so late, how will you eat? Come directly here!"

"Shall we bring a tiffin to your apartment?"

Again and again through our time in Ahmedabad, my cousin Prakash and his wife, Sonal, looked out for our nourishment. We had set up a minimal kitchen in our rented apartment, but I was soon revealed as an inadequate wife, stunning everyone who inquired after our food. For I never kneaded any sort of flour. I didn't briskly maneuver a rolling pin to make perfectly round *roṭlīs*; I could not pat heavier *roṭlās*. I didn't know how to spoon oil around the edges of a *parāṭhā*, evaluate the puff of a perfectly fried golden *pūrī*, or press savory *theplās* against a griddle.

"*But what do you eat?*" people asked, blanching. "Why don't you learn? You want to learn? Come, it's so easy . . ."

"Teach him," I'd sweetly say.

Could I possibly be serious? Whoever was cross-examining me paused for a confused moment, then burst into laughter.

Ken gamely received some flour-dusted lessons in a few households. But everyone remained alarmed about our nutrition, and especially Ken's. Though Ken had started out as a most respected brother-in-law, or "Jijaji," to Sonal and Prakash, he had soon become their "Jiju," and a darling Jiju was *supposed* to be indulged. Sonal was a fabulous cook, and whenever we visited, Ken's steel *thālī* was refilled again and again: more "hot-hot" food fresh from the stove, another round of pickles, more streams of ghee. Ken's saying, "*Bas bas*—enough!" or covering his *thālī* with outspread hands was dismissed as polite insincerity. I displayed my wifely shortcomings afresh when I intervened, earning a reputation as "the Police." Surely, given the deprived situation in our kitchen, Ken was famished! "Just one more!"

Prakash would murmur, laughing, slipping Ken another serving if my attention strayed. "Quick! The Police aren't looking."

Prakash and Sonal lived in Memnagar, a villagelike enclave within the larger city. We eventually mastered how to direct auto-rickshaw drivers from the mall and temple at the busy main road, through another turn, down a narrow lane lined with low apartment complexes and shacks where people might be sitting outdoors on rope cots. Along the front of Prakash's building, lined with a few small shops, a metal gate (welded

30. Sonal and Prakash, Ahmedabad, 2017. Photograph by Kirin Narayan.

for "the Society" by Prakash) opened into a deeply shadowed courtyard. Usually cluttered with scooters, motorbikes, and random furniture spilling from the apartments, this courtyard was sometimes cleared out and decorated with lights to become a staggeringly loud communal area for the Society to celebrate festivals.

Prakash and Sonal lived with his father and their son in a one-bedroom apartment on the ground floor. When they were home, the front door was always open. Their back door, looking out at a water-purification plant, was often open too, as workers heaved and stacked gigantic plastic bottles. Cross breezes, swarms of mosquitoes, and an occasional mouse or cat moved through these doors. Neighbors appeared and disappeared. They came by to distract a bored baby, borrow a stool, leave a key, use the facilities, display a new outfit, or inspect us. For however exotic we might be, as Society relatives, we belonged here too, amid all the informality of some women wearing long nightgowns through the day and men changing into baggy shorts when they came home through the dust, heat, and chaotic traffic.

On a Sunday soon after we arrived in Ahmedabad, we were invited to lunch. As we described the research project we were just beginning, Prakash listened intently, stroking his chin. I later came to recognize this as the same musing look as when he was trying to fix something: what missing part, what connection, what fine-tuning was needed. With the curtain to the narrow kitchen drawn open, Sonal stood by the stove, listening in to offer her own comments, hands in motion as she chopped, rolled, patted, flipped, and stirred.

After lunch, Prakash said that he'd thought of something that could help us.

"I'll be back," he said, briskly taking up his helmet and the keys to his scooter parked in the courtyard. It was almost dusk when he returned, hair plastered with perspiration, smile jubilant. The person he'd gone to find hadn't been home, so Prakash had followed the man's sociable Sunday trail all over town. Shining with the pleasure of having procured a key cog to get our research moving, Prakash handed over a slim Gujarati booklet with the title *The Knowledge and Religious Observances of the Vishwakarma Purana*.

The cover carried a color image of a white-bearded Vishwakarma and his youthful sons. Sponsored by an association called "The Spreading of Vishwakarma Dharma," with its office at "Shri Vishwakarma Plywood," the booklet was distributed for the cost of "Read and make others read." Prakash explained that it had been published in memory of his father's old friend and coworker at various Sarabhai family enterprises. This friend had been so devoted to Vishwakarma that he organized a yearly street procession with a framed painting of Vishwakarma, and composed hundreds of religious songs.

I was just beginning to learn to read Gujarati script. But already, flipping through these pages, I saw repeated mention of Ellora.

※

This gift from Prakash was the first of many dozens of contemporary Gujarati publications about Vishwakarma that people pressed on us through our stay. Such printed materials were brought out from somewhere near the household altar, or from a steel cupboard, or even from a back room after a long search.

"You can use this for your research," people would say. "Take it, take it! Don't worry, we can get another."

I had grown up imagining that my family's red book, distributed at the 1901 opening of the Bhorara temple, was singular. Yet as Vishwakarma-related texts in Gujarati slowly filled a whole shelf in our Ahmedabad apartment, I saw how our family book was just one early example of artisans asserting a community identity in print. All these Vishwakarma texts were privately printed for circumscribed circulation. They could be pamphlets of just a few pages, booklets between twenty-five and fifty pages long, or bound books of several hundred pages. The earlier books had been composed by scholarly Brahmins, with their names and titles—"Pandit," "Acharya," "Shastri," "Joshi," "Vyas"—offering a seal of Brahminical authority to the Vishwakarma lore, even as introductions revealed artisan patrons behind the project. In the late nineteenth century, it was rare for a community member like K. T. Gajjar to compile and author such materials, but this had become increasingly common. (I should add that across India, Vishwakarma-related groups also circulate newsletters and colorful magazines with reports and photographs of community events, matrimonial columns, lists of famous people of the Vishwakarma lineage, and more.)

Vishwakarma-related religious publications often honor the memory of departed relatives. While my grandfather's book had carried woodcut portraits of ancestors, those published later enshrined memorial photographs; Bhai, for example, showed us a nine-page pamphlet of Vishwakarma prayers that he had privately printed in 1976, from which his adored paternal grandmother Lachubai Tejshi, who had passed away in 1969, looked on through heavy spectacles. The cost for printing such texts was covered by individuals, extended families, businesses owned by community members, or community organizations. In the case of a thick 596-page Vishwakarma Purana sponsored by the Vishwakarma Charitable

Trust (based near Ellora) and composed by Bachubhai Vadgama, a retired carpenter in the industrial city of Rajkot, the foot of most pages carried information on a sponsor for that page—invariably a business—making the book both a religious text and a community business directory with information on tools, machines, manufacturing resources, and construction companies.

Most of these religious publications in Gujarati were styled as the Vishwakarma Purana, retellings of the Vishwakarma Purana, or extracted sections and practices associated with the Vishwakarma Purana. The very word *Purāṇa*, or "old," connotes antiquity. While there are usually reckoned to be eighteen major ancient Puranas and many hundreds of minor ones, a subcategory of Jati Puranas, containing stories about a *jāti's*, or caste's, origins and connections with a particular god, were generally composed to advance claims to a higher status.[1] The cluster of Gujarati texts characterized as the Vishwakarma Purana, linking artisans to their divine grandfather, clearly fall into the category of Jati Purana, with related sociopolitical aspirations.[2]

Soon after Bhai showed us his English materials on Ellora, he had brought out a thick Gujarati book (in clear plastic wrap), its bright cover displaying a seated grandfather Vishwakarma accompanied by sons and framed by stone pillars. *The Authentic Vishwakarma Purana*, published in Gujarati in 1965, was a compendium of mythological stories complemented by a few pages of hand-drawn illustrations.[3] Translated into Hindi in the early 1980s, this version turned out to be pivotal in circulating stories about Vishwakarma at Ellora beyond Gujarati readers (and perhaps inspiring artisans from other regions to also make the pilgrimage). Gently patting the volume with his finely shaped hand, Bhai said, "There is more about Ellora in here. But there is another Purana also, an older one. That is in the village."

After we had retrieved Bhai's books from the village, he arrived at our apartment one Thursday bearing the older Purana. Opening its pages, we immediately encountered a colored print honoring Vishwakarma as a guru.

"You can see how this picture brings out what is there at Ellora," Bhai observed.

We opened a laptop to find a photograph from Cave 10 for comparison. Instead of a statue in deep gray stone, in this colorful print Guru Vishwakarma is a fair, clean-shaven, neatly dressed young man. We all recognized the care with which the artist had depicted the Murti and standing attendants, the two lions with demurely raised paws beside the throne, other symmetrically arranged creatures, and celestial beings flying upward toward a crowning plant.

"Also, you can see the artist's imagination," Bhai said, leaning forward to peer through his spectacles.

140　Chapter 10

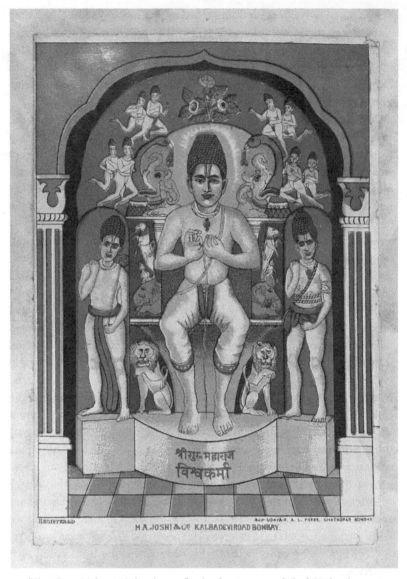

31. "Shri Guru Maharaj Vishwakarma," color frontispiece of Bhai's Vishwakarma Purana, 1926

The Murti's curly hair had become a beehivelike cap. He wore a cord with a red amulet around his neck, a sacred thread draped across his bare torso, and a yellow dhoti with a red border tucked around his waist. Both his attendants wore red. An elongated U-shaped red Vaishnava mark adorned his forehead, perhaps connecting to the Gujarat artisan community's drift to worshipping forms of Vishnu in the Swami Narayan and Pushtimarg sects. His hands displayed the teaching pose. The thumb and forefinger of his right hand simultaneously grasped the little finger of the left hand and dangled a long cord. This cord made him a literal depiction of a Sutradhar, connecting him more closely to his descendants, the Suthars, for whom the Purana had been composed.

"Just look at the date," Bhai said, handing us the fragile book, covered in brown paper, pages sepia with age. "My year!" This was one of the one thousand copies of the edition published in 1926, the year of Bhai's birth. He had grown up with this book always in the background. The book's title translated as *Vishwakarma's Deeds, Vishwakarma Purana, Vishwakarma's Stories*.[4] This was the second edition of the book; in the British Library we located the first edition from 1911, its frontispiece carrying a representation of Vishwakarma in black and white, and adding his location as Guru at the Mountain of Ellora (*Irour*).[5] (The image opens part III of this book.) The revised color print probably pointed not just to the increased availability of such technologies but also to more potential artisan readers.

The book's author, Vallabhram Surajram, had lived in the Raipur Pakhalini Pol, an enclave of Ahmedabad's old city. In the early twentieth century, this was a residential area for carpenters and blacksmiths migrating from their villages in search of work, and Ahmedabad's first Vishwakarma temple was made.

As a Sanskrit scholar with several books to his name, Surajram explained that an original Sanskrit text had been lost but he had reconstituted fragments from many places to form a new whole, which he presented in Gujarati, a more familiar language. He must have drawn on other texts or oral traditions, but he never specified his sources. We found this influential Purana, composed in verse in an older form of Gujarati with unusual spelling, outdated metaphors, and highly wrought emotions, particularly challenging to translate. As Bhai helped us understand key segments on his afternoon visits, he laughed aloud at some earthy expressions and observed, "With translation, you lose the charm."

I've spent much of my life thinking about myths, legends, and folktales circulating around the subcontinent, but frankly I didn't recognize many of the characters in these chapters. Sometimes I glimpsed characters and motifs I'd met before, configured afresh through a moralizing, high-caste male imagination. Surajram asserted that as Vishwakarma's progeny, carpenters were Brahmins and therefore should behave with appropriate decorum, ritual purity, and veneration for priestly Brahmins (like himself). He characterized Vishwakarma as forever celibate and without desire, with sons and daughters either adopted or miraculously produced from his own body.

Early on in the Purana's twenty-one chapters, when a goddess named Aakriti asks Vishwakarma for a boon—that she might always keep him company—he sternly turns her into his wooden measuring stick. Else, for Surajram, this goddess might seem a consort, and his Vishwakarma mostly views female characters as daughters, helping them out in various ways. Each favored one—to a woman!—enacts her virtue through not just through a daughterly devotion to Vishwakarma but a wifely attention to her husband's every need. The making of *roṭlīs* is surely too routine to be mentioned, but in these stories queens fast for the well-being of husbands, carry elderly husbands in cane baskets on pilgrimage, find ways for husbands to regain their vision. Even demon wives are so virtuous that they reform their wayward mates. And reappearing across these chapters is Ila, the serpent maiden (*nāg kanyā*) married to the mountain.

✳

In both Hindu and Buddhist mythologies, Naga serpents are guardian deities of place. They are associated with water sources, treasure troves, and the fertility of land and creatures. The serpent maiden Ila's role in these stories of Vishwakarma made us alert to Nagas in the exterior and interior of Cave 10.

Arriving in the courtyard, a visitor looks up to see flying figures accompanied by curiously snakelike long, curving ribbons on each side of the upstairs window on the façade. Pillars on the outer porch are inscribed with a snakelike knotted design, echoing pillars that more explicitly represent snakes at other Buddhist sites.[6] Inside the hall, each arching rafter is supported at both ends by Nagas, who manifest a human body above the waist, while their serpentine lower half remains submerged in rock. For every rafter, a male Naga joins palms at one end, while at the other end a buxom female Naga (also known as a Nagini) holds a flower or garland. These worshipping male and female Nagas alternate in a long series through the length of the hall, creating an ambience of worshipping serpents.

Early Buddhists in India often established shrines at the sites of local spirit cults, whether centered on nature spirits, Nagas, or ancestors.[7] At the Ajanta caves, the fifth-century Cave 16 depicts a serpent at its entrance, with an inscription noting that the cave was excavated in the mountain home of a Naga king.[8] Cave 10 has no such inscriptions mentioning serpents and no particular sculpture identified as Ila. But the serpent theme in the iconography offers a backdrop to the story of Ila bringing Vishwakarma to Ellora.

Meeting the story repeatedly in the many Gujarati community

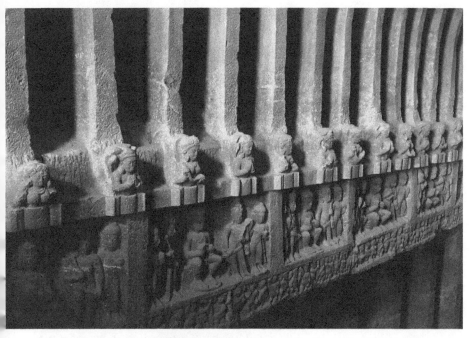

32. Female and male Nagas alternating at the base of each carved rafter, Cave 10, Ellora 2018. Photograph by Ken George.

publications that borrow from Surajram's text, I began to think of each retelling as another twist of a kaleidoscope: reconfiguring, elongating, sometimes adding tiny elements as others swam away in a multiply reflecting phantasmagorical ensemble. This is a long and quirky story; as I draw from many retellings to take my own turn with the kaleidoscope, I step back between episodes to reestablish my bearings.

VISHWAKARMA ARRIVES AT ELLORA 1: IRON PEAK TO GOLD PEAK

After its creation, the earth was unstable. To fix the wobbling, Vishwakarma placed eight huge mountains in eight cardinal points. He also made countless other mountains: some big, some small; some laden with stone, gems, or herbs; some on the surface of the earth, some submerged in the ocean.

Deep in the ocean, a mountain named Iron Peak (Loha Kut) gave refuge to many varied sea creatures who came and went through the caves. The mountain enjoyed this time underwater. He was a great friend of the Ocean, and the Ocean entrusted treasures to him.

At the time that gods and demons collaborated on churning the Ocean, the gods asked Iron Peak to help persuade the Ocean to give up choice treasures. As a reward, they—and in some cases Vishwakarma—promised Iron Peak that he would receive boons in future eras.

More mythological time passed. Naga serpents living in the underworld visited the earth, and sometimes they couldn't find their path home. Losing their way, they became vulnerable to human attack. They asked the gods for help to set up a marker for the place of passage between worlds.

The gods decided that this was the moment for Iron Peak to be rewarded: he would be brought out of the ocean to become a striking signpost for the Nagas.

Iron Peak was reluctant. Why should he leave his friend the Ocean to join land where he'd be trodden on, grazed over, and made a site of defecation? But he had no choice. The great Naga serpents together lifted Iron Peak and carried him out of the water. As they bore the mountain upward, the magical jewels on the serpents' foreheads rubbed against the heavy iron mass. By the time Iron Peak was resettled on earth, he had turned entirely into gold, becoming Gold Peak (Hem Kut).

....

The story begins by acknowledging Vishwakarma as the primordial maker of the world. His stabilizing the world through strategically placed mountains was sometimes said to have been accomplished on Maha Sud Dashami, the sixth of the annual nine-day Vishwakarma celebrations that culminate with Maha Sud Teras. The mountain of Ellora, also sometimes known as Charanadri, then persuades the ocean to give up treasures, gesturing toward the famous episode, retold in many Puranas, of the churning of the ocean by gods and demons. There is clearly alchemical imagery here too, as contact with the serpents' crest jewels transforms the iron mountain into gold. The boon of transformation extends even further. Reaching earth, this personified mountain not only becomes solid gold but gains the ability to take the form of a golden-bodied man. It is in this form that he crosses paths with Ila beside a pond on his own mountain.

.... ♨ ....

VISHWAKARMA ARRIVES AT ELLORA 2: ILA MARRIES THE MOUNTAIN

The great serpent king, Shesh Nag, was childless and did penance to Lord Shiva. Shiva appeared to offer a boon, and the serpent asked for a daughter so he could gain the merit of someday marrying her off. Ten months later, Ila was born.

Ila grew up. Coming and going with the other serpents between the

ILA THE SERPENT MAIDEN 145

underworld and the earth, she came one day, in the company of her girlfriends, to bathe in a pool on the mountain that was now Gold Peak.

Gold Peak happened to then be wandering around his own mountain and came face-to-face with the lovely serpent maiden. The moment Ila saw him, she was in love. She fell at his feet, pleading that he accept her as his wife so she could serve him.

Gold Peak responded that he couldn't just marry an unknown girl, but if her father were to give her away in marriage, he would be willing. Ila asked her serpent father to marry her to Gold Peak, and this was done with the appropriate rites.

When Ila came to live with her husband in a cave on the mountain, Gold Peak's name changed once more: he now became Ilachal, the Abode of Ila.

....

Surajram's retelling depicts Ila as destined for marriage. I was amused to see the elderly male romantic imagination in which a beautiful woman's longing to serve a husband makes her so forward that she herself proposes marriage (any impropriety being erased by the potential groom's show of restraint and etiquette in getting her father involved). Ila's power is then affirmed by the mountain becoming Ilachal to honor her presence. Yet as a stunningly beautiful serpent maiden, she catches the unwelcome attention of demons roaming the forest.

.... ⚘ ....

VISHWAKARMA ARRIVES AT ELLORA 3: ILA'S INVITATION AND DAUGHTERLY CARE

Ila was a most beautiful, virtuous, and devoted wife and helped her husband with his spiritual practices. Leaving him in the cave, she went each morning to collect flowers he could offer in worship. Seeing her, demons in the area became infatuated.

The wandering sage Narada happened to come by the mountain. He praised Ila for the wonderful ways she was serving her husband. He also initiated her into ritual practices so she could gain Vishwakarma's protection.

Ila was then kidnapped by a demon named Gidhmukh, Vulture Face. She prayed to Vishwakarma, and he instantly appeared along with his adopted son Vastu (the spirit of building sites). Vishwakarma rescued her and reunited her with her distraught husband. Moved by her devotion, Vishwakarma adopted Ila as his daughter. When she entreated him to come live with them on the mountain, he agreed.

146 *Chapter 10*

Arriving to live at Ellora, Vishwakarma looked around and, through the power of his vision, made three sacred bathing ponds: the Vishwa Kund, the Surya Kund, and the Chandra Kund—the Universe Pond, the Sun Pond, and the Moon Pond. The mountain attracted holy people of many orders, who found this a good place for undisturbed meditation. Hosts of other gods came to visit Vishwakarma at Ellora and to enjoy a dip in the holy ponds.

At Ellora, Vishwakarma made sons from his own body to continue his work of making, and later he produced daughters to be given in marriage. As a loving oldest sister, Ila looked out for all her younger siblings. She helped host family celebrations on the mountain, whether sacred thread ceremonies or weddings. When there were concerns about the expense for lavishly hosting the whole universe for her sister Randal's wedding to the sun god at Ellora, Ila appealed to her father Shesh Nag, who provided a philosopher's stone to generate unbounded wealth.

....

The 1965 prose Purana that Bhai had first showed us retold the story of Ila, and returned to her in its apocalyptic finale. With the world coming to an end, the waters rise, fierce winds whirl, and people scream in terror. Vishwakarma has withdrawn to the Himalayas. A group sets out to seek help from him and meets the sage Narada, always on the move, on the way back from a visit with Vishwakarma. Narada guides them to the Ellora mountain. Here they find Ila and Ilachal sitting in the company of Shesh Narayan, who has taken the form of a storyteller and is reciting the Vishwakarma Purana. All those who will survive the dissolution listen along with the serpent maiden and the mountain, suspended in stories until the waters clear and a new creation dawns.[9]

A 2013 retelling of the Surajram Purana for children ends with Ila's words. When Vishwakarma has finally left Ellora, his bereaved sons recall their father, already known as "Dada," or Grandfather. "How great our Dada was!" they say.

Ila arrives and emotionally corrects them, "Don't say 'our,' say 'my' Dada," she instructs her brothers. "There's a sense of motherhood and sweetness present in 'my' that isn't there in 'our.' For all of us, he is 'my Dada.' My Dada, yes, my Dada—Shri Vishwakarma."[10]

✸

Versions of the name "Ila" reappear in other texts relating to Ellora, often referring to very different characters. In her pioneering article about ancient traditions of veneration at Ellora, Micaela Soar identifies Ila/Aila as the older name of the mountain stream of Velganga that feeds the main waterfall at the caves. Soar observes that Ila was, in the Vedic period, a river goddess; in the subsequent period of the Brahmana texts, she became associated with the flow of incantations in sacrifice; in the yet later time of the Puranas, s/he was personified as a king and "alternating androgyne" (Ila/Ilā) who moves between genders.[11] In local Marathi versions, Ila is often a king who becomes a woman after entering the goddess's domain. As a handmaiden to the goddess, she bears a son to another prince, then, after dipping into sacred water, she becomes a man again. Or else, Ila is a king afflicted by maggots each night, cured by bathing in a mountain pond, who then builds the Kailash temple.

All these identities for Ila flow into the name for the sacred domain established on and around the mountain. If the Vishwakarma Purana draws on Ila to name the mountain Ilachal ("Abode of Ila") as well as Ilorgaṛh or Ilolgarh ("Hill fort of Ila"), in other mythological retellings, the name Ila/Eeloo/Yella can be recast as Elapura or Ilapur, Elichpur, Alaurapuri, Yelapur, Verul.[12]

While Ila takes many forms in the larger flows of mythological transformation across time and space—river, transgender king, king partly afflicted by past sins—in Vishwakarma mythology, she remains a devoted serpent maiden while her husband keeps changing forms and names until they connect. He is remade from iron to gold, moves from sea to earth, and is somehow simultaneously a mountain and a man. I wonder: might all this shape-shifting at a sacred place echo artisans' celebrating the transformations latent within matter?

We were intrigued to learn that Vishwakarma could apparently himself take a serpent form, as Shesh Nag. A booklet from the Vishwakarma temple in Jamnagar retells creation from the moment that "there was not a single god, human, or any living creature, no moon, sun or stars, and the earth was in the underworld with water spreading in four directions above." Then the Vast Vishwakarma manifested and "taking the form of Shesh Nag he brought up the earth, carrying the whole earth on his forehead to stabilize it."[13]

Historical materials about Ellora reveal other mentions of Nagas. The local Shivalaya Mahatmya (attributed to the Skanda Purana) eulogizes the area through different names for different cosmic eras. The last two are significant: while this was "City of Ila (*Elāpur*)" in the Treta Yuga, in the present degenerate Kali Yuga the area is said to carry the name "Place of Nagas (*Nāgasthān*)."[14] An early nineteenth-century summary of the Mahatmya traces this title to serpents having taken refuge behind the lingam in the nearby Ghrishneshwar Shiva temple during a mass slaughter of serpents by the legendary King Janamajeya, whose father had died of snakebite.[15]

This same summary of the Mahatmya describes how, after some time spent as a woman serving the goddess Parvati on the mountaintop, King "Yella" was again turned into a man. He then bathed in a series of pools along the "Yella Ganga" (Velganga) river, rebuilt the Ghrishneshwar shrine to Shiva, and "thence he went east to the Naga Jeree . . . [which has] sprung from the head of Shesha [Naga] and flows west in a rivulet for a quarter coss to join the Eela Ganga."[16]

The Naga Jadi or Serpent Rivulet flows through a pool in the area just above the Buddhist caves. The painter James Wales's description of an idyllic spring morning at the pool in 1795, with a cool breeze, waving bushes, and wild peafowl drinking water made me think of the mythology of Ila and her girlfriends coming to bathe. Wales also evoked how, with the monsoons, the scene would transform: the rushing water in the pool "like a boiling cauldron, till bursting from thence it runs with incredible swiftness down the smooth, rocky steep and darts its whole mass over a precipice ninety feet high, into the abyss below; when the gray fog veils it from sight. The spectator feels the solid rock tremble under his feet and is awed from the near approach."[17]

The force of that wild water during the monsoon wore away the exterior of the nearby Buddhist caves, and the rivulet is now carefully channeled away from the cave exteriors, with the depth of the plunge also reduced. Yet Wales was not present in the monsoon, and most likely, his vivid depiction of the waterfall is an imaginative projection.[18]

Ila's presence in Vishwakarma mythology seems to connect Cave 10's saluting serpents and serpent motifs with a local serpent cult associated with the nearby rivulet that was sometimes a trickle, sometimes a wild force. There's a logic, too, in Ila being characterized as a *female* serpent, for as we came to know when following stories of Randal, another of Vishwakarma's daughters, the Ellora mountain is also celebrated for manifestations of the goddess.

✳ 11 ✳

From Mantras to Tools

One of the Via-Via links that Prakash forged for us was with Jayantibhai Gajjar—his niece's father-in-law. "He knows all the stories," Prakash said in his reassuring way. "About Vishwakarma, about Ellora . . . everything; whatever you want to know, you just ask him!"

Jayantibhai lived to the east of the Sabarmati River, in the industrial part of Ahmedabad that people said had been wide-open stretches of land, a "jungle" until a few decades ago. One Sunday in November 2017, Prakash and Sonal accompanied us to that side of town for a celebration of the goddess Randal, Vishwakarma's daughter, at a community hall. (Since Randal is married to Surya, the sun god, Sundays are considered good days for her worship.) My cousin Yeshu had loaned me a tie-dyed sari to wear Gujarati-style with the final section draped forward. A few hundred Kathiawari Gujar Suthars, also all festively dressed, had gathered, and 54 representations of Randal were lined up in tiers. Because of her doubled form, this meant that 108 colored prints of her head and torso had been wrapped around coconuts balanced in waterpots. Each identical print showed her smiling, dressed in red and green, and adorned with a beaded crown. Standing nearby, a five-headed Vishwakarma statue looked on in several simultaneous directions.

Fifty-four families had signed up to participate in this group event. The morning started with representatives of the families sitting cross-legged on the ground in long rows, ritual implements and ingredients arranged on low trays before them. At the front of the hall, near the resplendent assembly of Randal images, a few Brahmin priests sat beside microphones, alternately chanting goddess prayers in Sanskrit and issuing ritual instructions in Gujarati. We joined the onlookers and elderly on folding chairs at one side.

After an hour or so, the Brahmins disappeared. The orderly gathering broke up into milling jollity as everyone began preparing for the ritual's next phase. Each of the fifty-four families was to honor a sequence of fourteen girls or married women with the ceremonial anointment of a toe, feeding with rice pudding (*khīr*) and wheat *roṭlīs*, and a small gift. Women moved between groups, taking pictures and excitedly calling to others. I put my notebook and camera away as Sonal summoned me over so her sister-in-law could pour water over my big toe and mark it with red *kumkum*.

33. Kirin preparing to step up during group worship of goddess Randal, Ahmedabad, 2017. Photograph by Ken George.

Toe anointed, a paper bowl with the sweet homemade *khīr* and *roṭlīs* was handed up to me, followed by a small brass oil lamp. Then I returned to being the anthropologist as another woman stepped forward.

When each family had wrapped up this phase of worship, everyone went downstairs to the courtyard for a buffet lunch. Loudspeakers played recorded music at eardrum-destroying decibels. Meal done, some people rested and caught up, shouting to be heard over the music; others started bending and stepping in big circles, or hopping and prancing forward and backward in the "horse dance," said to delight Randal. Prakash and Sonal disappeared into the sociable crowd while Ken and I were cornered by a young man wearing white, intent on sharing theories he was certain were essential to our research, such as Gujarati being the original language of the world ("Even dogs speak Gujarati. Don't you hear them say '*Bho-bho-bho?*'"). What a relief when Prakash showed up! He had organized a ride for us with a nephew, he said. We could go out for a few hours and still be back to observe the evening rituals.

As we started toward the entrance, another of Prakash's many nephews asked where we were headed. This nephew, who worked at the Ford assembly plant, was comfortable in English and, hearing that we were off to confer with Jayantibhai, exclaimed, "He is an *encyclopedia*!"

"Yes," Prakash continued in Gujarati. Always on the alert for ways to translate things into terms meaningful to us, he added, "Jayantibhai is very deep into these matters—like a *PhD*!"

Outdoors, as our ears recovered from the pounding music, the traffic seemed oddly muted. The usual haze of pollution washed color from the buildings and sky. We dropped Sonal off to visit with her mother, and set out toward Jayantibhai's place, moving through streams of honking vehicles, wayside vendors, and people on foot for Sunday errands. At the bottom of a traffic overpass, we turned off the main road, passed a set of gleaming new buildings with shops, banks, and restaurants, and came to a halt in a lane lined with low apartment complexes and paved courtyards.

Following Prakash up a narrow stairwell, we were greeted by a beaming family standing by the open door: Jayantibhai and his wife, his two sons and their wives, a teenaged granddaughter. We placed our sandals amid heaps of footwear on the landing and entered a tidy living room dominated (in traditional Gujarati fashion) by a bed-size wooden swing. Just by the door, atop the television, sat a small metal statue of Grandfather Vishwakarma dressed up in yellow cloth.

The women of the family bustled about, watching us with intent interest as they brought out tray after tray: glasses of water, cups of strong tea, plates of homemade Divali snacks and sweets. Jayantibhai settled onto the large swing, rocking a little. His silver hair combined with his slender build gave him an aura of ascetic refinement. He spoke in a low assured voice, mixing a little Hindi into his Gujarati for my benefit.

How could we prompt Jayantibhai to tell "all the stories" relevant to our project? Sitting with Prakash on a low sofa nearby, Ken began by asking about Vishwakarma temples around Ahmedabad.

Jayantibhai listed a few, then told us, "But the oldest Vishwakarma temple in all of India is at Ellora (*Iloṛgaṛh*). That is Vishwakarma's original residence."

To place Vishwakarma at Ellora, Jayantibhai started with the first stirring of creation. Primordial formless Brahm (Parabrahma), he said, had wanted to create, and the power of this desire manifested as a powerful goddess, Shakti. She made Vishwakarma from an egg encompassing three basic qualities (*guṇa*)—luminous clarity, active energy, and dense heaviness. Then she made the other great gods, Brahma, Vishnu, and Shiva, who each separately embody one of the three qualities. Vishwakarma himself went off to do spiritual austerities, and the stories of the other gods went on with twists and turns until Vishwakarma returned to stabilize the rocking earth by placing heavy mountains around so creation could proceed.

"See, every god has a specialty," Jayantibhai instructed. "Vishwakarma's is to make things. This entire universe was made by Vishwakarma through mantras. Also, he provided tools for every kind of work."

Jayantibhai used the Gujarati word *sādhan*, which means "tool" as well as the means or process by which a task is accomplished. As city cacophony rushed in through windows facing the overpass, Jayantibhai transported us to Ellora (*Iloṛgaṛh*) as the place where Vishwakarma's sons first gained their tools.

VISHWAKARMA MAKES SONS, AND A SON MAKES A MISTAKE

After the universe was created, then Vishwakarma came to live in Ellora as his sacred dwelling place (*dhām*) on earth. After some time, he started preparing to leave for his other place, in heaven. It's just like when I want to come home after a day at the factory; in the same way, Vishwakarma had finished his work of making everything, and he was ready to go to his own place.

But all the gods were worried. They wondered, "Who will make things and mend things if Vishwakarma goes away?" So then Vishwakarma made five sons from mantras. He lived with them for some time at Ellora.

Vishwakarma gave his sons the power to make things through mantras. He wanted his boys to be educated, and he sent them to other sages to learn more. One son was left behind in Ellora.

That boy made a big mistake. He wanted to try out that power of making. Using mantras, he instantly constructed a big fortress in the nearby forest. But he forgot to put in doors and windows. All the living creatures, even insects, were trapped. They couldn't breathe, and they all died.

Vishwakarma was very angry. He took away the power to make by mantras. But he gave the sons tools. "From now on, you'll have to work with your hands," he said.

....

"That is why we now have tools," Jayantibhai concluded.

Our talk returned to the present as Jayantibhai told us how he had worked as a carpenter, then a fabricator, an electrician, a foreman at a gold refinery. When replacement parts were required for foreign machines, he figured out how to manufacture them. When he didn't have a clear *nakshā*—a sketch, a method, a plan—Jayantibhai said that he appealed to Vishwakarma. "He instructs from the third eye," he told us, tapping the center of his forehead. "Then I get an idea of how to proceed."

Prakash vigorously nodded. "*Sixth sense*," he clarified for us in English.

More relatives had appeared through the open door to make the customary post-Divali visit to elders. After greetings, introductions, and further rounds of water, tea, snacks, and sweets, Jayantibhai and his sons began looking around the apartment to find old carpenters' tools kept in storage. They carried these out, carefully laying them on the table: a handsaw, a hand plane, a wood chisel, the head of an adze, a bow drill, and more. These tools had belonged to Jayantibhai's grandfather, who worked in a village in Junagarh district, Saurashtra, and Jayantibhai had used them when he was starting out. As we took photographs, the gathered group marveled at how the elders had done amazing work even in the days before power tools. Jayantibhai remembered how a cord would be attached to the bow drill, pulled back and forth by the user or a helper to generate more force.

Jayantibhai had used the word *dorī* for cord. Remembering the carpenter's cord in one of the derivations of Suthar/Sutradhar, I asked if this could also be termed *sūtra*.

Jayantibhai shook his head no, and reverently said, "The *sūtra* is *written!*"

He stood up to lift the brass statue of Vishwakarma off the television, bringing it closer to point out the treatise in Vishwakarma's lower right hand.

✳

Prakash had been listening intently. A few weeks later, when he and Sonal brought over a meal to our apartment, he shared his own thoughts about how to think of *sūtra*. Grasping for a way to translate *sūtra* into English, he lit on, not "code," but "formula," and "proof." To him, the term encompassed the tacit understanding of the appropriate process, combination, and ratios of elements.

"It's understanding how much of what material you need to bring together if you're going to make something right," Prakash said. In his quick eager way, he reached for a piece of paper to illustrate his words. He drew a right angle, marking the vertical line as ¾ of a meter and the horizontal line, 1 meter. Then, pen slashing at a downward angle, he marked the hypotenuse as 1¼ meter. "It's understanding *this* measurement," Prakash said, holding up the sheet. "This is one *sūtra*."

The 3–4–5 ratio of this triangle's sides is an instance of what's often known as the Pythagorean theorem. I was interested to find these same ratios associated with Vishwakarma and grounded in cosmology, in a handbook to an Indian craft exhibition in Delhi from the start of the twentieth century. Describing a Suthar at work on a wooden replica of part of the Bhavnagar palace, the British curator George Watt reported, "As the work progressed, he observed that the finger of God was pointing the way and that accordingly mistakes were impossible. In support of this belief, he quoted the ancient rules of his craft such as that if the nine planets, the twelve signs of the zodiac and the fifteen dates of the lunar month were kept in line together, Vishwakarma had told that they would subtend a right angle . . ."[1]

When I asked whether *sūtra* couldn't also mean "cord," Prakash emphatically disagreed.

"*Sūtra* practical *chhe!*" Prakash said. "It means practical knowledge! You have to know how thick a beam should be for a room of a certain size. You need to understand the angle of a roof to allow for rain. This understanding is what a *sūtra* is—it's not just some cord that you attach to a plumb bob for straight lines, or that you use to mark out plots. There's no intelligence in holding a plumb bob! It'll always show the same thing, whether you hold it high or low! The *sūtra* is the *tattva*—the principle, the essence, the code...." Casting about again for an English term, he said, "Look, it's our own *structural engineering*!"

Yet it turned out that the word *sūtra* could also encompass key tools associated with measurement and alignment. A sort of Vishwakarma catechism in Gujarati that was forwarded to us on WhatsApp at several

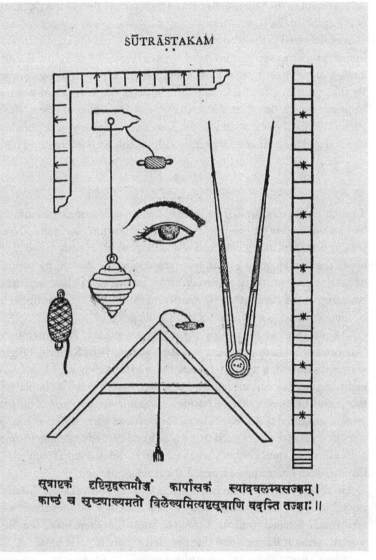

34. "Eight Sūtras," from an overview of building manuals, Lucknow, 1958. British Library Asia, Pacific and Africa V 15011.

different moments in our research included a question about the *sūtras* that Vishwakarma gave his sons. The list of seven started with "vision" and moved on to a footrule and cord followed by other tools. But in various Shilpa Shastras, or ancient building manuals, we noticed variations on a diagram often titled "Eight Sūtras." Professor D. N. Shukla's authoritative overview of texts on traditional forms of architecture begins with a dedication to Shiva temples, including the one at Ellora, as the "crowning achievement of the Indian artisans and their gurus." Beside this dedication is a diagram of the eight *sūtras*.[2]

As celebrated in the accompanying Sanskrit verse, the eight *sūtras* are a human eye, a measuring stick, cord twisted from wild *munjā* grass, cotton cord, a plumb bob, a set square, a level, and finally, a drawing compass. By distinguishing between two sorts of cord, the number of key tools becomes eight rather than the contemporary reckoning of seven. The capacity for visual perception is listed first. The human eye at the center of this assemblage connects outwardly visible tools with internalized codes.

✳

Though Ellora was familiar to Jayantibhai through stories, he had never had an opportunity to visit it. During the monsoon, we invited him to join us on a trip, along with our research assistant Hardik (who, as the nephew of his daughter-in-law, was a close relative). We had the privilege of hearing and recording stories about Vishwakarma at Ellora against the backdrop of the caves. Also, we learned more about how Jayantibhai had become enchanted by these stories as a village child.

"When I was small, I enjoyed reading everything," he remembered. "There was a Brahmin, a Shastri [scholar], who narrated Kathas—religious stories. I thought, why can't I recite these in the same way? I was about eight or nine. The Shastri felt a lot of compassion for me. As he narrated the stories, he used to seat me beside him, and I became a part of the gathering. I imagined that I would learn Sanskrit and narrate Kathas too. But our circumstances were such that my father didn't educate me. I wanted to be educated, but I couldn't get an education. So that didn't happen. But through such gatherings, I learned about religious texts."

He continued, "In those times, there was no Vishwakarma Purana in my village. My older brother Chagganbhai used to tell stories about Vishwakarma. I listened to those. I came to know that there was a temple of Vishwakarma at Ilorgarh and that people go there to meet him."

When he was eighteen, Jayantibhai moved to Ahmedabad, where he lived with his father's sister's family. Through Via-Via, he found a job as a

35. Jayantibhai Gajjar, Ken George, Hardik Siddhpura, Ellora, 2018. Photograph by Kirin Narayan.

carpenter, making bobbins, then brushes, for cloth mills. After three years, he was able to rent his own place. A carpenter living in the apartment upstairs learned of his interests and borrowed a Vishwakarma Purana from a relative so Jayantibhai could begin reading. "Slowly, slowly I began to have direct knowledge of these stories," he said. Eventually, he found his own copy in the shops that sold used books and religious texts near Ahmedabad's Ellis Bridge.

Almost a year after we met, Jayantibhai brought out a well-worn copy of Surajram's Vishwakarma Purana, the cover anointed with a red *tilak* on Vishwakarma's forehead. Recognizably the same book as Bhai's 1926 edition, this later edition from the 1970s was more reader-friendly: the verses had been indented rather than presented in a continuous, proselike flow, and a few illustrations had been added. The story of Vishwakarma granting his sons tools appeared in chapter 18.[3]

When Bhai later helped us translate this chapter into English, we recognized how closely Jayantibhai's retelling had drawn on the Purana. As background, Bhai explained that Vishwakarma had first given his sons the power of instantaneous making by mind and the use of mantras, possibly with a small sprinkle of water. Here is my summary of our translation.[4]

.... ☙ ....

THE EYE OF VISHWAKARMA

Vishwakarma and his sons were living peacefully and happily at Ellora. One day, Indra, king of the gods, arrived from heaven. He said that he didn't want to impose on Vishwakarma as an elder. But since the throne in his assembly hall had become shabby, he wondered if Vishwakarma could send a son to make a new throne.

Pleased by this humble petition (for Indra is notoriously high-handed), Vishwakarma sent four sons to heaven to make the throne. The fifth, Shilp, stayed behind at Ellora. He looked around at the big forest and decided to experiment with the power of making he'd received. So he sprinkled water and, simply imagining a fort, a gigantic fort appeared. But he hadn't thought to include a single door or window.

In the words of the Purana:

> Within the fort were trees and shrubs, animals and birds; various sorts of crawling and flying insects; and all kinds of snakes. Fresh air couldn't circulate, and all those living creatures were trapped. Some panicked, some died. As the air became foul, the creatures suffered. They began to thrash about and to fix their minds on Vishwakarma. Meditating, they wept. Vishwakarma became aware that something was afoot. Filled with great compassion, he went to find out what was happening in the forest.

Vishwakarma climbed the Ellora mountain peak for a good view. Seeing a huge fort without any openings for air, he instantly destroyed the monolith. As the fort collapsed, some creatures escaped. But he witnessed how inside, "there was no end to the thrashing creatures and their distress."

Vishwakarma sadly recognized that this must be his sons' doing. He issued a curse revoking the boys' power to make things by imagining them. In heaven, the four sons collaborating on Indra's new throne had begun painting it red, green, yellow, and pink. But suddenly everything they had made started disintegrating. Unable to proceed, the sons came back to Ellora.

With all his sons gathered, Vishwakarma berated them for their cruelty to the creatures of the forest. The sons who had been off working for Indra objected: they hadn't done anything, they were innocent, they would lose their very identity if they lost the power to make things! They begged their father to give them back the special knowledge.

Shilp confessed that he alone had been responsible. He implored Vishwakarma not to confiscate the sons' power of making with the mind.

But Vishwakarma wouldn't budge. A curse, he said, can't be undone. As further punishment, Shilp would be an outcaste from the group. Vishwakarma, though, still wanted to ensure his sons' futures and granted them a different token of his care: "But sons, I give you my blessing that you won't live amid troubles. Work with your hands, and that will be equivalent to the lost knowledge. Look, my sons: I have three eyes, and I will give you one. Many eyes are united through this eye that will remain in your families."

Promising this inner eye to all future generations, Vishwakarma assured them, "My eye will stay closed within you. But when I'm needed, take the measuring stick and the cord into your hands, and the eye will open. You'll see what you need to do. Mind moving fast as the wind, you'll know right away how to proceed."

In this retelling, intended for carpenters, Vishwakarma offered the four innocent sons the title "Sutar": "You'll be known as the Sutar of the Sutradhars. Even when your work is difficult, you'll be tough enough to overcome all obstacles."

Cast out from the group, Shilp rolled about on the ground, wailing. Ila arrived and intervened on her little brother's behalf. She reminded Vishwakarma that even good people make mistakes. Vishwakarma felt compassion for Shilp, and he counseled his sons on the human duty of compassion for other creatures:

> Be careful not to injure other creatures with your work. Just like we suffer, they suffer too. Whether animals or birds, whether crawling or flying insects, whether male or female; it's your human duty to be compassionate to them all. From now on, don't forget this teaching.

....

The story went on with the sons being given specializations. Assuring Shilp that he still loved him, Vishwakarma granted the boy a new identity as a Kadiya mason/bricklayer, segregated by caste from Sutar carpenters but working beside them. Vishwakarma also presented Shilp with a plumb bob, a level, and a trowel; the other brothers gave him a float to smooth plaster. (This story used the older spelling, "Sutar.")

Vishwakarma then blessed all the boys, saying that together they would make many sorts of residences, stepwells and ponds, vehicles, and machines: "Whenever making something new is undertaken, then you five will be honored." Seeing these other sons receive boons, Vastu, the adopted eldest son, felt left out. Vishwakarma put his hand on Vastu's head, blessing him. When the other sons made or renovated residences, Vishwakarma said, Vastu should first be recognized as the deity of harmonious place.

This story explained the origin of tools, the different occupational specializations of Vishwakarma's sons, and a fall in status. For while ancient Hindu texts assert, "The hand in the act of making is always pure,"[5] making by hand has generally been looked down on and associated with a lower-caste status. Historically, respected Brahmins and scholars made creations through words and by ritual action; those who used their hands for a livelihood were viewed as workers whose role was to offer practical service.

Vallabhram Surajram's version introduced "the eye of Vishwakarma," thought to be present within his descendants and capable of opening when tools are taken in hand: in particular, the sacred footrule and cord. If the two-armed Murti commissioned by my great-grandfather in Bhorara was holding a footrule and cord, perhaps that was intended to be a representation of Vishwakarma showing how the eye could be accessed. Other Vishwakarma Murtis—for example, at Dakor—prominently display a third eye.

As Jayantibhai said, "For us it's like this. Vishwakarma has given us this promise: 'whatever work you want to do, if you're stuck, when you can't see any kind of solution, at that time remember me. My third eye will instantly open; immediately your work will be done.'"

We heard versions of the story of the sons losing one power and gaining another two more times. On the morning we visited the workshop of the National Institute of Design in Ahmedabad, students weren't needing concerted supervision for their class projects and the technicians in charge chatted with us at length, revealing their own backgrounds as sons of Vishwakarma—some from assorted Suthar castes, others from Panchal metalworker and Soni goldsmith castes. In the corner of the large workshop filled with machine tools was an altar with a framed poster of Vishwakarma with tools and sons, alongside a larger image of the goddess Durga riding a tiger and carrying weapons in many of her eighteen outspread arms. A bespectacled technician from a hereditary goldsmith background launched into the story, and this was how I later wrote it down.

.... ☙ ....

ROOFING THE WORLD

Vishwakarma's sons had first made things just by imagining them. When they became fed up with shifts of weather—hot sunshine, heavy rain—they imagined a roof enclosing the whole world, and instantly the world was roofed.

At first they lived comfortably. But then all the plants, all sorts of animals, birds, and insects, even people, were choking and dying.

Vishwakarma was angry. He took away that marvelous power and, instead, he gave his sons tools.

....

Here the sons had collaborated in making a big roof to withstand the subcontinent's scorching sun and monsoon storms, thoughtlessly torturing all living creatures with this enclosure. But when we met the story again, at a local museum, Vastu, the adopted eldest son, played a key role.

When we asked about Vishwakarma, we were directed not to the museum's collection but to its in-house carpenter, a middle-aged man named Pravinbhai, of Gujar Suthar background. As he showed us his small workshop, Pravinbhai emphasized that he was, however, more than a carpenter: he was an "all-rounder" technician, cutting glass, improvising exhibit stands, working with cement, even replacing washers in sinks. On his wall hung a colored lithograph of a young Vishwakarma as Resident of Ellora (clearly adapted from the 1911 Vallabhram Surajram Purana frontispiece).

Pravinbhai showed us how he had set up the background of his smart phone to alternate between images of Vishwakarma in the two-armed Ellora form and the elderly four-armed form. He extended his phone to share other images he had collected or downloaded from the web. We too showed him unusual images we had located, and lifting his phone to the iPad, he added these photos to his archive. He then related how Vishwakarma's sons had received tools. His version emphasized the cross-caste collaborations traditionally involved in building, extending kinship to potters. Again, all sons suffer because of one son's thoughtlessness with the gift of mental making. Here the culprit is Vastu, overseeing the work of others.

.... ⚘ ....

VASTU MAKES A MISTAKE

At first, Vishwakarma's sons recited mantras and things were made. Vastu was the supervisor, and using mantras, the four Suthar carpenter sons made doors and windows, the Salat mason made walls, and a Prajapati potter joined in making tiles for roofs.

Then Indra asked for a palace. As supervisor, Vastu used the power of mantras but forgot all about doors and windows.

Vishwakarma was angry. "You will no longer be the supervisor. You will have to drive Surya's chariot and you will receive worship and be fed through pujas at the beginning of construction projects."

Then Vishwakarma took the power of making through mantras away from all his sons. He gave them tools and taught them how to use these tools.

....

"This is how from mantra, we moved to *yantra* [tools and machines]," concluded Pravinbhai.

He went on to advise us that tools should be treated with reverence, not left lying on the ground where they could inadvertently be disrespected by contact with feet. He described the central importance of the measuring stick (*gaj*), and how different gods resided at different inch marks. Before the museum closed, he carefully laid out his hand tools in an arrangement that his father had taught him for worship on Vishwakarma Teras and Dassera day. Each tool, he said, would then be honored with a red *tilak*, and *laḍḍus* of ghee, jaggery, and wheat or chickpea flour would be offered at the altar. As he explained, "We worship tools along with Vishwakarma because these are the source of our livelihood."

※

While Ellora was identified as the place where Vishwakarma bestowed tools, we also learned of a Rajasthani tradition of bringing tools to Ellora for blessing; if this was ever the case in Gujarat, no one has told us about it.

Our friend Walter Spink sent us an online link someone had forwarded to him, to a selection set at Ellora from the filmmaker Saeed Mirza's memoir. Mirza had been making a documentary about the caves in 1992. Seeking a location shot after the day's crowds had dispersed, his filming team had set up cameras outside a cave when a group of about ten men and women came to the cave's steps, put down a bundle, and began to pray.[6] The team waited. The group was reverentially taking its time, and the sun would soon set. So Mirza approached the turbaned men intending to ask how long they would take, and if they might speed up their prayers.

The pilgrims warmly engaged with Mirza. They said they were from Jaisalmer (a region within Marwar) in Rajasthan. They usually made the pilgrimage every two years, taking three days to come, a day to worship, and then three days to return. Mirza was curious if they visited all the caves, but one of the men explained that only this temple was close to their hearts, as their forefathers had made it. "We have been artisans for many, many generations," the man explained. "We might be illiterate, but we pass on our history from one generation to the next by telling them the stories of our past."

Mirza asked what was in the cloth bundle they were carrying and was shown an assortment of chisels, hammers, cutters, and wooden wedges. He was told, "These are our implements. We bring them with us and ask God to bless them so that we can do good work, just as our ancestors did."

Mirza decided that his team could film the shot the following day. As they lugged away their equipment, he looked back and saw that the pilgrims had settled down for a communal meal at their ancestral temple.

✳

For months, I'd felt uneasy about Vishwakarma traditions so enthusiastically celebrating all projects of building and making. Living amid the constant construction and extreme air pollution of Ahmedabad added poignancy to thinking about the trapped and choking creatures. The dense particulate matter in the air was indeed like a roof: I imagined a generation growing up thinking that gray was the sky's natural color and that asthma and other respiratory issues were routine parts of life. From our apartment I often watched the morning sun lift out of a darker band along the horizon, flushed a deep maroon, and though I had hung a prism in an east-facing window, the sunshine was too weak to make rainbows. Each time we got into a plane, lifting upward and out of the smoky soup, it seemed a surprise to find that the sky could still be blue. People kept remembering how there had once been many sparrows in the city; where had these common birds gone, let alone the rarer ones? People talked of birds falling from the sky and humans fainting on the pavement in the intensity of summer. With climate change, this pall hanging over all lives and felling the most vulnerable could only get worse.

The story of Vishwakarma withdrawing the power of instantaneous material creation didn't solve the problem of careless human action. Giving his sons tools, he only slowed down their actions, forcing them to physically interact with the materials they were transforming. Yet in this gap between conceptualizing and making, Vishwakarma opened a space for reflection on the ethical consequences of making. I remembered the slogan in my grandfather's book: "Nonviolence is the supreme way of life" (*ahimsā paramo dharma*). Even as Vishwakarma couldn't guarantee what his sons would do with the tools, he counseled them and all makers of the future to keep other creatures in mind: "Just like we suffer, they suffer too."

This compassionate attention to suffering, I realized, was very much in line with the Buddha's teachings. Perhaps the manifestation of "Guru" Vishwakarma in Cave 10 at Ellora, hands arranged in the pose to transmit wisdom, reminded artisan pilgrims to consider the suffering of other creatures as they went about their work.

✳ 12 ✳

An Injured Finger and Other Tokens of "Proof"

If the big, seated Murti in Cave 10 was perceived as Vishwakarma working through mantras rather than with tools, I could understand why, contrary to all other forms, at Ellora he had empty hands. But we soon discovered a set of stories that elaborated on the cave's iconography to identify a cord, and even conjure up an absent chisel. For those keen to find Vishwakarma, it seemed, his presence was affirmed all through the cave.

While the Murti's hands are now worn away, looking more like mittens, they are unmistakably arranged in the *dharmachakra* teaching pose—a pose repeated among the rows of similar Buddhas above the pillars. When Buddhists familiar with the iconographic meaning left the area, it seems, this pose drew imaginative elaboration. The right thumb and forefinger held the tip of the left little finger; didn't this seem a soothing gesture? And then, directly below the hand, something trailed toward the ground. Could that be a cord, establishing the figure as a Sutradhar with cord in hand? Or was it perhaps a trickle of blood from a wounded finger?[1]

✳

During our early months in Ahmedabad, we heard a Gujarati version of Grandfather (Dada) Vishwakarma's wounded finger. At a story event, on an afternoon of rituals honoring Vishwakarma's daughter, we started chatting with an older man babysitting his toddler granddaughter. We learned that he and his family had recently moved to the city, and he was named Pravinbhai (the same name as the museum carpenter of the last chapter). Further conversation revealed that his sister had married into the same village as Ba's sister Maushi, and in fact, was married to Maushi's grandson. I had not only met her but had once photographed her holding a framed photograph of her son on pilgrimage

36. Clear view of hands and edge of robe, Cave 10, Ellora, 2018. Photograph by Kirin Narayan.

to Ellora. Pravinbhai also knew all about Ba and her flamboyant visits to the village.

"But you are our relatives!" he exclaimed. With this connection established, we were immediately invited to dinner. Two evenings later, we joined the family in a small, immaculate apartment in the Vastral industrial region; nearby they had set up small workshops to manufacture aluminum hinges, latches, and sliders, as well as spectacle frames. As we were served tea, Pravinbhai brought out books of interest to us. Opening Bachubhai Vadgama's 2013 retelling of the Vishwakarma Purana with its color plates showing various forms of Vishwakarma, we were struck by a photograph of the Murti in Cave 10, labeled "Lord Vishwakarma in the cave of Ellora Mountain (*Ilāchal*)."

As Ken positioned an iPad over that image, the middle son, Mitulbhai, observed, "Our mother knows that story." His mother, Jyotsnaben, was just then busy making dinner with her eldest daughter-in-law, the scent of roasted red chilies and curry leaves wafting around us. We had to wait until after our dinner, eaten in a circle on the floor. After everything was tidied up, Mitulbhai urged his mother in Gujarati to retell the story of Cave 10: "The one about the mark on the forehead [*tilak*]," he prompted. I got my phone ready to record.

Jyotsnaben was in her fifties, wearing a bright sari with the end extending forward in the Gujarati style. Speaking at a brisk clip, she transported us to the sacred cave at Ellora.

.... ✤ ....

VISHWAKARMA REASSURES HIS SONS OF HIS PRESENCE

When Dada was leaving for his own heavenly place, his five sons asked him, "Dada, if you go off to your own place, who will take care of us?"

Vishwakarma said, "Just look, there's my Murti; it's right in front of you!"

The sons said, "But Dada, how are we going to know it's you in the Murti?"

Vishwakarma said, "If you cut the little finger of the Murti, blood will flow. Anoint my forehead with a *tilak* of that blood. If the finger is cut and blood flows, then that's the proof that your Vishwakarma Dada is here."

The sons said, "But Dada, that is Buddha!"

Vishwakarma said, "Buddha, that's fine. But if the finger is cut and blood flows, you'll know this is your Vishwakarma Dada."

....

The family went on to note the location as the "*dasvā* number *guphā, Ilorgarh*"—that is, Cave 10, Ellora.

"So, since they cut the finger and blood flowed, then that's Vishwakarma," Mitulbhai summarized.

Jyotsnaben agreed. "Yes, yes, Dada is present there."

Jyotsnaben wasn't sure how she had learned the story; maybe she'd read it somewhere. She told us that Suthars were advised to read Vishwakarma stories on "Vishwakarma Teras [Thirteen]" also known as Maha

Sud Teras, a lunar date that usually falls in late January or early February. She remembered how, when she'd gone on pilgrimage to Cave 10 some decades earlier, she'd seen a little box with *kumkum* placed at the side of the image so that a red *tilak* could be offered. (I didn't yet know to ask: where were the guards that day?)

No one else retold this story of the Murti to us, and the story was strikingly absent from contemporary publications like Bachubhai Vadgama's 2013 Purana, which after dinner, Pravinbhai's family insisted we take home. But an emotional version appears in Vallabhram Surajram's Vishwakarma Purana from about a century earlier, which might directly or indirectly have been Jyotsnaben's source. This story comes toward the Purana's end, as Vishwakarma prepares to leave Ellora, an event said to have occurred on the eleventh day of the bright half of the sacred month of Shravan (July/August).[2]

.... ॐ ....

VISHWAKARMA ESTABLISHES HIMSELF IN A MURTI

After years of living in Ellora with his sons, Vishwakarma departed for his own heavenly place. His five sons were disconsolate. They grieved so hard they couldn't work. So Vishwakarma came back to them.

His sons sobbed, tightly hugging him. They said, "Father, we can't let you go! How can we express the pain in our hearts? We can't live without seeing you; without you, we're miserable."

Then Vishwakarma established his own self within a Murti.

The sons asked, "Father, why did you do this? Tell us, what did you just do?"

Vishwakarma said, "You've made me happy, and I've made you this Murti. You'll be satisfied by viewing this Murti and you won't be so sad."

But the sons didn't think a stone statue was a good substitute. Real presence, they argued, was not the same as resemblance.

"Look, a thread of spittle can't tie up a bundle of grass!" the sons said. "If a donkey's droppings could be used to press papadam, no one would ask the price of lentils. If a mirage could quench thirst, people wouldn't care about rain. If the eye could see without light, no one would worship the sun. If thumb-sucking produced milk, no one would suckle a mother."

Vishwakarma insisted that the image wasn't just a stand-in. "I'm fully present in this Murti, so don't worry," he said. "I'll show you the proof. Watch the Murti closely. Believe that this initiation I'm giving you is true."

He cut the Murti's little finger, and blood immediately flowed.

Then all the sons were satisfied, and they believed his assurance. Vishwakarma was really present in that Murti!

...

In these Suthar myths, the finger is cut intentionally—by Vishwakarma, or at his request. The blood represents a promise: flowing from stone, it proves to Vishwakarma's descendants that the Murti is alive with their forefather's presence.

In other recorded versions, though, Vishwakarma's finger is wounded by mistake. I've already reproduced Charles Malet's summary of a story from the late eighteenth century tracing how, in a single, magically prolonged night, Vishwakarma was charged with excavating all the caves and then connecting them by tunnel to the Daulatabad fort. Interrupted by a cock crowing earlier than anticipated, "he retired, having wounded his finger, to . . . his hovel, in which state the figure in front of the entrance of this beautiful excavation is said to be a representation of him holding the wounded finger."[3]

A few years later, in 1808, in a fascinating manuscript report on Ellora (*Ellola*) prepared for the colonial surveyor Colin Mackenzie—about which I will say more later—the story reappears with a twist, establishing a connection between Cave 10 and the two caves immediately to the north. Cave 12 was the three-level residential cave where Chakradhar Swami had camped, and where the Buddha on the uppermost level had come to be worshipped as the deity Ram or Ramchandra; Cave 11 also started out with three stories, though through the centuries, debris had blocked the lowest floor. With only two levels visible, Cave 11 became known as "Two Levels" or even "Vishwakarma Two Levels," in contrast to Cave 12, "Three Levels."[4]

... ॐ ...

MAKING CAVE 11, VISHWAKARMA CUTS HIS FINGER

Viswacurmah having formed the Treetalla (or Three Heavens) in three different stories intended to form Images there [in Cave 11] & to finish the third story when he cut one of his fingers & the God Ramchundra told him "I live in Tree-Talla! you must not built its resemblance"; then Viswacurmah finding these bad omens removed from that place.

...

Here, Vishwakarma leaves Cave 11 unfinished because of an unexpected injury and because Ram would not like his habitation in Cave 12 to be exactly copied with the same three levels. Vishwakarma then moves south to Cave 10, the "Viswacurma Jhopadee," where he sits down to soothe his injured finger in the company of a concerned team of workers.

·· ❧ ··

VISHWAKARMA SITS IN CAVE 10, HOLDING HIS WOUNDED FINGER

Viswacurmah cut the form of a Jhopadee (or Cottage) out of the Bundah or Great Stone as an arched Muntapum [Pavilion] in which Viswacurmah is seated with his followers & servants around him, about 225 Figures; they are represented in grief for his wound & holding his wounded finger, some of them standing...

···

This mythological sequence of building is the opposite of how art historians trace the unfolding from Cave 10 to 11 to 12.[5] Another version of the same story was recorded two decades later from local Brahmins by W. H. Sykes, statistical recorder for the East India Company. Cave 11 was identified as the space where Vishwakarma cut his finger, and "he was compelled by pain to desist; whence 'Dookya Ghur' [House of the Pained]. On his recovery he sculptured himself in the next cave (Bisma Kurm) holding his finger to commemorate his accident."[6] The story still circulates in Marathi oral tradition as the key to identifying Vishwakarma in Cave 10.[7]

Why was Cave 11 seen as the site of an injury? It had been known with two levels for some centuries, until 1876, when the Ellora caves were being tidied for a visit from the Prince of Wales. Between six and twelve feet of silt were removed from some caves and their courtyards, and in Cave 11 the clearing revealed a landing with stairs leading downward; continued excavations in 1877 uncovered a long verandah, then cells and shrines.[8] This forgotten lowest (and necessarily last-made) level of Cave 11 was found to be asymmetrical and unfinished, containing a decapitated seated Buddha.[9] Had the artisans found that the rock had serious flaws or fissures and chosen not to continue? Had a terrible accident happened there, causing the stoneworkers to hastily withdraw? Whatever destructive event took place in that lowest level, it is possible that the artisans' sense of connection to what they had made translated into an injury experienced by Vishwakarma.[10]

The perception of an injury was extended by the fact that in Cave 10, the top part of the robe over the left shoulder of the Murti's torso is not visible (as in other Buddha statues in nearby caves), so the portion of the robe's edge that is seen, draped around the left wrist and falling toward the ground, seems self-contained. This robe edge displays regular notches, appearing like a cord or even possibly a serpent. For those who saw the disposition of the hands as nursing an injured finger, the robe edge became a flow of blood. At some points in the cave's history, this association was highlighted with color. A British army major's 1935 description of the cave, "much frequented by carpenters," notes, "It is, in fact, affirmed by the local devotees that the Brāhmanical cord which hangs from the thumb of the image is not a cord at all, but a stream of blood flowing from a wound inflicted during the course of the daily work as a carpenter, and for this reason it is painted red."[11]

Any artisan would recognize—and empathize with—the danger of a tool causing injury to the hands. But why focus on the little finger? Both a blacksmith and a carpenter have explained to me how, for a right-handed person, the sensing little finger of the left hand guides a tool through touch. The importance of this little finger among stone carvers too is confirmed in an aphoristic *sūtra* about the proper handling of chisels in a Sanskrit manual. The commentary elaborates: "Holding the chisel firmly in the left hand, it should be controlled by the little finger. . . . One should hold the mallet for carving in the right hand."[12]

Sometime in the mid-twentieth century, when the Bengali metal sculptor Meera Mukherjee was visiting Ellora, she asked stonemasons making repairs to Cave 16 whether their ancestors had made the caves. "They shook their heads," she reports, "and entreated me to look closely again into the Viswakarma Cave." Notice, they instructed her, how throughout the cave, figures repeat the central image's gesture, one hand holding the little finger of the other. "While cutting stones," they explained, "one of the artisans had lost his finger and all the other artisans felt the same hurt. This has been depicted in a frieze showing them to be holding their fingers which were hurt."[13]

Shifting focus from the central Murti toward all these smaller figures turns the whole hall into a massive, supportive gathering. These smaller figures in the panels above the pillars could be identified as Vishwakarma's "followers and servants . . . represented in grief for his wound & holding his wounded finger"; as "images of 360 Sutradhars seated together"; and even as Vishwakarma's "favourite servants . . . whom he thus honored by giving them a station from which they might view the place they themselves had assisted in forming."[14] The cave was seen as a space of artisans' solidarity, mutual sympathy, pride, and acknowledgment of a collective dependence on hands.

These locally told versions of Vishwakarma's injury in Cave 11 are threaded with motifs immediately familiar from Indian folklore: the night magically extended across many months;[15] the object left forever incomplete or roughly finished when an artisan is interrupted;[16] the patron who insists that his own monument be the greatest and who will not allow an artisan to copy or surpass that work (as happens in the Rudra Mal story).[17] But while the despotic patron in other stories may maim artisans' thumbs or hands, in these tales of Vishwakarma's injury, the slip is his own doing.

That Vishwakarma is perceived to adopt this lasting pose in the safe space of his own cave seems a reminder to all artisan pilgrims that hands are vulnerable to the tools they engage. If the story of Vishwakarma giving his sons tools underscores how built creations might cause suffering for other creatures, these stories point to how tools pose a danger to the user's own body.

❋

While the Murti's hands appear to be central inspiration for stories reconceptualizing the Buddha as Vishwakarma, Suthars also pointed to other aspects of the cave's iconography and architecture as evidence of Vishwakarma's presence.

For example, Bachubhai Vadgama, composer of the 2013 Vishwakarma Purana, had self-published a few earlier booklets. One of these carried a chapter titled "Lord Vishwakarma's Ilachal, Today's Ilorgarh," filled with tips for Vishwakarma's descendants seeking audience with their grandfather at Ellora. Vadgama extols Ellora as "Dada's Place of Work" (*karma bhūmi*) and essential "for anyone of Vishwakarma's lineage to visit once in their lifetime," then lists the reasons he personally thinks Cave 10 is associated with Vishwakarma.[18] "On the upper storey [entablature] there are 32 rectangular brackets and each one shows Vishwakarma present along with his four disciples or sons," he wrote. Here again is an assembly of Suthars, since in older Gujarati versions, the four castes of carpenters were four sons.

Vadgama goes on to interpret the stupa as a waterpot for ritual observances, "just as a pot put on a stool is believed to be a symbol of Vishwakarma." Counting the angled protrusions atop the stupa, he reasons, "This waterpot carries 64 corners and the Vishwakarma is expert in the 64 arts." Finally, adding the two figures flanking the Murti to the groups of four gathered around the similar smaller images in the entablature, he views the whole cave as a tribute to Vishwakarma "surrounded by six sons. That's why I believe the cave is Vishwakarma's and the Murti is Vishwakarma."[19]

I want now to add yet another possibility of why Cave 10 is connected to Vishwakarma: the number of pillars. First, though, I need to explain the sacredness of the *amās* day for Suthars. Learning about our research, upper-caste acquaintances in Ahmedabad often exclaimed, "Everyone knows one thing about carpenters! They won't work on an *amās*. They won't touch their tools for any kind of work on that day." In case our research had unearthed the reason for this peculiarity, we were quizzed: "Why is that? What does *amās* have to do with Vishwakarma?"

Amās derives from the Sanskrit *amavāsya*: *amā* "together" and *vāsya* "residing" refer to the sun and moon positioned in such close conjunction that the moon is not visible from earth. Gujarati lunar calendars count the fourteen waxing (*Sud*) days between a "no-moon" (or new moon) *amās* and a full moon, then fourteen waning (*Vad*) days back to the next *amās*, marked as "0." The *amās* is considered a powerful, dangerous time; not a good moment to embark on ventures. But as I mentioned earlier, it is a special time for ancestral observances. I was moved to read how the Kurma Purana describes ancestors coming to a descendant's door on this lunar day, to see what is offered to them; if nothing, they leave at sunset, "hungry, thirsty, despairing."[20]

If ancestors were to be remembered on an *amās*, it made sense to me that artisans considering themselves Sons of Vishwakarma would choose the day to honor Vishwakarma as the ultimate divine ancestor. In the little booklet Prakash found for us, Vishwakarma was further declared to have been born on an *amās* day, on a Wednesday in the winter month of Magh Sar, at Cave 10 in Ellora (*Ilorgarh*).[21] Another booklet from the Jamnagar Vishwakarma temple connected the *amās* to Vishwakarma's manifestation as the first glimmering of form and light within the inchoate darkness that preceded creation.[22]

.... ⚶ ....

THE GREATNESS OF AMĀS

When there was darkness all around, there was nothing: no earth, water, light, place, wind, sky, body, mind, intellect, gods; no Brahma-Vishnu-Mahesh. The days of the lunar months, days of the week, festivals and months had not been fixed. There was no sun, no stars, no moon, and everywhere only utterly empty emptiness.

Grandfather Vishwakarma manifested himself within this darkness and created the universe. As he made this creation, light emerged within the darkness. That day is the moment of the *amās*; a moment of happiness, light, brightness. That's why we of the Vishwakarma lineage celebrate the manifestation day of *amās*.

....

There are also other associations with *amās*. Our clan's Barot, for example, named that day as marking Vishwakarma's killing of the demon Lavanasura, a deed that forced him to undertake penance at Ellora. Bachubhai Vadgama's collection of Vishwakarma stories elaborates on this episode but connects the killing of the demon on an *amās* to the undoing of Vishwakarma's penance at Ellora, linking this to a different story involving the Rudramal temple prototype earlier made at Ellora.[23]

.... ψ ....

VISHWAKARMA'S PENANCE AT ELLORA

A Brahmin began bullying the gods, acting like a demon. Despite his high-caste origins, he got the name Lavanasura, "Briny Demon." He was invincible because of a boon from Brahma: no matter how he was injured, his body was made whole again. The distraught gods asked Vishwakarma to intervene.

Vishwakarma cut off Lavanasura's head, but the head rejoined the body and the demon sprang back to life. He tried and failed to kill him five times. On his sixth attempt, Vishwakarma placed powerful objects between the head and the body: proclamations from other gods, and his own measuring stick and cord. This time the head and body were unable to reunite, and Lavanasura died. This happened on an *amās* day.

Though Lavanasura was a demon, he was also still a Brahmin, and from that day onward the sin of killing a Brahmin stuck to Vishwakarma. Later, when Vishwakarma was furious at Narada for tricking him out of the barley seeds of prosperity (given by Indra in thanks for the Rudramal made at Ellora), Vishwakarma came to Ellora to find equilibrium through doing penance. He stood on one leg with one-pointed concentration. But with the earlier sin of killing Lavanasura clinging to him, he was vulnerable to distraction.

Vishwakarma's fierce penance accumulated such tremendous power that Indra became nervous about a challenge to his own preeminent position. So Indra sent a celestial nymph who danced in his royal court to perform before the meditating Vishwakarma. As she danced, limbs moving this way and that,

Vishwakarma's concentration was broken. His penance was over. He married this lovely dancer, and a son was born.

With his penance incomplete, Vishwakarma wondered how he might yet shed the sin of killing a Brahmin. He asked a storyteller, expert on the Puranas, for advice.

That storyteller advised that listening to stories about ancestors from one's genealogical book could wash away sin. So Vishwakarma arranged for such a reading. When the gods and sages assembled, the storyteller began narrating how, in the beginning, the Vast Vishwakarma manifested, and across time re-emerged in ten incarnations. As the audience reverently listened, Vishwakarma's young son began clowning around, making fun of the storyteller. Everyone broke out laughing. The offended storyteller closed the genealogical book, and stubbornly refused to continue his narration.

With the reading incomplete, Vishwakarma still hadn't wiped away the sin of killing a Brahmin. He asked the storyteller for an alternative solution. The storyteller referred to the authority of scriptures and told Vishwakarma he could be released from this sin if once a month, his descendants observed the *amās* day. On that day Vishwakarma's descendants should honor Vishwakarma and should not use their tools for livelihood.

....

A craftsman's observance (*anujā* or *akto*) is a time to rest one's tools and to honor Vishwakarma. For Suthars, the *amās* is the main observance, coming twelve times a year, and interspersed between these no-moons are other sacred dates marking Vishwakarma's actions on this earth (often involving Ellora) that his descendants are also enjoined to observe. Reading this story, I was particularly struck by the suggestion that listening to the stories of ancestors and observing a monthly remembrance could alleviate inauspicious energies passed onward across generations.

Seeing the importance of *amās*, I also began wondering whether the cave's layout could be read as evoking this sacred day. Could a spatial evocation of *amās* have influenced Suthars' choice of this configuration, over other possible *chaitya* "huts" evoking wood? The particular layout is legible in the cave's plan drawn by the archaeologist James Burgess's assistant, Ganpat Purshottam, in 1877. In the British Library, Ken and I had the opportunity to handle the original folios for plans and ink drawings, with their heavily creased paper.

Extending from the stupa, the projecting knees of the seated Murti face the brightness of the doorway. A visitor enters between two square pillars. The hall is lined by two rows of octagonal pillars, fourteen on each side.

37. Detail of Plan No 30 Visvakarma Cave by Ganpat Purshottam, 1877–1880 British Library WE 2215(15–16) in Burgess III Original Drawings Ellora Cave Temples.

These rows curve and meet just behind the stupa. A circumambulating visitor traces the row to the left of the Murti, following the turn it takes, behind the seated figure, after eleven pillars. Here, at the hall's far end, light begins to dwindle. Directly behind the stupa, the stone mass blocks out all illumination from the door and balcony window. Then, making the further turn, the visitor emerges and another line of pillars comes into view, growing brighter with each step.

Fourteen identical octagonal pillars; fourteen lunar days. The two square pillars flank the door like two light giving bodies—the sun and moon, standing together. Could the perfectly spaced sequence of pillars be read as a waning fortnight to the north, a waxing fortnight to the south? Could this passage behind the stupa, through total darkness, be enacting the bodily experience of the waning, then disappearing moon? The Buddhist monastic observance of *uposhadha* on new moon and full moon days might have been the original reference for the design, but for Suthars the focus would be on the *amās*.[24]

And one more thing—as Bhai would emphasize, "according to my own imagination." Looking closely at the Murti (or at the photograph that I've set at the beginning of this chapter), a set of parallel white streaks come into focus on the torso—a thicker band directly across the heart and arms, with two thinner, perfectly spaced stripes below—almost as though the dark rock were shot through with light. This is most likely a vesicular flow of chalcedony or calcite.[25] While the basalt at Ellora is in some places mixed with other minerals and even agates, rarely is the basalt so symmetrically patterned on a sculpted image.

The sculpture was most likely plastered over in earlier times, hiding these vesicular bands. But at the moment of making, as the sculptors cut into basalt, I wonder whether the emergence of a milky band just at the Murti's heart might have suggested that the rock itself was overflowing toward the chisel. Might this have seemed a revelation of grace to those long-ago makers, granting an awareness of the live presence of a deity emerging into form and overseeing their progress?

PART IV
Forms in Flux

38. "Cave X, Viskakarma [sic] at Ellora in Maharashtra, India," Henry Cousens, 1875 British Library 40/14, Granger.

✳ 13 ✳

Vestiges of Worship

Entering Cave 10 today, the arched interior appears to be of uniformly sculpted gray rock. Even as the eyes adjust, and each texture of basalt is seen to hold differently the natural light and shadows, there's a calming beauty in this austere rock. But as we explored older writings, we glimpsed how devotees had once filled this space with colors, scents, the warm light of flames, and chorused songs.

A compendium of Gujarati songs published in Ahmedabad in 1913 goes into some detail about the sequence of pilgrims' worship at Ellora (*Elolā*). Composed by an exponent of the Vishwakarma Purana named Goverdhanram Devram, the book was intended for "all those who have taken refuge in Vishwakarma—carpenters, masons, stonemasons, and blacksmiths whose income depends on Vishwakarma's craftsmanship."[1] The book's preface describes how Vishwakarma manifested in the southern region of the Ellora mountain, taking the position of "Head of the Artisans" (Shilpacharya); how, after transmitting artisan knowledge to his sons, he departed, leaving them to step into his role; and how they gradually grew distant from him. As "the Dear One," he could still be found at Ellora.[2]

> Come brothers, let's go to Ellora,
> Having audience, we'll all be happy.
> We'll go make requests to our Dear One.
> Come brothers let's go to Ellora. (*refrain*)
>
> Bathing in the Vishwa Kund is purifying.
> After that do various sorts of worship,
> offering him your lotus heart.
> Come brothers, let's go to Ellora . . .

Bathe the Lord with five nectars,[3]
keep meditating on him in your heart.
Bow before him each day.
    Come brothers, let's go to Ellora . . .

Apply musk and sandalwood paste,
rubbing this over god's body.
Present him with saffron clothes.
    Come brothers, let's go to Ellora . . .

Spreading rice paste on his forehead,
let go of all your anxiety and restlessness,
Offer all kinds of service to god.
    Come brothers, let's go to Ellora!

Place a flower garland on god's body,
Offer him scented flowers.
Always carry enthusiasm within your heart.
    Come brothers, let's go to Ellora . . .

Light incense and a lamp bringing happiness to your mind.
Hari will see the food being offered.
There's no one like him in this world.
    Come brothers, let's go to Ellora . . .

Wave lamps before him and sing his praises
So we can wander happily through this life
and cross the ocean of worldliness with ease.
    Come brothers, let's go to Ellora . . .

After a purifying dip in the nearby Vishwa Kund, pilgrims are advised to follow the usual steps for honoring a deity. But rather than go through a priestly intermediary, the pilgrims themselves are instructed to wash, anoint, dress, and garland the large image in the cave, and then to offer incense, lamps, and food. Carrying the fragrance of musk, sandalwood, flowers, and incense, this song fills the cave with yellowish sandalwood and white rice paste, saffron cloth, bright flowers, gray smoke, golden flames that flicker and spread warm light when waved. Some verses set up a mirroring, an aspect of ritual that intrigues me: the offering of outward action and the promise of inward transformation. Rice paste applied to the rock forehead is said to calm a devotee's anxious mind; lighting a lamp within this arched interior will illumine a devotee's own mind with gladness. Goverdhanram Devram goes on to extol how this pilgrimage to the divine family member at Ellora will wash away sins, grant liberation and purification, fulfill desires, and ease suffering.[4]

Another song carried the refrain "Sitting in Ellora, the Sutradhar sanctifies his family / again and again, he grants audience and blessings to his sons." The closing verses advised that for ongoing prosperity, a pilgrim should wash the Murti's feet and drink that sacred water, then circumambulate the space and prostrate.[5] Feet, after all, are commonly the focus of worship. Prominently inscribed atop the Murti's right foot is small pennant, shaped like an elongated, backward-facing "4."

I wondered: could this be an example of "mason's marks"—tiny tokens of a carver's identity or clan discreetly carved into many historical sites from the second century BCE to the seventeenth century CE (and present even in the Taj Mahal)?[6] But this location, visible to anyone facing the Murti, is hardly discreet. Since a fluttering pennant can mark a sacred site, it's more likely that some overzealous devotee took up a chisel to literally

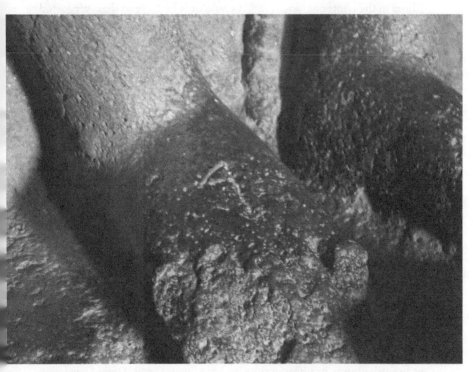

39. Pennant chiseled into Murti's right foot, Cave 10 Ellora, 2018, Photograph by Kirin Narayan.

flag his devotion. For centuries, those who considered themselves Vishwa-karma's descendants seem to have felt it their ancestral right and obligation to redecorate the rock surfaces of Cave 10 during visits with their grand-father. Tending to the Murti with the intimacy of touch, they also acted with a sense of familial entitlement to leave lasting tokens of their visits.

✳

Color flashes by in historical mentions. In 1758, the Murti was "gigantic and painted red";[7] in 1854, red paint appeared along with a *tilak* on the forehead;[8] a 1910 conservation report laments that carpenters have "given the idol a liberal coating of red paint and have picked out the leading fea-tures in black and white."[9] I have also already mentioned the account from 1935 pointing to how, through painting the cascading edge of the Buddha's robe red, what could also be seen as a dangling cord was transformed into blood from Vishwakarma's wounded finger.[10]

A particularly striking description appears in the travel diary of Walter Crane, a London-based Arts and Crafts artist and illustrator who visited Ellora in the winter of 1906–1907. It could only be Cave 10 that "suggested in its plan and form an apsidal basilica, and in detail a wooden structure, the roof being carved in close ribs, curved to the form of a pointed arch, supported by a horizontal cornice and columns set very close together. A colossal figure of the seated Buddha filled the view at the end of the nave, but there was an ambulatory behind it." This was all familiar, if drawn up in splendidly precise architectural terms. Then Crane went on: "The figure was painted a dark red with white drapery and black hair, the eyes, with strongly marked white and black pupils, had a fixed stare which carried the whole length of the Temple."[11]

Today's serene stone Murti has downcast, indrawn eyes; yet this "fixed stare" would have connected with a visitor's gaze in the mutual viewing of *darshan*.[12] While Gangaram Tambat's drawing shows these eyes, they recur in a few nineteenth-century photographs.

We first encountered eyes painted open in a photograph taken in 1880 by the archaeologist Henry Cousens, reproduced at the beginning of this section and available online through the British Library. The two atten-dants have painted eyes as well. A man in a white turban sits before them, gazing upward. Perhaps he is a Suthar communing with his grandfather, or perhaps he is an assistant enjoined to pose beside the image for scale.

Visiting the British Library ourselves, we came across Cave 10 again in bound albums of photographs by Lala Deen Dayal. Deen Dayal was a hereditary jeweler and trained engineer—both Vishwakarma-related professions—who became court photographer for the Nizam of Hyderabad in the 1880s, when Ellora was within the Nizam's territory.[13] In some of these Ellora photographs, the Murti's wide eyes are again enhanced by a white headdress and circular halo; the attendants on either side also have painted eyes.

40. Detail of "The Sutar-ki-Jhonpri [Visvakarma] Cave, Ellora, interior view" Raja Deen Dayal, 1880s. British Library Photo 430/6 (69) in Curzon Collection: Views of HH the Nizam's Dominions, Hyderabad, Deccan 1892.

While Deen Dayal photographed Vishwakarma's fine curling handlebar, Gangaram Tambat's drawing from about a century earlier displayed a long drooping mustache, and other photos showed no facial hair at all. By the time we came across a photograph by Alfred Plâté in the online archives of the Metropolitan Museum of Art, we were really confused. Were these all truly of the same image? Periodic applications of paint explain the changing mustaches and widening and narrowing eyes, but even the shape of the nose and the set of the jaw seemed different across old photographs. How could this be?

41. Detail of "Sutar ka Jhopda Cave Interior, Ellora Caves," Alfred Plâté 1890–1900. Image © The Metropolitan Museum of Art AR6190264. Art Resource, NY.

The explanation lies not just in paint but in plaster. At the time the caves were carved, rock surfaces were intended to be covered by layers of mud mortar and dolomitic lime plaster mixed with sand and cannabis sativa.[14] This plaster served as a ground for decorative painting: while at Ajanta, enchanting paintings can still be viewed on walls and ceilings, at Ellora, only occasional fragmentary paintings have survived.[15] After Buddhism receded from the area in the eighth century, further plaster and paint became a way for worshippers to make up a deity afresh, or even change its identity; the shapes and colors of stories consolidated those identifications.

Ritual specialists taking charge of caves could make them up afresh with plaster and paint, introducing visitors to their own chosen deities and stories. By the eighteenth century, caves north of Cave 10 were controlled by local Brahmins, while caves to the south were taken charge of by Guravs, or ritual specialists for the lower castes. The Buddhist caves south of Cave 10 became known as the "Dedhwada" and "Maharwada," linked with castes considered untouchable; members of high castes simply did not visit that area for fear of pollution.[16] Cave 10, at the fulcrum of the Brahmin and Gurav domains, seems to have remained "much frequented" by visiting carpenters who claimed it as their own.

Across the stretch of caves, British attempts to discredit the local identifications of deities often pointed to the plaster as evidence of fraud: the cantankerous Captain William Sykes, for example, lofted his walking stick to knock away what appeared to him as an anomalously large nose ring on the "Indrani"—actually a *yakshī*, or nature spirit—in Jain cave 32, to satisfy himself "that it was the addition of the workmen, who at one period had painted and chunamed [plastered] the whole of the caves at Ellora."[17] Similarly, in their archaeological work from the 1870s, Fergusson and Burgess describe how the central Buddha on the top floor of Cave 12, "which the natives persist in worshipping as Rama," received his face: "His nose and lips have long been wanting, but these as well as mustachios are supplied in plaster, and whenever they fall or are knocked off, their place is speedily restored by fresh ones."[18]

In Cave 10, the colors of paint could change, underlying plaster be refashioned, and the walls and pillars adapted into an open visitors' book. An 1884 account of the Nizam's dominions includes a report on Cave 10: "The walls and pillars are much disfigured by the names of the artisan visitors which have been carved and written upon them. The figure of Buddha is coloured with blue, yellow and green paint, which is applied to it upon all festive occasions. One of the pillars in the cave is inscribed with the date Shaka 1228, which is equivalent to A.D. 1306."[19]

188   *Chapter 13*

That date, 1306 CE, would be some decades after Chakradhar Swami's visit, and two years before the Yadava-ruled Devagiri near Ellora was annexed by the Delhi Sultanate (to be later renamed Daulatabad). The artisans' pilgrimage somehow continued across shifting political landscapes. I wondered: might any of my ancestor's names have been among the layers of paint recording visits on walls and pillars?

Whatever happened to all the paint? And under the paint, to the plaster?

*

After the Prince of Wales's visit in 1876, the Nizam of Hyderabad's archaeology department posted a police guard at the newly cleaned caves "to prevent, as far as possible, the wanton mutilation and defacement of the caves and the sculptures which they contain."[20] In his 1877 guidebook, James Burgess lamented that this guard seemed ineffective in stopping visitors from damaging, decorating, and inscribing their names on walls and sculpture.[21] By 1911, the supervising archaeologist A. H. Longhurst became focused not just on damage but on what he perceived of as faith-based disfigurements.

"I understand that it has been a practice of recent years to lease out caves to neighboring villages for religious and pecuniary purposes," wrote Longhurst. "The result of this is that a great number of interesting and valuable sculptures have been disfigured with daubs of red paint and grotesque ornament, obviously the work of the local artist. This practice should cease and every attempt should be made to remove these disfigurements by scrubbing down the sculptures with soap and hot water. There would be no objection to any of the caves or temples being used for religious purposes as long as the worshippers refrained from altering or disfiguring the caves or sculptures in any way."[22]

In this view, worship was fine, but material tokens needed be removed and henceforth banned. Longhurst went on to Cave 10: "I was amused to find that the local Hindu carpenters have appropriated the large image of Buddha in the Chaitya cave as their own special deity, to whom they make little offerings and daily worship. Needless to say they have given the idol a liberal coating of red paint and have picked out the leading features in black and white, producing a most ludicrous effect."

Yet as late as 1949, a committee appointed by the government of Hyderabad State reported that "some sculptures were disfigured by red paints and other greasy substances by religious enthusiasts who failed to appreciate the artistic beauty of them without such embellishment," adding that "prompt action of the Secretary, Archaeological Department" had resulted in the paint being removed.[23] Bhai had reminded us, too, how, even with guards on hand, a small donation might persuade them to briefly look the other way while tokens of devotion like red kumkum were offered.

With fresh plaster and paint no longer applied, the Murti's face changed entirely. In my mother's cherished copy of Heinrich Zimmer's two-volume *The Art of Indian Asia*, I found two photographs of Cave 10 taken by the American photographer Eliot Elisofon in 1949.[24] Here the face appeared in two shades, features skeletally sharp and recessed. What had happened to the face so long concealed by plaster? The rock itself could have worn away with water seeping through the hillside across centuries.[25] Or a hostile wounding of the face might have occurred at some unrecorded time. After all, other caves in the vicinity, particularly Cave 14, show signs of intentional damage to deities' faces. We saw a different view of the asymmetrical face when our landlords in Ahmedabad invited us over to view their slides from Ellora. These were undated, unattributed slides they had bought at the caves decades ago. The ravaged face surfaced again, in a blurry way, in an undated set of twenty-one postcards put out by the Nizam of Hyderabad's archaeology department that we handled in the British Library. This would place the postcards sometime in the years before the 1951 ceding of the Nizam's dominions to the four-year-old Republic of India.

When the Archaeological Survey of India began repairs and reconstructions at Ellora after 1953, the explicit policy was to retain the "authenticity" of the ancient site and leave broken sculpture unmended. But in the late 1950s, some repairs were undertaken for fallen pillars and for the structural elements of a few sculptures, using concrete reconstruction. The reshaped forms were ingeniously followed by "a duly-tinted layer of cement plaster mixed with the required grade of sand . . . for finishing by chisel to bring out the effect of rock."[26]

We haven't been able to access Archaeological Survey of India records, but we guess that sometime in the 1950s—certainly by the time of the photograph linked to my parents' visit—a professional sculptor had been brought in to refashion the Murti's face in Cave 10. This reconstruction seems to have occurred a second time too, for photographs from the 1950s onward are to our eyes subtly different in their proportions from the present face. Today, the long history of mobile plastered and painted faces has withdrawn into the shadows, and a classically heavy-lidded, full-lipped Buddha absorbs visitors with a sense of timeless, tranquil beauty.

❋

The painted signatures of Suthars that once filled the cave have long since been scrubbed away. But in the far-flung Via-Via of generous scholars

190   *Chapter 13*

sharing leads, we were introduced to a short article in Marathi by Brahmanand Deshpande focusing on an inscription chiseled into a pillar in Cave 10 by visiting Sutradhars.[27] Reproducing the inscription's five lines in the Nagari script, Deshpande suggested a possible date of 1036 CE. This inscription, he argued, illustrated the antiquity and continuity of Vishwakarma worship in the cave. He retold the legend of a wounded finger, recast the Buddha Murti as Vishwakarma, and described Rajasthani carpenter pilgrims who brought newlyweds, along with entire marriage parties, to prostrate before the Murti for blessings. When Desphande had suggested to one group of pilgrims that this was Buddha, not Vishwakarma, he had been showered with abuse.

Saili Datar-Palande, who gave us Deshpande's article, accompanied us to Ellora in August 2019 with the express purpose of locating this inscription. Other visitors stopped to watch, puzzled as we started moving around Cave 10 with a powerful lamp to cast bright beams on the pillars. A low wooden fence had now been put up around the Murti, for as a guard explained, "people kept wanting to sit in the Buddha's lap for photographs." We needed permission now to walk behind the stupa for a circumambulation allowing us to look closely at the pillars usually shrouded in darkness.

The guard clearly thought we were deranged. "There is no writing here," he flatly said in Marathi, then repeated in Hindi. "If you want writing, just go upstairs. There is some writing on the balcony there."[28]

As we continued to scan the rock, the guard repeated, "I'm telling you—there is *no writing*."

But then, on the seventh pillar from the door, we spotted the lines of writing. These were positioned so that if someone standing a few feet away to face the Murti were to look over a right shoulder, the words would be at about eye level. A few letters of the inscription trailed like an addendum onto the adjacent pillar facet.

Coming into view, the inscription seemed so obvious that none of us could understand how we hadn't noticed it earlier. Saili tilted the lamp. Ken raised the iPad; I pulled out a notebook and began transcribing. The guard, now convinced, also stood beside us and helped spell out letters.

For anyone who can read the contemporary Devanagari script, the inscription is legible, even though it doesn't connect letters into words by drawing a flat "roof" above each word. Looking at these letters, we had to partly guess at words from their spacing. Strangely, what Saili and I discerned didn't quite match how the words were reproduced in Deshpande's article.

VESTIGES OF WORSHIP 191

42. Pillar inscription recording Sutradhar's visit, Cave 10, Ellora, 2019. Photograph by Kirin Narayan.

I've showed these intriguing lines of text to knowledgeable friends across the world. A Sanskritist said, "Look, this isn't Sanskrit, it's Sanskritish." Other readers of relevant languages using the Devanagari script—Hindi, Rajasthani, Marathi—have also been confused. I looked in assorted dictionaries and debated possibilities with friends. Just as the face kept changing, might some residual plaster at the time of Deshpande's reading have recast how the letters appeared?

Partly because the meaning is still unresolved, I reproduce both readings for any knowledgeable person who might want to join in this detective work.

LINE	DESHPANDE'S READING	OUR 2019 READING	
1	samvat 1121 varshe sūtra	samvat 1721 varshe sūtra	
2	dhār 5 gotra. parāsar ta[d] vam	dhār 5 gotra : parāsar sūtra	sūtra netā
3	she tākasā gotra bhāradvās	petā kanā : gotra bhāradvās	
4	sūtra kan bhopā ta. Sīs +	sūtra kan : gopāl sīrohī	
5	metā	mahā netā	

Sūtradhār is clearly split across the first two lines, and just *"sūtra"*—seemingly an abbreviation—is repeated in line 4. We discerned an additional *"sūtra"* in line 2, and another trailing to the other pillar facet in line 2.5, which Deshpande had not mentioned. Both readings concur on two mentions of *gotra*, the patrilineally transmitted affiliation with a particular great *rishi* or seer. One's *gotra* mostly comes up in ritual contexts, when a chanting Brahmin pauses to ask your *gotra*, then announces you as a member of that affiliation undertaking the ritual; you might know your mother's original *gotra* from before marriage too. Prakash explained *gotra* to us "as one kind of DNA" but couldn't remember what his was. He was about to consult his father when he said, "I think it's Bharadvaj"—coincidentally a *gotra* mentioned on the pillar. That the number 5 precedes the first mention of *gotras* is perhaps significant because of Vishwakarma's five sons.

Bharadvaj (*Bharadvas*) and Parashar (*Parasar*) are the names of ancient seers and their associated *gotras*; Parashar is sometimes also a first name. As an epithet of Krishna, "Gopal" is also a man's name, and here Sirohi seems to refer to the small princely state once tucked between the larger Marwar and Mewar states in Rajasthan. Sirohi is important to artisans both for high-quality iron used in swords and chisels and because the state's dominions included Mount Abu with its famed Dilwara Jain temples, intricately chiseled from white marble between the eleventh and thirteenth centuries. We thought that maybe the five gotras of Sutradhars were making a pilgrimage from Sirohi, or were originally from Sirohi and were involved in building projects in the area.

But when? Deshpande acknowledged that the date of the inscription was hard to decipher. He thought that the number specifying the year could be read as either 1221 or 1121, and decided on 1121.[29] As we scrutinized the numbers, it was also the second digit that puzzled us: if it were a "1" or a "2," as Deshpande thought, shouldn't it match the "1" that preceded it or the "2" that followed? Staring from different angles, I began wondering if it might be a Devanagari "7" positioned vertically rather than at the usual tilt. After all, an engraver starting to tap out a number at an angle couldn't erase what was begun. Like an ascetic doing penance, the number would be frozen in its unusual posture.

VS 1721 would be 1664 CE, during Mughal rule, two years before Jean de Thevenot arrived by bullock cart. At this point, artisans originally from Sirohi might well have been living in the area, drawn by the construction of mosques and tombs in Khuldabad or Aurangabad. For keen to "find good work and do good work," artisans were often nonpartisan about the religious orientation of the structures they made; one text attributed to Vishwakarma, the *Rehemana Prasada*, was structured as his instructions to a son, Jaya, on the proper way to build a mosque.[30]

Back in Ahmedabad, Bhai peered at the five and a half lines on the iPad and in my handwritten transcription. "This is a father and son visiting together," he said.

"What?" I asked, simultaneously bewildered and moved, remembering that Bhai had never had the opportunity to accompany his own father on such a visit. "Why?"

Bhai pointed to *petā*, seeing this as possibly *pitā* (father). If his reading holds, the addition spilling to the pillar's other face might also offer an elaboration that the father of the Sūtradhars was also the leader of the Sūtradhars (*sūtra petā/sūtra netā*). We discussed another possibility too, that the hand of the inexperienced engraver had slipped and so he had attempted a correction at the pillar's edge.

Just after the word *petā* was *kanā*, a word that my Hindi dictionary reveals as "the dark fortnight of the month of Aśvin" (roughly September/October), explaining that this is an astrological time auspicious for ritual, and particularly ceremonies to honor ancestors. The same dictionary page also holds a possible meaning for the word *kan*, which appears in the inscription's next line. It means "a particle, a small fragment" and could also be related to the Sanskrit *kanati*, "to shine, desire, go or approach."[31]

Based on a range of conversations with many patient friends, here is how I—in no way trained as an epigrapher—might imagine a very provisional translation:

In the Samvat year 1721 [1664 CE] rainy season, 5 gotras of Sūtradhars were here to honor Parashar the Sūtra[dhar] leader, Sūtra[dhar] father, part of Sūtra [dhars] of Bharadvaj gotra.

[signed] Gopal of Sirohi, great leader

We had already learned how Rajasthani artisans sometimes brought tools to be blessed at Ellora, which could explain why the visiting Sutradhars had tools on hand. All the same, knowing that other artisan pilgrims painted their names, what inspired this group to chisel an inscription? Could these men at the same time have chiseled the pennant on the Murti's foot? I wondered: did hereditary Sirohi-connected artisans of those *gotras* still visit Ellora, looking for traces of their ancestors' devotion on this pillar? Were these marks on the rock commemorated in another family's stories?

✳ 14 ✳

Transformations through Water

As I'd heard from Pa, the pilgrimage to Ellora involved more than just a visit with Vishwakarma. The artisan men also bathed in the nearby Vishwa Kund pond and put on a sacred thread.

Where was this pond? Before leaving Canberra in 2017, I looked about online and could find no clues.

As usual, Bhai was able to help. He explained that the pond wasn't actually at the caves but near the Ghrishneshwar Shiva temple in the Verul village. The name "Vishwa Kund," he said, was only used among Vishwakarma's descendants, maybe as an abbreviation for "Vishwakarma Kund." To others it was known as the "Ahilyabai Holkar Kund," in honor of the eighteenth-century queen who sponsored its rebuilding in 1769, or else the "Shivalaya Tirth," drawing on an association with the nearby Shiva temple.[1]

"See, the Holkar queen Ahilyabai renovated the temple and Kund in a most beautiful way," said Bhai, smoothing open an art book.

For years, I'd had a vague image of ancestors wading into a round pool at the foot of a temple. But the Vishwa Kund is a self-enclosed stone structure of squares within narrowing squares—its steps periodically punctuated by wider platforms—all moving downward into a square pool of water. Along one of these lower platforms, symmetrically placed shrines with pyramidal roofs point upward toward the sky.

Somehow, I'd imagined groups of artisan pilgrims visiting the Vishwa Kund *after* meeting with Vishwakarma in Cave 10. But in Devram's 1921 book, various songs described bathing there *before* proceeding to the cave. Extolling Vishwakarma as the Vishwa Kund's maker, these songs also celebrated the presence of other gods at the sacred site. One long song praised Ellora (*Elola*) as Vishnu's heaven, where the god Indra came for audience accompanied by all the other gods, "delighting the

43. Vishwa Kund, sacred pond central to artisans' pilgrimage to Ellora, Verul, 2018. Photograph by Kirin Narayan.

mind of the Sutradhar." Presented as Vishnu's incarnation, Vishwakarma was said to have been granted a sacred place as Sutradhar on the Ellora mountain.

The same song described Shiva visiting the Kund to drink its water and soothe his throat after he saved the universe by swallowing destructive poison; then, having drunk these sacred waters, he decided to settle at his Ghrishneshwar temple nearby. The song also extolled the wonderful effects of a dip in the pond for pilgrims and their ancestors.[2]

> Go to Ellora for *darshan*
> Seeing the Murti, you'll gain blessings (*refrain*).
>
> Through the power of his vision, he [Vishwakarma] made the Kund
> The Lord made this water pure as the Ganga.
>   Go to Ellora for *darshan* . . .

Those who go there and make offerings to ancestors
truly uplift seven previous generations.
   Go to Ellora for *darshan* ...

The sins of many births remaining in the body
wash off after bathing there and giving gifts.
   Go to Ellora for *darshan* ...

The one who bathes there and then goes to worship Father's body
with feelings of devotion, offering gifts—
   Go to Ellora for *darshan* ...

That son is very dear to the Lord.
Gaining good fortune and prosperity, his lineage will benefit.
   Go to Ellora for *darshan* ...

For one who goes to the mountain for *darshan*,
both sides of his family will be purified.
   Go to Ellora for *darshan* ...

His mother and father will say "Well done! Bravo!"
Through blessings and devotion, all bodily sins will be erased.
   Go to Ellora for *darshan* ...

With all these benefits available, the song's composer, Goverdhan, took a dim view of anyone who missed out on a chance to visit: "A person of the Sutradhar family who doesn't go there / Is an idiot and partner in sin."[3]

Gujarati Vishwakarma Puranas often grouped the Vishwa Kund with two other smaller ponds in the locality: the Surya (Sun) Kund and Chandra (Moon) Kund. The 1965 Purana described how, after moving to the Ellora mountain at Ila's invitation, Vishwakarma looked around and, with the very power of his roaming glance, "in an instant he made the kind of enchanting creation that even the gods would grow attached to. For the welfare of all creatures he made the three Kunds ... by bathing in them, suffering, poverty and difficulties are removed and people gain every sort of happiness. Peace of mind is regained after illness and all kinds of troubles. If a person bathes in these Kunds, 71 generations of ancestors will have a good onward journey. If they have become restless ghosts, they will be freed."[4]

While all the Kunds were considered sacred, the Vishwakarma Puranas tended to focus particularly on the Vishwa Kund as a miraculous site of transformation. It was only this Kund that offered bathing artisans the right to wear a sacred thread of the upper castes.

*

I'd grown up hearing from relatives that we were artisans *and* that we were Brahmins: Vishwakarma Brahmins or Vishwabrahmins. As a half-American city child, I didn't think much about what this meant. Yes, as a child visiting the Ramji Mistri Bungalow, I was aware of how Brahmins were honored, even as Brahmins seemed to be of many sorts, of more or less learning and prestige: for example, the Brahmin priest who came in each morning to offer worship in my grandfather's small shrine room was given more honor than the Brahmin cook who maintained rules of purity and pollution in the upstairs kitchen. Pa didn't wear a sacred thread, but the sacred thread worn by his own father, Ramji Seth, was central to a story of how Pa's older half-brothers had once snipped off keys tied to the thread while Ramji Seth napped, then looted his safes.

As a teenager visiting a Kangra village, I'd been startled when, halfway through lunch at the home of a friend, her father Shastriji, the local Brahmin Sanskrit teacher, asked my caste. I still remember my seat on the floor, the mound of rice before me, the hot mustard oil–flavored dal I was mixing in with my right hand. I earnestly assured Shastriji that in my family we did not observe caste. I trotted out what I had been told: that my father came from a family of Brahmins, Vishwakarma Brahmins. I noticed the look of sharp amusement that passed between my host and his wife and felt I had said something wrong.

But what exactly?

A few years later, as a new graduate student in anthropology at Berkeley, I found myself in a used bookstore on Telegraph Avenue, debating whether to invest in a book on Indian society written by one of my professors, David Mandelbaum. Flipping through the pages, I came to a chapter about the mobility aspirations of different caste groups (*jātīs*). "Artisans, in many villages of the South, show a special kind of mobility striving," wrote Mandelbaum. "The five allied jatis of artisans have made long and insistent claims to being Brahmins. They say that they are Brahmins of a special and most superior kind, descended from the god *Visvakarman*, builder and architect of the heavenly realm."[5]

Yes, of course.

But then what I thought I knew diverged from Mandelbaum's description like a stuck page liner in an old photograph album being pulled away, rustling and crackling. What was this, that even when artisans wore the sacred thread and adopted orthodox ways, "they are not taken as equal to proper Brahmins by their neighbors"; that while they "adapted culturally to the Brahmin category," they "failed socially" in persuading others?[6] So the claim to being Brahmins wasn't true? I was perplexed enough to buy this volume (for $1.85).

In those days, discussions of caste hierarchy were all the rage in the anthropology of India. I dutifully took a class laying out various debates and charting the complex ways that the fourfold categories of *varṇa* (roughly translated as priests, warriors, merchants, and workers) historically connected with many thousands of *jātīs*, or particular in-marrying, occupationally specialized caste groups. At that time, I was intending to do my fieldwork in the Himalayan foothills and thought mostly about caste hierarchies in that setting. Yet the next summer, when I was visiting India and relatives descended on the Ramji Mistri Bungalow for a ritual honoring Vishwakarma's daughter, I felt that to establish myself as a bona fide anthropologist, I must somehow address the topic of caste with them. I asked a visiting Kutchi village schoolteacher which *varṇa* category the *jātī* (or *jnātī*, as my relatives said) Gujar Suthars would be allied with.

She paused, reflected, then said, just a little uncertainly, looking around at others present. "We are Shudras, right?"

"No, no, Brahmins!" others jumped in. "We are Brahmins!"

"Shudras . . ."

"Brahmins . . ."

As the debate flew onward, unresolved, in Gujarati, I fled downstairs and reported this to Pa, who was reading in his armchair, shortwave radio playing beside him. "We are the sons of Vishwakarma!" he said emphatically, even angrily. "We are Vishwakarma Brahmins." He returned to his reading, and by the time I made my way back up the wooden stairs, my relatives' conversation had moved on.

Yet Brahminical law books decisively relegate artisans to the category of Shudras—the worker castes obliged to offer services to the three upper "twice born" groups whose males received a second birth through initiation marked by the sacred thread. To be grouped as Shudra is not as cruel as being considered altogether outside the system—"untouchable." But the term nonetheless implies innate inferiority, relative impurity, limited rights, and customary deference to the higher-ranked *varṇas*. Some Brahminical texts rail on about how Shudras should have molten metal poured into their ears if they hear the Vedas, let alone attempt to recite them.

Artisans appear to have first made the bold claim to a higher position within the caste hierarchies of South India, and by the early nineteenth century were asserting this through legal cases. Sons of Vishwakarma insisted that they had the right to serve as their own priests, without Brahmin intermediaries. Sometimes they went further, declaring themselves to be the authentic Brahmins, dispossessed by the impostor "Cow Brahmins" who had tricked them out of their previously high status.[7] The claims of unfairly fallen status spread across regions, crystallizing around a renewed commitment to Vishwakarma. As the sociologist Satish Saberwal, who did fieldwork in 1969 among Ramgarhia Sikhs in Punjab—who also worship Vishwakarma—writes, "From Ceylon in the south to Punjab in the north, during the late nineteenth and early twentieth centuries artisan communities everywhere asserted the great importance of their deity, Vishvakarma the Lord of Industry; and relying upon some Vedic and other scriptural references assigning high status to artisan groups claimed to be Brahmins: 'because of the caliber of our work,' one informant said, 'not because we go around begging food from others for eating ourselves.'"[8] (This last remark about "begging" was a direct sting aimed at priestly Brahmins, who might receive alms and donations for ritual services.)

In some regions, "Vishwabrahmins" declared themselves different from and even superior to priestly Brahmins, but in Gujarat the caste mobilization of Vishwakarma's sons seems to have occurred with the cooperation of Brahmins, who collated or freshly composed authorizing texts—like my great-grandfather's friend, the Acharya from Morbi, or Vallabhram Surajram of Ahmedabad, author of the earliest verse Gujarati Vishwakarma Purana, or Ramashankar Muktashankar Joshi of Khambhat, whose prose Purana went on to be translated into Hindi. All these Brahmins presented the community of Suthars as having lost touch with an original Brahmin identity. Vallabhram Surajram even elaborated on the Ellora mountain as the place where Vishwakarma first arranged for his sons' sacred thread ceremony.[9]

VISHWAKARMA'S SONS RECEIVE THE SACRED THREAD AT ELLORA

After Vishwakarma tried to leave this world the first time, all the other gods were distressed. They urged him to stay. Else who would make things and mend things for eras to come? Vishwakarma agreed to stay longer. He manifested sons from his own body, and said that these boys and their descendants would eventually take over for him. The boys lived with their father at Ellora.

One of the boys went out exploring and came to Brahma's place. Brahma sent Vishwakarma a message to tell him his son was safe, and the boy stayed on. Then Brahma was invited to a huge fire sacrifice performed by a sage learned in three Vedas, and the boy tagged along. But when the ritual was done and food offerings were being distributed, the sage ridiculed the boy. "You're not supposed to eat this *prasād* as you're not wearing a sacred thread."

The boy returned to Ellora in tears. When he told his father what had happened, Vishwakarma set about organizing a sacred thread ceremony for all five sons.

To receive all the guests, Vishwakarma made a massive tent on the mountain, using some hitherto unknown material: not metal, gem, stone, or wood. The tent shone with a radiance unlike that of the sun, moon, and stars and was brightly colored and decorated with flowers and vines.

After receiving their sacred thread initiation, four of the sons went off to study with different sages and eventually married those sages' daughters, while one son stayed home to look after their father.

Affirming how Vishwakarma's work was continued by his descendants, this story dramatizes the indignity of being mocked and barred from full participation in upper-caste rituals. As a caring father, Vishwakarma is concerned to remedy this for his sons. The novel material from which Vishwakarma makes a tent for hosting the celebration seems to represent the new social formation of the artisan Brahmins.

As artisan communities circulated textual, legal, and census-affirmed claims to Brahminhood across regional languages, they often used the term Vishwakarma Brahmin or Vishwabrahmin. Pa gave me a book in Marathi from the early twentieth century, with cracking yellowed pages, that he had found on a ramble with his brother-in-law in Ahmedabad. (As one of his letters recalls, *About 10 or 12 years ago, I went to 2nd hand book market with Sukhlal where I saw and purchased old books referring to our caste and Vishwakarma* [April 11, 1989].) This book offered a mythohistorical overview of Vishwabrahmins and reproduced translated legal briefs in the history of Vishwabrahmin litigation. Its frontispiece saluted an image of the five-headed Vishwakarma with assorted tools in his ten arms. Later, in the British Library, we found an earlier edition in which the print of this image is clearer.[10]

44. Five-headed Vishwakarma on title page of Marathi history of Vishwabrahmins, Poona, 1906. British Library 14058 cc 8.

Closely tied to Vishwabrahmin claims, the five-headed form of Vishwakarma symbolizes the five caste groups that came together in a "Panchala" identity (from *pānch*, five): blacksmiths, carpenters, braziers, goldsmiths, and stonemasons. But the form is also associated with Shiva, who can be depicted with five heads. One Suthar community publication in Gujarati recounts how, after Vishwakarma had done spiritual practices honoring Shiva, Shiva granted him the boon of making his own form. Blessing Vishwakarma with five heads and fifteen eyes, Shiva said, "In this form, you will be known as the source of the Vishwabrahmakul—the family of Vishwabrahmins—and an avatar of Shiva."[11]

This five-headed form, connecting Shiva, Vishwakarma, and Vishwabrahmins also became associated with the Vishwa Kund. A 1957 Gujarati book that Bhai unearthed from his village library in Kutch reproduced the history of Vishwabrahmin litigation and opened with another representation of the five-headed form of Vast Vishwakarma.[12]

45. Vishwakarma with goddesses in Gujarati history of Vishwakarma and descendants, Anjar, 1957.

In this print, Vishwakarma stands holding tools and implements on a raised platform under a banyan tree. The crescent moon hovers over his pot of water; the face of the sun spreads rays to his pot of flames. Vishnu and Shiva look on as two beautiful, crowned women in saris bend before Vishwakarma, pouring water over his feet. I thought these must be his daughters. Yet the Sanskrit verses reproduced overleaf, with Gujarati translation, praise the goddesses Lakshmi and Saraswati as serving Vishwakarma in his five-faced joyous form.

The site at which Vishwakarma is honored by these goddesses is for some the Vishwa Kund. In his overview of Ellora for pilgrims, Vadgama writes, "Lakshmi and Saraswati carried divine nectar from the realm of the gods here to the Ellora mountain and right beside the Vishwa Kund made by Vishwakarma, they washed Vishwakarma's feet and worshipped him. This nectar filled the Vishwa Kund."[13]

The Vishwa Kund features prominently in the long story of Vishwaavasu, which stretches like a superhero franchise across three chapters of the 1965 Vishwakarma Purana.[14] Vishwaavasu is identified as of Vishwabrahmin lineage, from a distinguished family of royal Pandits who also serve as the kingdom's architects. Born paralyzed, mute, and deaf, he is brought as a boy on pilgrimage to Vishwakarma at Ellora. He happens to fall into the Vishwa Kund, then instantly walks out, salutes, and chats with his astounded parents. Offering thanks to Vishwakarma, the boy stays on after the parents go home and, sitting by the edge of the pond, performs extensive spiritual practices to honor Vishwakarma. Here is a quick summary of what happened next.

VISHWAAVASU AND THE VISHWA KUND: THE MANIFESTATION OF VISHWAKARMA

Sitting beside the Vishwa Kund, Vishwaavasu faced Vishwakarma's temple and focused on spiritual practices. A year went by, and then, as Vishwaavasu was meditating, Vishwakarma manifested as a big flash of light. Vishwaavasu opened his eyes and saw that Vishwakarma was present at the edge of the Vishwa Kund.

Vishwakarma sat on a throne in the dense shade of a banyan tree. He was in his five-faced, ten-armed Shiva form, wearing bejeweled crowns on all his heads, a sacred thread across one shoulder, and yellow garments. He held a splendid tool in each of his many hands, and he blessed Vishwaavasu.

Through the power of these blessings, the boy began acquiring every sort of esoteric building knowledge at Ellora—even the magical knowledge of Maya Danav, architect of the underworld.[15] Later he used this knowledge to rout rival Pandits claiming the position of royal architects through their knowledge of texts rather than of making. Sprinkling water from the Kund, Vishwaavasu miraculously reconstructed broken buildings and upheld his family's honor.

The Kund's centrality for healing and pilgrimage was emphasized in the report on "*Ellola*" prepared for the colonial surveyor Colin Mackenzie by two Brahmins, Narrain Row and Anunda Row, who visited in 1806, three decades after Ahilyabai Holkar's renovation. They composed their account by referring to the Shivalaya Mahatmya (the Sanskrit text extolling this sacred space) and gathering oral traditions from local Brahmins and lower-caste Gurav priests. While they worked in Marathi, the report was translated and written out in beautiful English cursive by their colleague Sooba Row, eventually landing in the Mackenzie collection at the British Library. Over two centuries later, we eagerly read these pages for clues to Cave 10.

The Rows' overview begins with the Vishwa Kund, identified as the Shivalaya Tirtha. Again suggesting that the sacredness of the larger area emanates from the water in this Kund, the Rows summarize a sequence of stories about the water's fabulous transformative powers across different cosmic eras. The water was at different times golden, white, blue, and the color of a peacock's tail; it offered salvation, washed away sins, cured disease. Destroyed and drained by Yama, God of Death (as too many souls were gaining salvation after a dip rather than coming before him), the Kund shrank to the size of a cow's hoof, then became the site of Yama's penance and his worship of Shiva. Later, the Kund's rebuilding by King Ila (Yella Raja) resulted in the area being known as Ellora.[16]

Charles Malet had also spoken to a local Brahmin who referred to the Shivalaya Mahatmya to narrate how King Ila (EELOO rajah) had been cured of an awful skin disease by the holy water.[17]

THE KUND AND CAVES 16 THROUGH 10

EELOO raja's body was afflicted with maggots, and in quest of a cure, he came to the famous purifying water named Sewa Lye, or, as it is commonly called, Sewalla [Shivalaya].... In this water, EELOO dipped a cloth, and cleansed with it his face and hands, which clear him of the maggots. He then built [the] Koond (or cistern) and bathing therein, his whole body was purified; so that, looking on the place as holy, he first constructed the temple called Keylmas [Kailash], &c. to the place of Biskurma [Vishwakarma].

....

In this version, the key excavations at the caves—including Cave 10 itself—were undertaken primarily *because* of the Kund's miraculous powers.

According to Captain Seely, in the early nineteenth century the Vishwa Kund was off-limits to non-Brahmins: "No one but a Brahman of the highest order is allowed to touch the water, and to dispense the miraculous liquid to the devout and faithful."[18] For artisans, it seems, to bathe in the Vishwa Kund, controlled by Brahmins, and put on a sacred thread right there, was a way of enacting Brahminhood in conjunction with the existing pilgrimage to Cave 10.

Some of the Vishwakarma booklets we were given contained mantras to recite while putting on the sacred thread; occasionally someone would pull out an old, folded sheet of paper printed with a sacred thread mantra, the Brahminical Gayatri mantra, and Vishwakarma mantras. Yet as far as I can follow, not all Vishwakarma's descendants in Gujarat ever became involved in wearing the sacred thread—among the four subgroups of carpenters, it was mostly the Mevadas who had made this a regular practice.

By the time our research began in 2017, the Vishwa Kund's association with sacred threads seemed to have waned. With state-legislated affirmative action since the 1990s for historically underprivileged "OBCs" (Other Backward Castes, which in some cases include artisans), the allure of claiming Brahminhood had dissipated. The author of a community booklet from 2016 observed that currently Vishwakarma's male offspring usually don't wear the thread, or wear it only for short times, but he seemed to affirm what Pa had once told me, noting, "There is also a belief in Gujarat that only those who have visited Ellora (*Ilol garh*) can wear the sacred thread."[19]

✳

Ken and I visited the Vishwa Kund on a hot afternoon in January 2018. A waiter at our hotel had connected us to his older relative, Anna Bhau, who drove an auto-rickshaw and brought us along the main road to the Kund. Even as he was parking, people squatting near the southern entrance stood up expectantly. By the time we climbed out of the rickshaw, a teenaged boy had come rushing toward us. He was wearing a grimy, oversize T-shirt, his pants were rolled up toward his calves, and in his left hand he held a bowl of what looked like white paste, while with his right hand he reached out what looked like a tiny metal prong. Before we could object, he had stamped something onto our foreheads.

What was this? Was this the custom of the place?

I had to look over at Ken to figure out what we might now be sporting on our faces. Just above the bridge of his glasses, I recognized a very miniature version of the three parallel white lines that indicate an affiliation to Shiva; usually drawn with ash, these would stretch across the whole forehead. For this mini stamp of instant piety, the boy demanded a donation.

Was he a hereditary priest of this site in contemporary attire? Was he a bored teenager who'd figured out a way to trick pilgrims? Confused and hassled, I reached into my purse.

Immediately, the boy insisted that we produce more money. He urged us to buy a basket of flowers, a coconut, and a stick of incense from an older woman who'd appeared beside him, possibly his mother. Then he led us into the walled area, downward along the steps of the Kund toward the wide platform with eight shrines. The stone symmetries of the Kund had absorbed the afternoon heat, and the immaculately laid blocks were griddles beneath our bare feet. Plastic trash, dried bits of flowers, balled paper, and candy wrappers were scattered over the steps and in the courtyard. Framed images of gods were propped up in some shrines, and the boy urged us to set down more money (which he instantly pocketed).

What were we doing here, I wondered, following the boy in a daze as he led to another shrine, and another. Other men who had set up camp in the remaining shrines were beckoning us forward. Our guide vehemently steered us away.

"Don't go there! Follow me. This is where to put the money. Here, right here."

"Don't listen to him!" the others yelled.

Squabbles, exchanges of abuse, and even a shoving match broke out in these competitions for our small rupee coins and notes. From every direction, people began exhorting us to donate something. The holy water was flecked green with algae. Though I didn't yet know of the assurance in one recent Vishwakarma Purana that the water of this Kund would heal any wounds made by tools, suggesting that a bottle be kept always on hand, I resisted stepping downward for an anointment.[20]

Eventually, we extracted ourselves and were left alone to photograph.

We'd planned to proceed to the Ghrishneshwar temple, just a short distance up the road. But what were the chances that we'd be accosted there by similar characters? Instead we went straight back to our hotel for some afternoon tea and notes before evening prayers to Shiva from the scratchy temple loudspeaker began rolling across the valley.

Eight months later, we were back in Ellora, bringing Jayantibhai Gajjar, who for years had been telling stories about Vishwakarma's sojourn at Ellora but had never himself visited. As our research assistant, Hardik Siddhpura, held a video camera, Jayantibhai retold some of his favorite stories at the caves or sitting outdoors at the nearby guesthouse, a waterfall cascading down the mountain behind him. After a morning of storytelling, Jayantibhai was delighted when we suggested an afternoon visit to the Vishwa Kund.

This time, we knew to ward off anyone trying to take charge of us, and the four of us sailed right through the entrance. The ambience was very different from that of the hot January afternoon. With monsoon showers, the air was mild, the steps of the Kund seemed freshly washed, and the water was clear. A group of women squatted by the water, wetting their heads; a few male pilgrims had stripped down to shorts and were wading in.

Jayantibhai had been conferring by mobile phone with friends in Ahmedabad who were more familiar with Ellora. He told us that under the visible stone steps were hidden, submerged steps made of beautifully preserved wood. He speculated that the water went very deep, possibly to the underworld.

"Vishwakarma's footprint will be right there, beside the water," Jayantibhai announced. He climbed down to the pool's edge, and sure enough, there was a single carved footprint. "See?" he called up to us.

Ken and I stood at a distance, photographing. Shifting my attention to the Vishwa Kund had helped me glimpse how the pilgrimage to Vishwakarma at Ellora had become knitted into local traditions of Shiva worship and the transregional mobility aspirations of artisans, but somehow I felt at an emotional remove. Was it wariness after our first visit? I had grown up with the privilege of not thinking about caste—was the Kund's square framing of caste issues making me squirm? I still don't quite know.

Dipping his right hand into the water, Jayantibhai anointed his gray hair. He recited Vishwakarma mantras with Brahminical flair: "Holding a footrule, a cord, a waterpot, and a book with the Code of knowledge, he sits on a swan, has three eyes, wears an auspicious crown, his body expansive and ancient . . ."

Then Jayantibhai posed, beaming, for a photograph that we sent by WhatsApp to his family back in the industrial suburbs of Ahmedabad.

* 15 *

Locating the Goddess

Sonal, wife of my cousin Prakash, was the first to tell us that Vishwakarma's daughter, the goddess Randal, also has a presence at Ellora.

A smile played across Sonal's face as she recalled a community pilgrimage in 2014. To honor the memory of a relative, someone in Ahmedabad had organized a six-day bus tour of sacred sites in Maharashtra. This was just before the spring full moon of Holi, and Ellora was the key destination. Maybe 150 people—all members of the caste (*jnātwālās*) and mostly women—set out, along with a cook. At Ellora, they stayed in the dormitories of a new Vishwakarma temple beside the highway, where a professional storyteller was telling Vishwakarma stories.

"We were like one big family!" Sonal reported. "Everyone looked after each other. At Ellora (*Ilorgarh*) we went to the original temple of Vishwakarma. We went all around. We saw that big stone where Randal Ma's palanquin was placed at the time of her marriage."

Where was this stone marking Randal's wedding? Sonal couldn't offer further details. The women with her had observed that the stone was just like a ceremonial footstool (*bājoṭ*). Such low, four-legged stools, I knew, are often used to welcome a deity and to lay out offerings for rituals.

As with Vishwakarma, I'd grown up aware of Randal's worship, but I came to know her more through research. Her doubled form intrigued and inspired me; dual identities, her form seemed to say, could calmly coexist. Before our fieldwork began, I'd assembled whatever I could learn about her and more generally about Vishwakarma in relation to goddesses, and was immediately reminded that the Gujar Suthar's protective lineage goddess (*kul devī*) Chamunda of Chotila hill also manifested in a doubled form.[1]

In the shrine of the largest community temple in Ahmedabad, for example, the two doubled goddesses flank Vishwakarma. On the left, two aspects of Chamunda Mata, both bearing tridents, lean toward each other, keeping company with their muscular yellow lion, just as they do on their shrine atop Chotila hill, near Rajkot. These two sides of Chamunda Mata are her fierce and benevolent forms. On the right, two identical faces of Randal and her shadow self look warmly ahead from their shared torso. (Vishwakarma's sons are also present as small boys with joined palms barely reaching their father's knees, partly hidden by his garments. Beak respectfully lowered, Vishwakarma's signature goose/swan completes the gathering.)

Across India, Vishwakarma is associated with goddesses; who these goddesses are and how they are related to him are grounded in different regional stories.[2] The contemporary worship of Randal as Vishwakarma's daughter seems to be peculiar to Gujarat, and especially to the Saurashtra (Kathiawar) area of Gujarat where sun worship has been prevalent, for Randal is married to the sun god.[3] Yet, known by other names across the centuries and mentioned in the Rig Veda, Randal is a very ancient goddess; it has astonished me to see very Randal-like forms in museums, for example, in the British Museum, two small conjoined figurines from the Eye Temple in Syria, dating to about 3300–3000 BCE. In Gujarat, when Randal is invited from the sky for rituals, she manifests in the form of two coconuts set atop waterpots, which are then given faces of clay,

46. Vishwakarma with goddesses in temple sanctum, Ahmedabad 2018. Photograph by Ken George.

metal, or preprinted plastic, and brightly dressed and ornamented. She is also honored with songs and dances that include grown women prancing like horses and women worshipping fourteen other women. While other Gujarati castes also seek her blessings, particularly for fertility, for Gujar Suthars she is cherished as a daughter of the lineage and as a benevolent visiting aunty.

Since Randal is largely unknown outside of Gujarat, it was news to us that she could be found at Ellora. When Ken and I visited the first time, we looked around Cave 10 but didn't see anything resembling a footstool. Hoping for more information, we went to the more contemporary Vishwakarma temple that Sonal had described along the highway north of Verul village and that the taxi driver bringing us from the airport had mentioned. The resident holy man, Mahendra Bapu, was away just then, but the assistant who received us said that Randal's temple was "up on the mountain."

"Randal?" When we got back into our motor rickshaw, our driver, Anna Bhau, was perplexed. This was not a name he had heard before. But he agreed that yes, there were goddess temples higher up the mountain; we could go look.

The next day, we set off to find Randal. Wind whipping into the rickshaw, we moved past Khuldabad with its Sufi shrines and tombs, rattling higher and higher along the road north to the Mhaismal plateau. Anna Bhau pulled up at the temple to the goddess Girija (another name for Parvati, "daughter of the mountains," who is Shiva's wife). This temple was right by the road, beside the Velganga river, running west toward the caves. We wandered around the temple, then stood in line to enter the shrine overseen by male priests. The goddess's enormous painted face with eyebrows sloping at the sides carried an expression of sweet concern, and she was swathed in saris and garlands. But we couldn't discern any connection to Randal.

Anna Bhau next suggested that we try the old Girija temple to the east. This time he turned off the main road and jolted along an unpaved path through barren scrub and open fields. Walking the last stretch, we found ourselves within what seemed like a small forest sanctuary. This shrine was beside the Girija rivulet, which flows east from the origin it shares with the Velganga. Amid a cluster of trees and near a trickling waterfall, a few orange-painted rocks were adorned with eyes and red garments. A contemporary cement statue of a multiarmed goddess with wide eyes gave splendid audience within an open-air shed.

A female priest came from a nearby house to greet us. This goddess was Girija, she said; she didn't know anything about Vishwakarma's daughter.

We returned to Ahmedabad, perplexed. Where could Randal be at Ellora? When we were next invited over for one of Sonal's wonderful meals, we tried to get more details. "That footstool of Randal is just there, at the caves," was all she could tell us.

✳

We hadn't found Randal, but venturing higher up to the goddess temples on the Mhaismal plateau reminded us how the mountain is pervaded with a divine female presence that is often linked to waterways. The Ellora caves of all three faiths—Buddhist, Hindu, and Jain—house many memorably beautiful goddesses, sometimes with consorts, sometimes in groups, sometimes alone.

In the Buddhist caves, the goddesses mark the emergence of Vajrayana, a Tantric form of Buddhism that was still finding iconographic expression at the time of the caves' making.[4] Goddess emanations of Bodhisattva energies reappear across the stretch of Buddhist caves. At first glance, the large Murti in Cave 10 is male, with male attendants on either side and male figures in the friezes above the pillars. But look again, and within Cave 10's hall, balcony, façade, and cells, female figures come into focus: the goddesses Bhrikuti, Mayamayuri, and Prajnaparamita, flying celestial women bringing offerings, female serpent-beings saluting, women intertwined with male partners as auspicious loving couples. Just around the corner, in Cave 9, stands Tara, the goddess who watches over travelers, reminding us of how rock-cut Buddhist caves were often located along ancient trade routes.

Though in his grandfatherly form Vishwakarma is usually perceived as resolutely celibate, it seemed appropriate that some older Gujarati texts depict him as marrying the goddess Kriti at Ellora.[5] Kriti personifies the Sanskrit word *kriti*—"the act of doing, making, performing, manufacturing, composing."[6] Bhai commented that this could be glossed as "doing your work." (As he liked to say, for our artisan ancestors, what mattered most was "finding good work and doing good work.") *Kriti* can also refer to a creation, like a piece of music or work of art. I realized that a verse in a goddess hymn I'd learned as a child celebrated the mother goddess with this name: "Salutations to the Goddess established in the universe as creative action."[7]

The frame story in my grandfather's 1901 red book describes Vishnu's urging Vishwakarma to create offspring. And so, with the goddess Kriti, he has a son—the Shilpacharya who shared these teachings with descendants. That book also advises worshippers to present Vishwakarma with flowers while reciting in Sanskrit:

> I meditate on Shree Vishwakarma,
> accompanied by his wife Kriti.
> Creating images and all sorts of dwellings
> he is the Adept god.[8]

In the British Library, we discovered a fragile pamphlet about ways to worship and praise Vishwakarma, written in Gujarati and published in an edition of 125 copies by the Gujar Suthar community in Karachi in 1921. The author/compiler was Harji Lakhoo Desharia—clearly a Dahisaria clan relative and possibly someone present at the opening of the Karachi Suthar school sponsored by my grandfather. Kriti appears as Vishwakarma's activities at Ellora are extolled:

> You made this very special creation
> of heaven, earth and underworld.
> You settled in Ellora,
>   you who hold the measuring stick and cord.
> You married Kriti,
>   taking on a unique form.
> You purified the earth:
> Vishwakarma, source of happiness.
> You made Ellora
>   equal to the seven great pilgrimage cities,
> And all the gods settled there and
>   hugely enjoyed themselves.[9]

After making the larger creation, Vishwakarma is said here to settle on earth at Ellora, where he marries Kriti, takes on a unique form, and makes the magnificent dwelling space of the caves for other happy gods. Another section of the booklet narrates this arrival at Ellora after the first stirring of creation, when "the formless had the desire to take form," and a Vast Person came into being.[10]

THE THIRD VISHWAKARMA, KRITI, AND THEIR SONS

The Vast Person made the universe, gods, sages, and seers. Then he vanished and was remembered as Vishwakarma.

But the beings he had made didn't know the right ways to behave, so he returned to teach them. Then he disappeared again.

He reappeared a third time at Ellora (Ilorgaṛh), where he married Kriti. Five sons were born to them. The sons worked on the creation, made temples for gods, and begot offspring.

When Vishwakarma was ready to depart again, he instructed his sons and grandsons to travel north to the Pavagadh (Pāvāgaṛh) mountain (in Gujarat). To celebrate their mother Kriti, who birthed the universe, Vishwakarma instructed his descendants to make a temple in the name of Kali.

....

I tried to learn more about the goddess Kriti, but no one in the twenty-first century seemed to have heard of her. Others acknowledged, yes, in some previous incarnations, Vishwakarma might have been married, but they didn't think that "Kriti" was the right name. Surely, I meant "Prakriti" (primordial nature), since Vishwakarma needed to partner with primordial nature to make all things? Or might I mean "Aakriti" (form and appearance), since all his work involved the creation of form?

I hadn't yet learned of Kriti when, standing before the Ahmedabad shrine where Vishwakarma is joined by the two doubled goddesses, we chatted with the Brahmin priest. I asked, had he ever visited Ellora? He shook his head, no. He hadn't had *darshan* of the Murti in Vishwakarma's original place, he said, but he had heard that at Ellora, just as at Pavagadh, the true Murti of the deity was situated deep inside the mountain. "There's a secret path that only a few very fortunate people know about," he said, "and only they are able to have the true *darshan*."

I became curious about the analogy made between Ellora and Pavagadh, the volcanic mountain that became Kriti's destination and the site of a celebrated Kali temple.[11] Like Ellora, Pavagadh is a multireligious space (with Hindu, Jain, and Islamic places of worship). There too, the marvelous skills of past artisans are on display, though in buildings rather than caves. At this site, past inhabitants also constructed an elaborate system of water conservation, with cisterns and ponds.

Kriti, like Chamunda Mata, appears to be a form of the goddess Kali associated with the power of time and transformation—for artisans, the transformation of matter by the action of tools.[12]

✳

Even if no one these days had heard of Kriti, everyone knew Randal. Bhai was surprised to hear of Randal's association with Ellora, but some contemporary Vishwakarma worshippers shared their knowledge. These urban Suthars seemed familiar not just with Cave 10 but with the entire complex of caves, reeling off cave numbers and hypothesizing about iconography. As Ken said, you could think of these close alternative readings of Ellora as a form of "subaltern art history."

Narrotam Kaka, a retired engine mechanic from Surat visiting his son in Ahmedabad, told us that Randal's wedding had taken place at Cave 5, "the big cave near the second waterfall"—that is, the waterfall in the Buddhist set of caves. Cave 5 is a residential Buddhist hall, with cells and a central shrine where the Buddha sits in the same teaching pose as in Cave 10. The central passage toward that shrine is lined with two low benchlike platforms. For a seated monk, these platforms would be the right height to assemble texts for study, to engage in chanting, or even to enjoy a meal. But to Narottam Kaka, the platforms had clearly been set up for the wedding ritual. "See, *all* the caves," he emphasized, "were made for the wedding guests to stay."

On the other hand, Jayantibhai's friend Kantibhai was certain that Randal's wedding had taken place further north along the stretch of caves. He too located this near a waterfall—on the Velganga, amid the Hindu caves—but used a different line of deduction.

"In Cave 25, when you look up, you'll see signs of Randal Ma's wedding," Kantibhai told us one baking April evening in Jayantibhai's apartment. The rock ceiling of Cave 25—also known as "Sureshwar," from Surya—carries an image of Surya in his chariot. He is flanked by two attending goddesses, energetically shooting arrows with outstretched arms (aspects of the dawn driving away darkness). This then, was where Surya was believed to have arrived for the wedding—matching up with a local title for Cave 26: "Janawasa," or place for a bridegroom's party to stay.

Kantibhai continued, "Above Cave 28, higher on the mountain, there is the wedding canopy and the footstool near a Kund. It's all deserted, as people rarely go up there."

Cave 28 lies deeper in the ravine, behind the spectacular waterfall made by the Velganga river in the monsoon. The cave is a goddess shrine, with the river goddesses Ganga and Yamuna on either side of the door and an eight-armed goddess inside.[13]

But what cave, "higher up" the mountain and beside a pond, was associated with Randal? Sitting cross-legged on a sofa, with pictures of Vishwakarma around him, grandchildren coming and going, Narottam Kaka gave us precise directions before we again traveled to Ellora in August

2018. In the process, he also told us that the locations of the Surya Kund and the Chandra Kund, usually said to be on the nearby Sulibhanjan hill, could be debated.

"Behind Cave 22, keep to the pipeline, and go upward," said Narottam Kaka. "You will pass the Ganesh caves. There are seven ponds there. On the left side of the stream is the true Surya Kund, and where the water then descends is the Chandra Kund. You will find Randal Ma there. People also know this as the Jogeshwari cave, the Jogeshwari temple."

Finally we had a local name: Jogeshwari.

The twelfth-century shrine to the goddess Jogeshwari isn't within the World Heritage precinct, and guidebooks don't usually mention it. Most historical sources also focus on the sequence of caves carved along the mountain's base, omitting the caves carved uphill, along the banks of the Velganga River. Since Jogeshwari is a form of Parvati doing *tapas*—intensive ascetic practices that generate great heat and transformative power—it is appropriate that she be located in a somewhat out-of-the-way place.[14] The Rows' early nineteenth-century account mentions Jogeshwari as a two-chambered dwelling situated along the Velganga, with an image of Jogeshwari to the west, and pillar oil lamps on the other bank.[15] Drawing again on the Shivalaya Mahatmya text, the Rows retell the story of Jogeshwari's presence on the mountain.[16]

The story begins with Shiva and Parvati (Girija) playing a dice game at their home on Mount Kailash in the Himalayas—a scene rendered in several different sculpted caves at Ellora, all drawing on a complex of Puranic tales about Shiva and Parvati's dice games as shifts in cosmological power.[17] When Parvati loses the third game and is required to serve Shiva like his attendant bull, Nandi, she is offended. Taking Nandi to the river for a drink, she vanishes into the water and reemerges in the Godavari River at Toka, southwest of Ellora. She makes her way to the mountain above Ellora, bathing and worshipping at various sacred places. Arriving on the mountain, she starts her austerities and pronounces that all male creatures entering the forest around her will become female. Intent on yoga, she becomes "Jogeshwari."

King Ila, or "Yella Raja," appears again in this story, this time without a skin condition or a queen. Coming to hunt on the mountain, he turns into a woman named Ila (pronounced with a long *a*), who devotes herself to serving Parvati. Eventually, Shiva delegates his other wife, Ganga, to serve as go-between and Parvati cools down. Parvati then decides that since the area around Ellora has become desolate, it is time for her attendant Ila

LOCATING THE GODDESS 217

to turn back into a man, rebuild the Shivalaya Tirth, and reestablish the village. This is where Vishwakarma comes in.

.... ✤ ....

THE KUND IS REBUILT, PARVATI AND SHIVA REUNITE, AND VISHWAKARMA ARRIVES

At Parvati's request, Ila bathed in a sacred pool on the mountain, once again becoming King Ila. Witnessing the transformation, Parvati shed tears of joy that became two streams, one flowing east as the Girija Nadi, the other west as the Ila Ganga (Velganga). King Ila then prayed to all the river goddesses in various parts of India and started traveling downstream along the Ila Ganga. Moving west along this waterway, he bathed in different pools, including the pool at the base of the waterfall. He then repaired the Shivalaya Teerth [or Vishwa Kund] and gave the place the name "Ellola" or Ellora.

With these sacred places splendidly restored, Parvati sent Ganga north with a message inviting Shiva to join her. Shiva traveled to Ellora with a grand entourage of thirty-three million gods, sixty-four Siddhas or perfected beings, assorted Nath holy men, and Vishwakarma. The group arrived at the sacred pool, and Shiva and Parvati were happily reconciled.

Brahma suggested that the couple be remarried. So Shiva asked Vishwakarma to prepare Shiva's own residence (Cave 16), make a place for the wedding, and also excavate places for all the gods to stay on at the mountain.

Following Shiva's request, Vishwakarma carved the mountain and made many dwellings for gods.

....

In the Rows' words, since then, Shiva and Parvati "have both remained at Ellola; and the Davahs [gods] also placed Images resembling their several shapes in their separate Residences."[18] Again, the splendid residences that Vishwakarma made are seen has having induced gods to stay and to establish their own Murtis in different caves.

Gujarati Vishwakarma Puranas also celebrate the mountain as the site of a wedding with caves made to host wedding guests. These stories, though, feature Randal marrying the Sun. In fact, Randal's very manifestation is said to occur so the family can host a wedding on the mountain. For this to happen, Vishwakarma, who has already made sons, manifests daughters from each of his two hands.[19] When the girls come of age, he arranges the marriage of his older daughter Randal (or Samgnya) to the Sun. The mountain draws guests from across the universe, and magically expands so they can all be hosted amid abundance. The younger daughter Brihasmati's wedding isn't planned just then, and she feels left out; noticing this, her sympathetic sister Ila urges Vishwakarma to allow the girl to choose her own mate from the lineup of handsome kings who have arrived as wedding guests.[20]

························· ⚘ ·························

RANDAL'S WEDDING AT ELLORA

Great multitudes of beings flowed toward the Ellora mountain to celebrate the wedding. The guest list included "gods, humans, nature spirits, celestial musicians, snakes, serpents, eagles, ancestors, nymphs, saints, bards, seers and sages, and many animals, birds, insects, butterflies and moths, mountains, rivers, seas, sacred places, and plants etc. and the entire immovable and movable creation...."

The guests kept arriving and the Ilachal mountain expanded, growing larger and larger to accommodate them all; new spaces were made to host and feed them. Celebratory sounds of songs and chants resounded across the slopes. For the wedding feast, holy rivers served water, and sacred mountains parceled out food. With his own hands, the mountain Ilachal distributed a variety of tasty fried pakoras made from ingredients like sweet potato, squash, eggplant, pumpkin, and chili pepper.

Since the ritual of giving away a daughter should be performed by a father and mother together, Vishwakarma emanated a mother from himself. His female form, who personified this wish to greet a groom, performed a welcome ceremony for Randal's shining groom, Surya Narayan.

···

The Murti's smooth cheeks in Cave 10, it turns out, could be explained as Vishwakarma's maternal form created for the wedding. As Jayantibhai told us, "Vishwakarma in Gujarat has a beard, but in Ellora, he is clean-shaven. Why? It is because when his daughter needed to be married, she had no mother, and he had to split himself into two forms. He shaved off his beard. That way, at the wedding, he could be father *and* mother at the same time."

While Parvati did penance *before* she was remarried at Ellora, Randal's appearance as Jogeshwari comes *after* the wedding celebration at the caves. Usually, the site of her penance is said to be in the region of Uttarkuru far

LOCATING THE GODDESS 219

to the subcontinent's north, but for some this is transposed to the Ellora mountainside. Here is a widely told story of Randal.

.... ⚘ ....

RANDAL, THE SUN, AND THE SHADOW

After Randal's wedding, she found the Sun was hot, bright, and easily angered. They had three children together, and his scorching brilliance became unbearable. So, as Vishwakarma's ingenious daughter, she shaped her own shadow into her perfect double. She asked this enlivened shadow-self, "Chhaya," to take her place.

Randal went home to her father and told Vishwakarma of her troubles. Then she withdrew to the forest to focus on her own spiritual practices. So that she wouldn't be bothered by anyone, she took the form of a mare.

In her shadow coolness, Chhaya wasn't affected by the heat that caused Randal such distress. She was such a perfect replica that Surya and the children didn't notice that Randal was gone. Three more children were born. But when one of the older children, Yama, misbehaved, Chhaya cursed him. Yama guessed that she wasn't really his mother and alerted Surya. When Surya asked Chhaya who she really was, she admitted that she was the Shadow.

Surya went to Vishwakarma. "Where's your daughter and my wife?" he asked.

Vishwakarma told Surya that Randal couldn't bear his intense heat.

Surya asked for a solution. After all, blinding heat was his nature. Then Vishwakarma put his son-in-law on a lathe and shaved off some of his brightness so he would be more pleasing to Randal. The entire scorched earth was relieved. Later, Vishwakarma reworked those sun shavings into dazzling weapons for all the gods.

Then Surya went in search of Randal in the forest. Taking the form of a stallion, he danced and pranced as he approached her, pleasing Randal. Randal's austerities had borne fruit: her husband was transformed and bearable.

Reunited in their horse forms, the couple had three more children including the horse-headed, healing Ashwin twins. Since then, Randal has been honored in the doubled, conjoined form of her original self and her perfect shadow replica.

....

While Chhaya, emerging from Randal, is a goddess, Sanskrit treatises on making discuss how art arises when unmanifest divine light coalesces into conceptual form, then through an artist's skill manifests as the "Shadow" of outward form.[21] From this perspective, the stretch of caves, temples, and shrines at Ellora are all manifestations of Shadow, echoing Chakradhar Swami's revelation of the "Shadow of the Maker."

✳

Arriving at Ellora with Jayantibhai and Hardik, we set about following Narottam Kaka's directions to find the Jogeshwari cave. We first found the pipeline near Cave 22 and called Narottam Kaka, just to be sure. We also checked with a group of guards taking a tea break, and one of the young men in uniform volunteered to show us the way.

With the monsoon, the mountain was bejeweled. The facades of caves were darkened and glistening. Trees, shrubs, and grass were freshly green and washed; the two waterfalls swung their spray in gusting winds. All around us, water glinted, trickling, joining into larger flows.

We started climbing a muddy path on the southern bank of the rushing Velganga river. Sure enough, we first came to a set of small caves housing forms of Shiva and Ganesh. Crossing a cement bridge to the other side, we found a further warren of small residential caves, some quite dilapidated.

47. View of Jogeshwari cave beside sacred Velganga river during monsoon, Ellora, 2018. Photograph by Ken George.

Beaded curtains of dripping water hung across some cave entrances, and a few courtyards had turned into shallow pools. We had clearly stepped beyond the archaeological upkeep and constant hubbub of crowds at the World Heritage site.

The grassy path took a hairpin turn along the northern side of the watercourse. Climbing higher, we saw a flagpole with orange-red pennants: the sign of a shrine by the stream. We discerned the indent of a cave with a wide stretch of steps leading to the water, and a single lampstand pillar on the other bank. A few young men were swimming in the pool below, but as we neared, they went scampering upstream. The guard escorting us mentioned that a holy man lived in the Jogeshwari cave and tended

48. Goddess in Jogeshwari cave, 2018. Photograph by Kirin Narayan.

the shrine. At that hour, though, he most likely would have gone to the village for alms.

The goddess was alone when we arrived. Set atop a pedestal base, she faced the stream, her vermillion-plastered image suggesting a seated form with the right knee raised, perhaps holding something with both left and right hands. Her silver eyes gleamed in the light cast by the flame of an oil lamp and the brightness of the view she looked out on. Her lips and a horizontal tilak were inscribed with deep maroon *kumkum* powder. She seemed to be smiling.

In this shrine filled with the music of flowing water, we glimpsed what the other caves might once have looked like when they were still places of worship: painted walls, a plastered and painted image with prominent eyes, a burning oil lamp, and streaks from what might have been the water of coconuts broken open as offerings. At the same time, active worship meant updates. The tall, square base that we thought must be the "footstool" had been tiled over; as in many contemporary temples, these tiles had been installed to facilitate bathing the deity and cleaning up after worship.

Below the long steps, the stream bed had been carved into a few deeper square pools. Exposed rocks contained small pink and blue chunks of colored minerals, echoing the color scheme of pink and blue-green paint on the shrine walls. Orange dragonflies darted about, now and then alighting on the rocks as we sat down to enjoy the shifting patterns and the sounds of the rushing river.

✻ 16 ✻

On the Move

As we went around Ellora in August 2018, the four of us presented a puzzling spectacle. Our group was composed of Jayantibhai, some days dressed in a flowing kurta and dhoti, a shawl around his neck, worship marks on his forehead; Hardik, in his generation's transnational uniform of T-shirt and jeans, holding a video camera; visibly foreign Ken, with a roomy buttoned shirt, jeans, backpack, and an iPad; and me, in block-printed Ahmedabad matronly fashion, yet suspiciously light-skinned with short, hennaed hair.

Who were we, where were we from, why could we possibly be together?

Other visitors stopped to stare, invite us to pose for photographs with them, and ask questions. When Hardik told one inquisitive group that Ken and I were researchers from Australia, the young men assumed that Hardik himself was Indian-Australian. Even as he protested, laughing, he was peppered with queries about cricketers, educational opportunities, and the best procedures for immigration.

We were traipsing yet again into the Cave 10 courtyard when a man sprinted past, then looked back over his shoulder in a double take. Before he reached the steps, he stopped short.

"Idhar se yā udhar se?" he swiveled around to ask me. "From Here or from There?"

Apparently, I was the hinge, the visible half-and-half, as Jayantibhai and Hardik proceeded ahead of me and Ken lagged behind, taking another image of the exterior.

"Donon se," I responded. "From both."

"Achchaaaa!" he nodded. "Alright . . . !"

Off he went, past the guard at the doorway, and disappeared into the main hall of Cave 10.

The first time we had slowly wandered together through the cave, a small group of men in white dhotis and women in brightly colored saris approached us on the outer verandah along the courtyard. Perhaps they were drawn by Jayantibhai's pilgrimage attire, which gave him the aura of a spiritual guide.

"Where is Vishwakarma?" they asked. They were carpenters from Madhya Pradesh, they said, and couldn't figure out where to pay their respects.

"Vishwakarma is over there," Jayantibhai said with easy authority.

But he wasn't pointing to the Murti in the main hall at all. He was indicating a shrine at the far end of the verandah, to the right of the main door.

The Madhya Pradesh carpenter pilgrims flocked toward this southern shrine, and we tagged along. I was curious to see what they would do. In this recessed space of semidarkness, a serene, smooth-cheeked deity looked on with widened eyes and elongated earlobes. Someone had already marked the forehead with a long orange *tilak*. The carpenters placed offerings on this Murti's upturned left foot, then turned around to pose for a photograph of themselves with the god.

This deity sits on a raised lotus seat, right leg bent to the ground, left knee angling sideways. He wears a turbanlike headdress, a garment tucked at his waist, and what could be interpreted as a sacred thread draped from the left shoulder to the right hip. The fingers of his open right hand gesture downward as though pouring blessings. His left hand grasps the stem of a blossoming lotus, its central carpel at almost the same level and of almost the same size as his eyes. To art historians, he is a compassionate Bodhisattva Avalokiteshvara, "eyes dilated with joy."[1] He is also known as Padmapani for the lotus that he carries. But now, for some, he is recognized as Vishwakarma.

Jayantibhai had come from Ahmedabad with this identification squarely planted in his mind. This was where his friends had told him he would find Vishwakarma, and this was the location they confirmed when he called on his mobile phone from the Cave 10 courtyard.

"But what about the Murti in the main hall?" I asked.

"*That* Murti is Buddha," Jayantibhai said, enunciating each word with patient care. "*This* is Vishwakarma."

"But *how* is this Vishwakarma?"

"Just look at the hammer!"

The blossoming lotus had morphed into a round hammer; after all, Vishwakarma would hold a tool. Jayantibhai reminded us that Grandfather Vishwakarma usually sat on a throne in the same posture (the comfortable pose known as *lalitāsana*). As further evidence, not only did his friends point to this location, but this was where guards were ushering anyone who asked about Vishwakarma. "Over here," the guard on duty had said, bringing along a big steel flashlight to light up the image in the shadowed rock cell.

49. Padmapani or Vishwakarma? Deity with offerings in eastern cell of Cave 10, 2018. Photograph by Kirin Narayan.

Back in the guesthouse, we brought out a laptop to show Jayantibhai a sequence of late nineteenth-century photographs of the Murti with big painted eyes. Jayantibhai bent forward, carefully examining the images.

"But how is *this* Vishwakarma?" he bluntly asked.

We located the print labeled "Shree Guru Maharaj Vishwakarma," clearly an interpretation of the Murti in Cave 10, that served as a frontispiece for Bhai's 1926 edition of Surajram's Vishwakarma Purana.

"This is from the Purana!" I said, knowing his reverence for the book that had supplied him with many of his stories.

Jayantibhai nodded, thinking this over but clearly unconvinced.

A few months later, we came across another token that this newer identification of Padmapani as Vishwakarma was moving into wider circulation. We had hired a taxi for the day to visit Vishwakarma temples around Ahmedabad. At the city's northwestern edge, in a building supply district, we located a small temple with a banner crafted with women's bright beadwork saluting Vishwakarma over the door. Inside, a framed poster of a white-bearded grandfather presided at the altar.

But just to the left as we entered, a loudspeaker had been emblazoned with an overexposed photograph, clearly the Murti with widened eyes from the side shrine of Cave 10. "The Resident of Ellora, Honored Vishwakarma" (*Ilorgarh Nivāsī Śrī Viśvakarmā*) read the Gujarati label.

＊

"There *used* to be a board outside Cave 10 saying this was Vishwakarma's cave! Why did the government take it down?"

We kept hearing versions of this complaint from Vishwakarma devotees in Gujarat who felt themselves connected to Ellora. Sometimes the conversation veered off toward letters of protest addressed to the Archaeological Survey of India, none of which had ever received a reply. At the time of our visits, a large indigo board with white lettering propped up by the doorway of Cave 10 offered an official archaeological overview in Hindi and in English. The cave was identified as a Buddhist *chaitya*, with Buddha resident inside. In keeping with a colonial heritage framework that downplayed complex multireligious sites across India to emphasize a singular identity, there was no mention of this space ever having been associated with Vishwakarma.[2]

An extensive local Buddhist presence returned to Maharashtra in roughly the same period that the Archaeological Survey of India was consolidating the care and preservation of the caves. In 1956, the great Dalit leader Dr. Bhimrao Ambedkar led about half a million people in a mass conversion to Buddhism from backgrounds previously deemed "untouchable" in Maharashtra. His 1934 essay *The Annihilation of Caste* had powerfully argued that the caste system was integral to Hinduism, and that only conversion to a more egalitarian religion would bring true hope for social reform. Since then, growing numbers of Maharashtrian Buddhists have joined with Buddhist pilgrims from elsewhere in India and around the world to visit "Ajanta-Ellora" with a sense of personal connection. "This is our Gautama Buddha!" a young woman explained one morning in January 2018 as I stood by a pillar, watching many generations organize themselves for a group photograph posed around the image. One afternoon soon after, orange-robed Buddhist monks and lay followers from Indonesia sat chanting on the floor, facing the Murti as the setting sun lit up the rafters. Other tourists who happened to come into the cave just then also settled down with bent heads and reverentially joined palms, drawn into the reverberating swell of Pali sounds.

One guard recalled a "guru from Japan" who each spring would bring an entourage to honor the Buddha in Cave 10. They would bathe the statue with water, then all sit together for meditation. The guard remembered how, in the silence, the guru had received some direct inspiration that caused him to laugh aloud with joy, though what it was, the guard never knew, for everything had transpired in Japanese.

If the Buddha was now splendidly present in the main hall of Cave 10, Vishwakarma's relocation to the southern shrine could allow for an amicable coexistence. But not all Suthars were convinced. "Why can't a Murti be both [*banne*] Buddha and Vishwakarma?" one elderly Suthar asked. Others alleged that this alternate identification was a scheme thought up by guards: "This is all a way for those guards to make some money! They won't allow us to do proper worship, and still they want the money. So *they* made a different Vishwakarma."

Guards were kept busy attending to what was going on in the large central hall and were either unable to monitor or willingly overlooked worship in the little cell shrine tucked off to the side, in semidarkness. This smaller Murti's forehead was often visibly anointed with red or orange, its face or body rubbed with what looked like oil, darkening the rock. We saw flowers, cash, or other offerings placed on the upturned left sole, or atop the "hammer." One evening, at closing time, I observed a guard running his fingertips over the top of that lotus/hammer, then slipping a rolled note into his shirt pocket. Yes, it seemed that Vishwakarma's move carried potential benefits all around.

Offering worship was, after all, a central concern for pilgrims seeking audience with Vishwakarma. I got a sense of how strongly pilgrims might feel about worship being prohibited at an archaeological site when, before our first trip to Ellora, we'd met with Vhalabhai, a hereditary carpenter of about fifty who worked as a folk musician and event organizer. He was a tall man with a humorous manner and powerful voice, much in demand as an MC at storytelling events. Since the sacred nine days associated with Ila's propitiation of Vishwakarma were coming up, I had asked Vhalabhai whether any events might take place at Cave 10.

"*Kucch nahin*, absolutely nothing!" he emphatically answered. "You're not going to find any sort of worship on that day, or on any day! That cave isn't a temple anymore. It's a *Heritage Site*. Nobody is allowed to worship. You can't decorate the image. No *ārati* lamps waved in the morning and evening, nothing. Then too, you must pay to enter."

Still, Vhalabhai acknowledged that even without active worship in Cave 10, "The Murti has a powerful force. There's no doubt: you feel something."

Like others, he pointed to Vishwakarma's descendants' need for a place to honor their ancestor in the ways they saw fit. This, we were often told, was the rationale for making a Vishwakarma temple to the north end of Verul village.

The new temple was the brainchild of a hereditary Suthar, Mahendrabhai Mistri, widely known as "Bapu" or "Father." As the biographical sketch included in a recent Vishwakarma Purana relates, Bapu was born in a village near Surat, then worked in Bombay, where "he pursued Vishwakarma devotion and ways to spread accurate and clear information about Vishwakarma among his descendants. Eventually he took the road to Ellora [*Ilorgaṛh*]."[3] Bapu established the Shree Vishwakarma Teerthdham Charitable Trust in 1998. Investing his own life savings to buy land in Verul as Vishwakarma's sacred pilgrimage center (*tīrthdhām*), he worked through the trust to raise community funds and oversee construction projects, with some community members like Narrotam Kaka and his sons volunteering their labor and expertise. The temple to Vishwakarma was inaugurated in 2000. With an adjoining large dormitory for community members on pilgrimage, this offered a place close to the caves for hosting community gatherings and big storytelling events.

A senior guard at the caves recalled how, at the time of the new temple's inauguration, a Suthar group had come with a waterpot to transport life from the Murti in Cave 10 to the Murti at the temple. "Vishwakarma isn't in Cave 10 anymore," this guard assured us. "He has been taken away."

The temple is about a twenty-minute rickshaw ride north of the caves. We set out on the main road through the village, passing the Grishneshwar temple and Vishwa Kund on the right. (We also passed a turnoff on the left to another, smaller modern Vishwakarma temple behind a gate with a large metal lock; it was closed, we were told, because of a land dispute, but we never learned the full details of who had built it and when.) Traveling further along the Kannad highway, we arrived at a large gateway with a temple visible just beyond, a two-story building further back, and the sacred mountain in the distance.

As the four of us entered the compound, we noticed an uncompleted cylindrical structure that was Mahendra Bapu's cherished next project: a 108-foot Shiva lingam surrounded with replicas of the twelve *jyotirling* sacred sites, of which the Grishneshwara temple was one. He had taken a vow not to speak until this project was completed.

We had called ahead to say we were coming, and Mahendra Bapu was waiting for us, sitting at a low desk in the temple. He had a kind, open face, clipped white hair and beard, and was wearing a white lungi and a simple white cotton kurta with "Jai Viśvakarmā" embroidered in red Gujarati script on the pocket over his heart. A white marble Murti of a regal, straight-backed, white-bearded Vishwakarma looked on, surrounded by his five sons. On the wall were posters of Randal, Chamunda Mata, the five-pointed star of the Vishwakarma *yantra*, and texts of devotional songs.

Jayantibhai was keen to make a donation. Mahendra Bapu issued a handwritten receipt and then led us into the larger building for tea. He lifted plastic chairs out of a stack so we could all sit down and brought out a low table to lay out the collection of Vishwakarma materials that Ken and I had examined on our previous visit: antique posters, a few old books, and some fragments of manuscripts. This was an informal archive that Bapu had assembled, even as his charitable trust sponsored the publication of older Vishwakarma texts (like my great-grandfather's book, minus the introduction containing the family story) and newer texts like Bachubhai Vadgama's Vishwakarma Purana with its many color prints.

Mahendra Bapu was welcoming, even as we found it an unusual research challenge to talk with someone who had vowed silence. When agreeing with something, he affirmed, "Hmm, hmm, hmm, hmm!" Disagreeing, he shook his head no, "Hmm-Hmm." He sometimes picked up a little pad to scribble short notes in Gujarati that his assistant was able to decipher; if the words were correctly read aloud, Bapu nodded along: "Hmm. Hmm. Hmm."

As Vhalabhai emphasized, the new temple affirmed the presence of Vishwakarma in this sacred region. "It's the same mountain," he assured us. "Whether in the cave, or in the temple, it's all still Vishwakarma's original place—it's Ellora [*Ilorgaṛh*]!"

✳

The morning before we were to return to Ahmedabad, Jayantibhai said that he had been reconsidering the identity of Vishwakarma in Cave 10.

"I've been thinking about it," he said. "I used to hear how people went and stood on the knees to make a *tilak*. You can't stand on the knees of that Murti at the side."

As Jayantibhai noted, anyone making a *tilak* on the forehead of the Murti in the side shrine could just extend a hand: no need to scramble onto a knee. He was now reconsidering his certainty about the identity of the Murti in the main hall.

After breakfast we bought our tickets to enter the World Heritage site, first wandering around the Kailash complex before crowds gathered for the day. Then we went on to Cave 10. Jayantibhai stood inside the ribbed cavern, near the Murti's left elbow, looking upward into the face. As usual, two large brown and tan signs that we did not see in any other caves were propped near the base of the seated figure. "WARNING," the boards exhorted in Hindi, Marathi, and English: "DON'T SIT OR CLIMB OVER THE SCULPTURES." A guard leaned against the doorway to ensure that we followed these instructions.

"This is where we used to do the *tilak*," Jayantibhai said, pointing toward the huge forehead. He spoke in a low voice, as though sharing a secret. His words stretched and echoed in the shadows. "But doing this was only possible for someone who's a descendant of Vishwakarma. Otherwise, even if a tall man tried to make that mark, the Murti would grow larger, and he wouldn't be able to reach the forehead. Yet if they were of the Vishwakarma lineage, even small children, six or seven years old, would climb on the knees and be able to offer the *tilak*. This was the miraculous power of the Murti, that it could grow big or small."

I was charmed by the idea of the Murti's playful complicity with descendants. At the same time, this belief insisted that the Murti somehow remained perpetually out of reach for others. I couldn't help wondering if in the past, other communities beyond Suthars ever attempted to mark the Murti's forehead: it's easy to say others can't when they don't.

"That *used* to be the proof," Jayantibhai said, looking up at the serene face. He seemed resigned that like many miraculous things, this shape-shifting had come to a halt. "But now, there is no proof. There was once a portion [*amsh*] of Vishwakarma here. This is Buddha. But there is no doubt that in the past this was Vishwakarma's form."

"This," he authoritatively concluded, "is what is said in the Purana."

*

After we flew back to Ahmedabad with Jayantibhai and Hardik, I began to see Pa on a terrace rooftop that we faced from the living room window of our seventh-floor apartment.

Pa sat in a low chair that faced away at an angle, toward the southeast. I saw him in the mornings, before we drew our heavy blinds across the window to keep out the heat, and I saw him in the evenings, when the air had cooled and we could again let in the view. I could see the back of Pa's head and the edge of his black-framed glasses. I could picture the way he raised his chin to read, the widow's peak at his forehead, his protruding lower lip. He seemed absorbed, turned away, yet somehow beside me, a consciousness in my present.

At first, I kept this to myself. One morning I was sitting by the window, journal open in my lap, when Ken came out, laptop in hand. "Can I show you where I see Pa sitting?" I asked.

Ken was half-asleep. He hadn't yet had coffee, and the latest dystopian news was on his screen. "Pa?" he asked.

"Yes, Pa. I see him sitting here every day, day after day." I gestured through the window streaked with pigeon droppings.

"I guess I need my glasses," said Ken.

Glasses on, he stood beside me. We looked out the window across the road where solitary dogs and dedicated walkers were now stirring and where every form of transport would soon be moving and blasting horns.

"Do you see that roof with the peacock sitting on it?" I asked. There were a few peacocks out, so I had to point.

"Yes—the peacock at the top of the red tiles."

"Beyond there, slightly to the left, there's our very own Ahmedabad mini–Eiffel Tower in the far distance. Now look at the roofs directly below the tower."

"Yes, I see that."

"OK, now slide left down the roof, to the terrace. Do you see the person sitting there?"

"Yes, I do."

"That's Pa."

Since Pa was facing away, I couldn't make out just what he was doing. He probably had his morning fruit sliced on the table beside him. Maybe he was reading the newspaper. If he was looking out, he was seeing what we saw from a different vantage. Maybe he too was witnessing the peacock flipping its tail open into a splendid fan, then turning slowly to be admired from all sides even as the peahens studiously ignored the show. Did he also notice the vultures circling beyond the crisscross of wires on the skyline, the clusters of high apartment buildings, some with billboards plastered along their sides? Even if, like us, he couldn't see as far as the huge mountain of trash, Mount Pirana, across the river—with its mica-like glitter of plastic bags, trucks ascending, tiny figures of ragpickers bent over with their sacks—did he also sniff its presence in the wind?

When Prakash and Sonal came over, laden with a steel tiffin filled with hot food, I pointed out this figure on the balcony to Prakash.

"Ho!" he agreed in his jovial way. "Yes, I see Uncle [*Māmā*] there."

Prakash stood beside me and considered. He didn't think Pa was looking at the view at all; he was quite sure that Pa was reading.

"He was always reading, always reading," Prakash remembered. "He had so many books!" Prakash went on to recall other things about Pa: how he had dressed "like a European," eaten fried eggs and toast for breakfast, and when he talked, come up with such great jokes that everyone around him was always laughing.

Pa remained there until October, when the things stored up on that terrace were rearranged. The chair disappeared. At the terrace's other end, an inchoate pile rose higher.

With matter reorganized, Pa had vanished.

✳

Though Ken and I couldn't continue our pace of research travels after March 2020, friends across the world continued to send us materials relating to Ellora. From Ahmedabad, Vhalabhai shared regular WhatsApp updates on musical events where he was a performer or MC, links to his Youtube recitations of the Vishwakarma Purana, and announcements for pilgrimages he was organizing in his new venture as a leader of tour groups.

In August 2021, Vhalabhai sent out a WhatsApp message in Gujarati advertising a bus tour that would set out from Ahmedabad for a Vishwakarma Katha, a multiday storytelling performance, at Bapu's temple. The storyteller was to be a young woman of the Gujar Suthar community who performed under the name "Ranna Didi." Aspiring pilgrims could join the weeklong outing for the cost of 5,100 rupees (about $65). After a night journey, the schedule for four key days summarized many themes I'd been struggling to write about:

Sunday, August 15. 10 AM to 12 PM: Pilgrimage of the sacred book, lighting of lamps, start of the story. Afternoon after 2 PM: Pilgrimage to Ellora Vishwa Kund, Grishneshwar, Ellora caves, Vishwakarma cave, Kailash cave.

Monday, August 16. Storytelling 9 AM–12 PM and 3:30–6:30 PM: a celebration of Vishwakarma's manifestation and the greatness of Ellora.

Tuesday, August 17. 7 AM–9 AM: Worshipping waterpots of Randal. 9 AM–12 PM: Celebration of Randal's manifestation. 4 PM–6 PM: Randal's wedding celebration.

Wednesday August 18. Anniversary of Vishwakarma's departure for his own place. 7 AM–9 AM: Prayer and worship for the peace of the departed. 10 AM–12 PM: Vishwakarma *yajna* (fire ceremony) and storytelling. 4 PM–7 PM: Finale.

Vishwakarma stories, sacred sites, and ancestral observances at Ellora all came together in this program. Another message added that for 1,100 rupees special rituals could be sponsored, "in the sacred Shravan month in Vishwakarma's region of Ilorgaṛh, for the good onward passage of Vishwakarma's descendants who have died of corona [virus]."

The message went on to explain:

The 11th day of the bright lunar month of Shravan is the anniversary of Vishwakarma's departure for his own place. It's a special day for ritual observance. On this day, the organizers will do peace recitations for all Vishwakarma's descendants who have died. In addition to hearing the Katha, they will observe silence and pray with rosaries.

For those who wish to perform peace recitations and prayers for the good onward passage and liberation of beloved departed family members at this Katha, send the deceased's photo, name, village, date of birth, date of death, and the sender's family name or personal name. A banner with the photo, name etc. will be placed where the story or worship is taking place and can also be used for advertising. You can see this live on Youtube.

If any family cannot afford this amount, then the organizers will bear the expenses.

Words might come to rest in a book. But the pilgrimage to Ellora by those who consider themselves Vishwakarma's descendants continues forward: shifting, adapting, moving to new locations and situations, carried outward by new media.

Hands inside Hands

"If you really want to know why you're doing this project, you need to think about Sethji," said my mother through the laptop screen. She was in her adobe home near Dharamshala, and I was in Canberra. This was during the pandemic in 2020, when I had no chance of travel to India. I'd been sorting through a jumble of materials—memories, letters, notes, stories, histories—to compose short segments that I thought of as "chunklets"—not yet chapters—while I tried to figure out how to order these along a cord of story. I didn't quite know what sort of book was emerging. In the meantime, Ma read drafts and offered comments.

Entering her nineties, my mother, Didi Contractor, was a celebrated vernacular architect. While she'd always considered herself a designer, by her early sixties she'd found ways to pursue her lifelong interest in building; by her late eighties she was winning awards and recognition for this new career. She had always thrived on sociability, and before the pandemic, people from across the world who were interested in building and sustainability appeared at her home even as she often hosted architectural interns. With the pandemic, she was bored. She visited us by screen practically every day, and as my preliminary chunklets found form, she discussed Vishwakarma traditions in relation to her understanding of the family she'd married into, her interest in art history, and her own experience of bringing dwellings into form. Ma was especially drawn to the story of Vishwakarma insisting to his sons that they needed to be mindful of how carelessly changed environments could bring suffering to all life-forms. "Write it up so I can refer to it in talks," she urged.

I could guess why, in relation to this project, Ma advised me to think about my grandfather Ramji Seth. But I wanted to hear her reasoning afresh. Keeping my eyes on the screen, I groped about for a pen and the blank side of the latest *New Yorker* international mailing sheet lying on the kitchen table beside me.

50. Ma on her eighty-ninth birthday, Kangra, 2018. Photograph by Kirin Narayan.

"Why, Ma? Can you just explain a little more?"

I was sure that Ma would retell the story of how she had visited her father-in-law's deathbed and felt his plea to be reborn. I never mind hearing stories again, knowing that each retelling might add a new drop of detail that slowly unfurls, infusing understanding with fresh colors. Instead, she said, and I scribbled: *You have to think of the impulses that a person carries onward. His interest in Vishwakarma, and his interest in the status of the community. You're doing this too: carrying out an ancestral obligation to the Vishwakarma lineage.*

"So, you really think I'm his reincarnation?" I persisted.

My hand was rushing across paper, but she'd pulled back from that familiar story to articulate what she saw as larger guiding patterns: *We're all carrying several layers of reality simultaneously: realities within and without ourselves. You carry these ancestral impulses in your being. Look, the "I" is also mythological; it's metaphysical. It carries a certain coherence we can't see. This also has a tide, and the tide pulls us into it like a hand inside a puppet. Something else works through us, a hand inside a hand.*

There's a lot to ponder in these enigmatic words. I reread them now and am still not sure that I understand. But as Ma spoke of "ancestral obligation" and then "ancestral impulses," I was thinking of how this applied to pilgrimages and stories of Vishwakarma at Ellora. Hadn't we been told, after all, that our research was brought about through the blessings of ancestors—hands within the hands dispensing research funds and organizing our travels? And wasn't my quest partly a way of situating intriguing family stories amid multiple other connected stories? I looked around again to locate a verse that had struck me when we interpreted portions of the oldest Gujarati Vishwakarma Purana in Bhai's company. These lines came toward the end of the calamitous chapter that described how Vishwakarma had been enraged by suffering caused to other creatures and had taken away his sons' power of instantaneous making by mind:

> Those who listen to stories of their own family
> wash away the sins of those who came before.
> Ancestors and gods are pleased:
> This is of the greatest importance.[1]

Family stories, it seems to me, are themselves a form of ancestral observance, establishing a cord of imaginative connection to those who came before. Listening closely, dominant histories might stretch to include voices and visions of the less powerful—like the artisans coming long distances on pilgrimage to Ellora. Simultaneously, within families, a renewed attunement to family stories can dislodge their set form, revealing other stories in the shadows.

✳

I now wonder: when Pa urged me to write that multivolume saga—*Ramji and Sons*—did he sense that looking into family history might help me understand him—one of those sons—a little better? For in the course of researching Vishwakarma's presence at Ellora, I became aware of stories that remained mostly unspoken within the family yet were retold by others. Through my childhood, the Ramji Mistri Bungalow—with its two stories, three wings, wide courtyard, well with clear drinking water, garden of flowering trees, and farm filled with mango trees—had seemed a monument to my grandfather's fabulous success. Now I learned of the ruins over which that monument was raised.

After losing two wives, Ramji Seth had married a third time. This was around 1920, I think; he was probably in his early fifties. His business in Bombay was flourishing. He had an apartment in what was then the fancy suburb of Byculla (later a wasteland of abandoned mills and big bristling rats). The woman he married was a distant cousin with whom he had fallen in love.

But caste elders decreed that this violated some rule. In one version, she was said to be too close a relative. Yes, everyone married within the community, but there were strictures around clans and *gotras*. The couple's kin connection wasn't close enough for them to have known this was inappropriate at the time of the marriage. Or was there some other disregard of convention? I wonder: as my grandfather continued to surprise everyone with his business acumen, might envy have played some role in this invocation of caste orthodoxy?

The couple was outcasted. To be outcaste was to find yourself severed from all social relations with members of your caste: no coming and going of relatives, no eating with the community, no exchanges of gifts, no marriages arranged with your children. One of Pa's letters had actually described outcasting without mention of how close it had struck: *To not be invited by the Panchayat or barred in joining any celebrations was castigation, and people in old days committed suicide, if such a thing happened to the family* (April 20, 1980).

Bhai, then ninety-two, and his exuberant ninety-eight-year-old friend Jayrambhai (who still liked to ride a bicycle in the Mumbai suburbs when he wasn't tinkering with electronics in a home workshop), had volunteered fragments of this story. Fragments, not details. Both said that they knew only parts of this sad story from overhearing their own elders; sorry, they didn't know more.

"No one would visit Byculla," said Jayrambhai. "No one would come if he held a feast."

Ramji Seth had his contracting work to absorb him. But she—whose name never emerges in any stories—she became deeply depressed.

"Her heart was broken," Bhai said, voice saturated with sympathy. "She died."

From Jayrambhai: "She died by fire."

I'd been living with allusions to these events without really registering what they meant. One of my notebooks records my aunt Manuphui saying, "An old woman told me that a woman in our house died by fire."

From childhood memories: "One of Dada's wives died while cooking."

From someone—who?—the possibility of foul play by relatives concerned about their own position.

This death at a time of social shunning and inner despair hovers, unresolved. She died without children: no son to perform funeral rites with the possibility of ancestral observances across generations. A husband would then do the last rites, but did any community member dare accompany my heartbroken grandfather to the cremation grounds?

How at the time of this dissolution of his known life, did my grandfather go forward?

He is said to have been very ill for a long time. He paid a fine of 5,000 rupees to the caste—as people emphasized, "In the rupees of *those* days!" Eventually he was reintegrated, but as Bhai pointed out, Ramji Seth's name had been taken off the community hall he built and was never put back. Ramji Seth also found an alternate community, deepening his connection with the Swami Narayan sect, "from one of his wives"—maybe this third one? When he sought blessings from the sect's guru, Shastriji Maharaj said to him: "Face northeast, and start a new life."

Holding his guru's words close, a benediction, Ramji Mistri went northeast from Bombay to buy land in Nasik. Around the age of sixty, he married a fourth time. This was to my grandmother Ba. Being a Kathiawari (not Kutchi) Gujar Suthar, she was from outside the circles that had outcasted him.

Ba, it turns out, was escaping her own painful past. She never spoke about this in her lifetime, but a few years after her death, records of a divorce seeped out from court papers buried deep inside a locked safe. These typed foolscap pages record a legal battle between Ramji Mistri and his two older sons, who in 1936 tried to prove that since Ba was already married, her children didn't bear a right to their father's fortune. Ramji Mistri's solicitors produced a statement from the first husband, another Suthar from Zinzri, a village near hers, employed at the textile mills in Bhavnagar.

Yes, his translated testimony read, he had been married in 1916 to Kadvi or Kamalabai, the daughter of Hirji Velji: "My marriage w/ the sd. Kamlabai was not happy. Disputes and differences arose between us, and ultimately with a view to put an end to these disputes I applied to my caste to have my marriage with Kamlabai dissolved."

Disputes and differences! I could see how the intrepid will and sharp tongue that made Ba "a character" in old age would not have been appreciated in a young girl of her times.

He went on to say that in October 1923, "My complaint was investigated by the members of the caste, and after both the parties met the members of the caste decided to dissolve my marriage with Kamlabai and directed that the sd. Hirji Velji the father of Kamlabai should pay to me a sum of Rs. 300/– or thereabouts and that in consideration thereof I should pass a *Fargati* [resolution] in favor of Kamlabai releasing all my claims as a husband . . ."

The case was resolved by the male caste elders, and it was Ba's father who paid the fine. In his deposition, the ex-husband attested that according to custom, after this resolution, both were "free to marry again and any children begotten are considered legitimate and can inherit property, etc." Those were the key words that Ramji Seth was looking for—that his children with Ba were legitimate heirs.

Ba was often vague about her age. Now I can see how the story that she had married at sixteen was true, while neatly erasing some missing years by not clarifying just whom she had married at that age. If she was born in 1900, and Pa in 1927, something didn't quite compute. Court papers can of course be concocted and doctored, but if the millworker-husband's affidavit was true, she'd lived with him between the ages of sixteen and twenty-three.

When I visited India in January 2009, my aunt Chandaphui unexpectedly began lamenting that she was eighty years old and had never seen her mother's village. Ba, she said, had always insisted that the village was overrun by dangerous witches, and wouldn't risk taking her children since *she alone* was strong enough to withstand them! Chandaphui knew the name of the village, Untadi. She also knew that, sending funds from afar, Ba had sponsored the building of a Shiva temple there.

I hired a car, and off we went, along with Chandaphui's sister-in-law, Pramilaben. Enlisting help from Ba's sister Maushi's descendants, we found the village. I was photographing the small temple when a local man, curious about visitors, came by and told us about the temple, built by a "Suthar auntie":

There had once been a Suthar girl called Kadviben born in this village. The girl's husband had died. Returning to her parents' home, she was so distraught that she jumped into the well to die. But she lived, and prayed to the local Shiva, "If you save me and if you find me a good home to marry into, I will build you a temple." She was rescued. Then she was married to a rich Seth from Nasik. To show her gratitude to Shiva, she arranged for this temple to be built.

Oral tradition had claimed Ba's story, recasting some events, maintaining others. The man showed us the place just by the temple where a big well had dried up and then been filled in. By then others had come to investigate and we were invited to have tea.

When the word went out that Kadviben's descendants had arrived, as though from the mists of legend, Chandaphui and I were led around the village. We were shown the humble home where Ba was raised, which was now rented out. Her brothers' descendants were away, we were told. Then a schoolteacher who served as village historian squatted at the edge of a raised porch, interviewing Chandaphui, as crowds looked on. She stood, recounting the names and transnational locations of Ba's descendants; our very existence, it seemed, was, for the onlookers, evidence of their local Shiva's miraculous powers.

With her remarriage, Ba had escaped the village, but in the city, she was at first scorned by Ramji Mistri's existing sons. "She was the Black Sheep of her family," read my old notes. "It wasn't even a regular marriage—it was the sort where you bring a *ṭīkā* [forehead mark] and you bring her

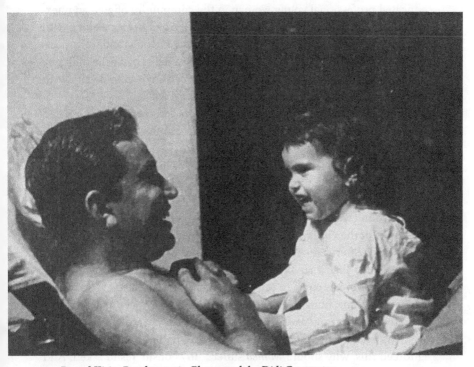

51. Pa and Kirin, Bombay, 1962. Photograph by Didi Contractor.

back. She had no manners; she didn't know how to properly wear a sari. She had to be taught everything: how to talk, what to eat."

Ba was unfazed. As she always liked to say, "I might be illiterate, but it doesn't mean I have no brains!" She sharpened her brusque manners and did what she pleased. She rode around in a white Buick with red leather seats and learned to play cards while servants cooked and cleaned. If anyone dared ask about Ramji Seth's earlier wives in Ba's presence, she retorted, "I'm the fourth, and I'm not interested in the other three!" Her elderly husband was amused by his "Mad Girl." Her feisty carapace, I think, helped him start a new life and establish a safe space beyond community disapproval. My grandfather might once have been outcasted, but through his success and largesse, he could powerfully display that he was the Pride of the Vishwakarma Lineage.

If not for their courage to start again, I would not be here. For no Pa would exist for me to have become his daughter.

✳

In December 2018, a few weeks before we returned to Australia, a college-educated professional young woman in the community offered an unexpected perspective on these family silences. We had been speaking with her family about Vishwakarma, Ellora, and caste histories and were meeting her for the first time. I don't know what problems had been afflicting her, but she said that to ease them, she had been advised to do rituals to bring peace to the soul of my grandfather's third wife.

Her mother explained, "See, the curse of that woman who immolated herself in her home sticks to daughters of the community; they can have an unhappy life."

I was stunned. Maybe self-immolation had been hinted at. But a curse? Was this worry of the third wife's curse falling on community daughters a way to acknowledge the profound harm inflicted by outcasting?

The young woman described how her brother had traveled with her to the banks of the Godavari River in Nashik, where death rituals are often performed. After fasting, the young woman did the *puja*; as a male, her brother made the ritual offerings. A soul is said to have accepted the offerings when crows come to eat. But she recalled how the two had waited a long, long time, hungry and thirsty, before any crow would descend.

Later, I asked women of my own family: had they heard of difficulties in women's lives set into motion by a curse? They hadn't. "If it was men who enforced this, why should *women* suffer?" my cousin Yeshu asked. And yet, when I looked again at my old notebooks, I find a mysterious line in reminiscences about my grandfather: *He went and performed prayers for girls of the family, near Bhavnagar.* Now, I realize these prayers were also perhaps his attempt to bring peace to that sorrowful wife's soul.

It was Bhai, an observer from the margins, who revealed an unexpected connection between the tragedy of Ramji Seth's third wife and Pa's bent toward self-destruction. I've written in an earlier book about the long shadow Pa's drinking cast over my childhood, but Bhai offered a new thread of understanding.

Returning from Colorado to set up his own engineering business in Bombay, Pa had worked through Via-Via—like so many caste members before him. The older relative who took Pa under his wing supplied him with collaborations and contacts—and made heavy drinking part of business routines. He plied the younger man with great quantities of alcohol and entangled him in dubious building ventures. I suspect that for Pa, alcohol became, in part, a way to numb the shame when things weren't quite right or went altogether wrong.

Why did Pa stick with his corrupt mentor? From my child's perspective, this relative had seemed a gray-haired bogeyman, blackheads speckling the bags under his eyes, whose appearance at night could mean finding his sidekicks lying in their own vomit in the living room as we prepared for school in the morning. Any story has multiple perspectives and angles of causality, but it's surely significant that this "mentor" had been the third wife's nephew.

Pa never enjoyed his work as a civil engineer and periodically tried out other business ventures. In these ventures too, the pattern of being fleeced by opportunistic relatives and hangers-on would be repeated. Across the years, Pa seemed easily mesmerized, allowing others, including uncomfortably close relatives, to relieve him and his children of the ever-dwindling remnants of his father's fortune. I now wonder if, each time he urged me to write *Ramji and Sons,* and I asked "What about the daughters?" his silence came partly from his ambivalence, as a son of Ramji, regarding ancestral obligations related to construction. As his letters make so clear, what he really enjoyed was using language to carve open the constricted present and shape bright, expansive spaces. A daughter needn't acquire skills as a carpenter, a contractor, an engineer, or an architect: she could be urged to take on the work of a different sort of Sutradhar, chiseling stories from words.

"So, what *really* happened?" I'm sometimes asked (as in: *cut to the chase*). "Is what your father told you actually true?"

I think again of the goddess Randal's doubled form. I know, and I don't know. This research has affirmed multiplicity and coexisting truths over rigid certainties. Yes, Cave 10 at Ellora, a Buddhist chaitya, has also been known as "Vishwakarma" and "the Carpenter's Hut." But I can't say when artisans' devotion to the cave began. Had "stone-carpenters" already found something sacred about the cave as they were excavating it? Or, more likely, was it only after Buddhists left Ellora in the eighth century that the cave was repurposed and became known first as the home of Kokas the carpenter—a manifestation of Vishwakarma—and then as the dwelling of Vishwakarma himself? The astounding Kailash complex nearby may have influenced the Suthars/Sutradhars who chose this arched cave for its chaitya form, reproducing wooden artistry in stone, and on account of the imposing seated Murti extending from the stupa. The layout of pillars matching lunar patterns with a "no-moon" observance and the gathered assembly of figures were likely also key. Whether perceived to be teaching, holding a cord, or drawing attention to a wounded finger, the Murti's hands became a focus for artisans whose livelihood depended on their hands.

Were these pilgrims to the Carpenter's Hut only carpenters? The many construction skills associated with Suthars/Sutradhars, and the periodic retraining and shifts between materials, likely meant that visitors included carpenters, sculptors, and metalsmiths of various sorts. As far as we know, mostly pilgrims from Gujarat and Rajasthan have honored Vishwakarma and his sons at the caves. With Ellora as a focal point, the caves, mountain, and surrounding locale became the backdrop for Suthar stories about the marvels and the hazards of making things, making progeny, and making selves. Ellora was invoked too in the nineteenth-century caste mobilization claiming Brahminhood, with the Vishwa Kund granting artisans the right to wear a sacred thread. The claim that "we" made the caves seems to refer more to lines of shared stories across time than to a genealogy that might be proved through strands of DNA.

I don't have access to any of Ramji Seth's once legendary property, but I have been granted a trove of family stories, including these that led me to Ellora. If Ramji Seth and his brothers fulfilled their father's wishes to make a temple for Vishwakarma away from Ellora, in following Pa's stories, I've ended up housing Vishwakarma and Ellora within a different sort of dwelling. I hope that this book, made from words, adorned with images, stands in for some version of that multivolume saga Pa envisioned.

※

The pandemic continued, and Australia's borders remained closed. I couldn't visit India for more research, and I couldn't go when Ma fell ill in February 2021. As she drifted into increasing pain and disorientation, the once-daily calls became infrequent. "How's the book?" she said in one of our last conversations. As though adding her stake to the ancestral obligations, she said, "Finish it for me, okay?"

"I'm trying, Ma."

She took her last breath in July of that year, with three generations of her descendants present by screen.

Grounded in Canberra, I tried to stay in contact with people who'd helped our research. With Bhai, this was a challenge.

As Bhai moved forward into his nineties, he was growing weaker and was largely confined to a wheelchair. He didn't have his own phone, so I called Yeshu and she carried her phone to him for a video call. The internet connection wasn't always stable in his room, though. He wasn't practiced with using screens to chat, and he couldn't hear well. Ken and I often addressed the top of his forehead, viewed his chin from below, or strained to make out his features against the brightness of the open window behind his reading chair. Our conversations were conducted partly through mime and loudly enunciated requests: "We can't see you! Can you shift the phone higher? What did you say? Can you say that again?"

Sometimes, when the connection was strong, we could enjoy a conversation. Early on, as I confessed I was struggling with writing, he advised, "You must write a *novel* book."

"Bhai, this won't be a novel! This is all about our research."

Bhai's chin rose, lean face filling the little screen as he laughed.

"*Arre*, I am not saying to write a *novel*! I am saying write a *novel book*. Something unusual. You have gathered so many rare materials, things we can't even imagine now. So you must write this in some new way."

"I'm trying, Bhai."

Working out solutions to problems of design, materials, and construction had, after all, always been prized among the ingenious Sutradhars turned Suthars. To get the advice to experiment from Bhai, a connoisseur of books, made me work all the harder. I was keen to get this book in its entirety into his hands.

But for me, books always take much longer than what I imagine as I start. "How is the book?" Bhai called out across the continents every few weeks.

In December 2021, the book *still* wasn't finished, but I decided to send Bhai a preview: a few early chapters bound with a dedication.

When Yeshu texted that the package had arrived, I called and she took her phone in to Bhai's room. He had only begun leafing through the pages. I held the copy I'd retained toward the screen to hear his thoughts on images. "*Hān*, there is *Bāpā*!" he said on seeing Ramji Seth. Bhai seemed to grasp the many stages behind this first draft. "So much traveling, collecting, selecting, summarizing!" he sympathetically said. "It is tedious work. You might find one story one place and then later somewhere else, and you have to compare."

Two weeks later, when I called to wish Bhai a Happy New Year, he had read more. With characteristic humility, he emphasized all that he was learning even as I protested that really, this was thanks to leads he'd shared.

"You have created something new," he affirmed.

Something *new*! Something *novel*! I was so glad to receive this stamp of approval.

We could hear each other well that day. After Bhai and Ken talked, I propped the phone on a cushion and sat opposite to ease into a longer conversation. Bhai reminded me that the next day, January 2, was an *amās*, a no-moon day. He said he would be honoring Vishwakarma by reading a booklet of Vishwakarma prayers he'd printed in memory of his grandmother.

I confided that I had begun to light a ghee lamp and make an offering of rice pudding (*khīr*) on the *amās*. Through the course of our research, I had come to think of this day as a time to pause and to remember ancestors, and as a moment of potentiality betwixt and between cycles of time, with darkness before emergence into light invoking the space directly behind the Murti in Cave 10.

I tried to explain to Bhai how, in my eccentric twenty-first-century, New Age way, I'd adapted this observance. While carpenters put down their tools, I still use my tools of writing: pens, notebooks, keyboards, screens. And while I honor my bodily ancestors—those revealed by stories, and unknown others, too—I try to remember, as well, at least some of the honorary ancestors who have shaped me, making me who I am. I've gained these other ancestors in various ways: from long friendships, coexistence, shared interests, and even research. Among these are the "topsy-turvy" Swamiji, whose stories helped me gain a PhD; my older brother Rahoul and our shared godmother Stella Snead; wise women storytellers and singers in the Himalayan foothills; Anton Chekhov. Claimed by so many fellow writers across time, space, and languages, Chekhov offers a powerful reminder that it's not just through children that someone becomes an ancestor.

I also tried to express my deepest hope to Bhai: that though this book explores a family heritage coming to me from my—and his—ancestors, assembling these stories in a written form might allow them to be shared by all people who see themselves as makers.

"See Bhai, just like Ellora is a World Heritage site, I'd like to offer these stories about Vishwakarma at Ellora as part of our human heritage, to anyone who's interested. I'd like it to be for anyone who's thinking about the mysteries of making things, both the joys and the dangers; what this making means to us and also for other creatures."

I wasn't taking notes on my own words, but this is more or less what I was hoping to say. I felt a little tongue-tied and audacious.

"Oh ho! You are becoming a philosopher?" Bhai smiled his radiant smile.

He seemed to accept my awkward rush of words. "Very good, very good," he nodded. He raised a palm to the screen in blessing: "I wish you happiness all the days of the year. Vishwakarma Dada is helping us."

I joined my own palms and fingers, bending my head to accept this benediction. I didn't know then that this would be our last conversation. Bhai stepped toward the ancestors in the early hours of January 28, 2022. He was in his own room, books organized in his grandfather's large cupboard nearby.

I keep thinking about Bhai's farewell gesture of the raised palm, remembering Ma's mysterious allusion to hands. Hands inside hands could also mean hands in communication, responding to other hands. I looked again at Bhai's story of how our distant ancestor Gangadhar was advised by his guru to compose the final inscription for the Rudra Mal. Along with the obligatory celebration of the patron king, he was told to include "the names of your ancestors who hold your hand as you carve," and also "a short description of all the people who gave advice and did the labor. . . . We should know it is the imagination of all of these persons together."

The imaginative people behind this book stretch out in a multitude: those we met in person or through their creations, sending us onward to others in chains of Via-Via, and the many ancestors present in this book's writing. Holding a pen, smoothing paper, tapping at a keyboard, taking up a pencil to edit, my hands assembling these words carry traces of my parents' hands, each with their own pleasures in writing. Ancestors from Europe and North America reside in these hands too, but they are mostly invisible since I don't really know their stories. Thanks to family storytellers and what I've learned through research, I can best imagine Sutradhar-Suthar hands that migrated, reskilled, took on different identities, gestured in concert with stories. These were hands that grasped at measuring ropes, footrules, chisels of many shapes; hands that mixed masalas, stirred utensils, tended the young and the infirm, composed embroideries with mirrors catching light.

Some of these hands once joined together in the tenth cave from the south at Ellora: in greeting and in prayer.

Acknowledgments

First, thanks to immediate elders and ancestors who smiled upon this undertaking: Narayan Ramji Contractor, Didi Contractor, and Kapret Kumar Dahisaria. From here my thanks extend to Kamlabai Ramji, Chandaben Gundecha, Narmada Contractor, and Pramilaben Pinara. Thanks also to Maya Narayan, Devendra Contractor, Alina Borsa, Yashodra Dahisaria, Prakash and Sonal Dasadia, and Rima and Rashmin Dahisaria.

This research was made possible for me and Ken George by funding from the Australian Research Council (DP 170104212); the American Institute for Indian Studies, which awarded us both Senior Fellowships; and the Fulbright Foundation, which sponsored an extra year of Ken's research with a Fulbright-Nehru Academic and Professional Excellence Award, granted by USIEF. We are indebted to colleagues who warmly welcomed us and helped us refine ideas at the Maharaja Sayajirao University of Baroda; the Centre for Environmental Planning and Technology (CEPT); the National Institute of Design; the Dhirubhai Ambani Institute of Information and Communication; the University of Calcutta; the Indian Institute of Technology–Guwahati; the Centre for the Study of Developing Societies; the Australian National University; the University of Sydney; Yale–National University of Singapore; the University of Colorado–Boulder; the University of Pennsylvania; Cornell University; Duke University; the University of North Carolina–Chapel Hill; MF Norwegian School of Theology, Religion and Society; the University of Oslo; and the University of Copenhagen.

We are so grateful for the hospitality and insights of friends in Ahmedabad, including Rashmi and Dinesh Korjan, Tara and Siddharth Sinha, Ashoke Chatterji, Tridip Suhrud, Abhijit and Rita Kothari, and Alka Parikh and Ranjit Konkar. For help with the Ellora quest, particular thanks to Hardik Siddhpura, our research assistant, and his parents Bina and Sanjay, and to Jayantibhai Gajjar and family; Mahendra Bapu; Jayantibhai

Shastri; Vhalabhai Gajjar; Pravinbhai Vadgama, Jyotsnaben, and family; Narottam Kaka; Hiteshbhai Bhatt; and Vasantbhai and Shardaben Voralia.

We couldn't have been luckier in connecting with colleagues from across the world who shared their expertise on Ellora and allied sites in person, by email, and by screen: Pia Brancaccio, Carl Ernst, Deepak Kannal, Geri Malandra, Lisa Owen, Saili Palande-Datar, Holly Shaffer, Mahesh Sharma, Micaela Soar, Pushkar Sohoni, and Walter Spink.

We are grateful to those who assisted us with lengthy translations from different Indian languages, including Nayana Desai, Murtaza Gandhi, Uday Shelat, Anand Kale, Dnyaneshwari Kamath, and Bina Siddhpura. Devadatta Kali, Peter Friedlander, Narayana Rao, and McComas Taylor have generously responded across the years to many queries about shades of meaning around words. Special thanks to David Shulman for translating the Baroda copper plates as poetry.

Many friends have lightened and brightened the work on this book through conversations, comments on chapters, and help in choosing photographs; in beginning to name them, I fear that I am likely to leave someone out. But let me try, with advance apologies to all who may find themselves missing: Annette Aronowicz, Amrita Basu, André Bernard, Regina Bendix, Shameem Black, Sean Downes, Kathryn Dwan, Judy Ernst, Chris Goad, Marian Goad, Ramachandra Guha, Anne Haggerson, Deborah Hart, Ian Hannah Holland, Rosanne Kennedy, Brigitte Luchesi, Tryna Lyons, Rob Magrath, Sue McIntyre, Dane Varkavisser, Uma Visser, and Helen Wottiez. Thank you all! Thanks also to Jenny Sheehan of the CartoGIS team at ANU, who prepared the book's maps.

Enormous thanks to friends who patiently read and commented on the entire manuscript: Helle Bundgard, Dipesh Chakrabarty, Debjani Ganguly, Rana Ganguly, Ann Gold, Claudia Hyles, Anthony Lovenheim Irwin, Geri Malandra, Cynthia Packert, Geoffrey Piggott, Leela Prasad, Ronit Ricci, Helena Wulff—and anonymous readers. For this last stage of bringing the book into form, I am so grateful to Alan Thomas, Dylan Montanari, Fabiola Enríquez Flores, and Joel Score at the University of Chicago Press.

Ken George, my dear friend, colleague, and partner, has made this journey from curiosity to completed pages possible in myriad, multifaceted ways. The most encompassing of thanks to Ken.

Maps

MAP 1. Key locations across India

MAP 2. Sites of ancestral histories in Western India

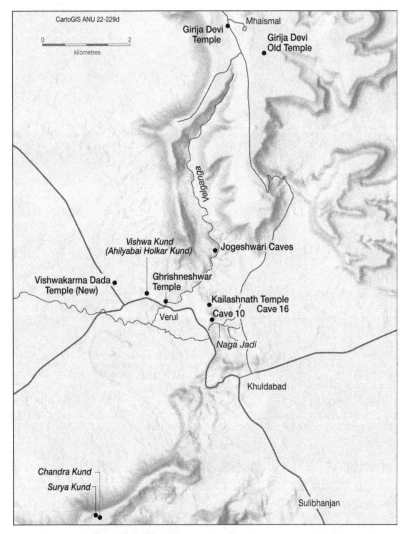

MAP 3. Sacred sites around the Ellora Caves

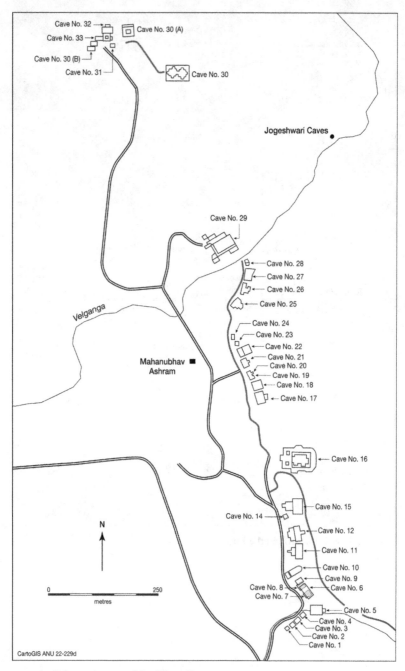

MAP 4. Schematic map of the Ellora Caves

Notes

Chapter 1

1. James Burgess, *The Rock Temples of Elurā or Verul* (Bombay: Education Society's Press, 1877), 25. For more of Burgess's authoritative writings on Ellora, see James Fergusson and James Burgess, *The Cave Temples of India* (London: W. H. Allen and Co, 1880); James Burgess, *Report on the Elura Cave Temples and the Brahmanical and Jaina Caves in Western India* (London: Trubner and Company, 1883).

2. A meticulous reader might notice that Pa's letter described a hand raised in blessing rather than a waterpot. Another variation we observed was a snake in the hand instead of a cord.

3. While the goose (*hans*) was depicted in older Indian iconography, modern interpretations often feature a swan. See Jean Philippe Vogel, *The Goose in Indian Literature and Art* (Leiden: Brill, 1962).

4. Alice Boner, S. R. Sarma, and B. Baumer, *Vāstusūtra Upaniṣad: The Essence of Form in Sacred Art* (Delhi: Motilal Banarsidas, 1982), 42. In Sanskrit, the words are *vrittajnānam rekhājnānam cha yo jānāti sthāpakah*.

5. R. E. Enthoven, *The Tribes and Castes of Bombay* (Bombay: Government Central Press, 1920), 3:355.

6. Enthoven, *Tribes and Castes*, 3:358.

7. The challenge in locating information about Vishwakarma is exemplified in the nearly identical titles of two books published twenty-five years apart: the sculptor Meera Mukherjee's personal quest *In Search of Viswakarma* (self-published, 1995), and the historian Vijaya Ramaswamy's volume, emerging from a symposium, *In Search of Vishwakarma* (Delhi: Primus Books, 2019). Vishwakarma's names are transcribed into English with a confusing range of spelling, with and without diacritics, thoroughly confounding online search engines. Following Vishwakarma toward Ellora, we found him called, for example, Viśvakarmaṇ, Viśvakarmā, Viswakarma, Biswakarma, Visvacarma, Biskurma, Bisma Kurm, and Viswacurma.

8. The iconography of tools in Vishwakarma and Freemasons' posters can be uncannily similar—a place of transcultural exchange that I hope someone else might someday research.

9. See Stephanie Jamison and Joel P. Brereton, *The Rigveda: The Earliest Religious Poetry of India* (New York: Oxford University Press, 2014), 3:1513–17 (hymns X:81 and X:82 to Viśvakarman), 1:51 (overview of hymns mentioning Tvaṣṭar).

256 NOTES TO PAGES 20-30

10. Much of this overview is summarized in Kirin Narayan and Kenneth M. George, "Vishwakarma: Hindu God of Technology," in *Technology and Religion in Historical and Contemporary South Asia*, ed. Knut Jacobsen and Krishtina Myrvold (New York: Routledge, 2018), 8–24. For the variation in regional forms of worship, see K. Narayan and K. George, "Tools and World-Making in the Worship of Vishwakarma," *South Asian History and Culture* 8 (2017): 478–92. For how industrial technologies can be aligned with Vishwakarma, see K. George and K. Narayan, "Technophany and Its Publics: Artisans, Technicians and the Rise of Vishwakarma Worship in India," *Journal of Asian Studies* 81, no. 1 (2022): 1–19.

11. All of these are available online at the Wisdom Library, https://www.wisdomlib .org/buddhism/book/jataka-tales-english. See especially Hatthipāla Jātaka (509) and also Kudāla Jātaka (70), Culla-Sutasoma-Jātaka (525), Ayoghara-Jātaka (510), Somanassa Jātaka (505), Mūga-Pakkha Jātaka (538), Sarabhanga Jātaka (522), Sāma Jātaka (540), and Vessantara Jātaka (547).

12. Suruci Jātaka (489); Mūga-Pakkha Jātaka (538).

13. Sarabha-Miga Jātaka (483).

14. Kalyanadasa Bhanabhai Gajjar, *Viśvakarmājnāna: Śilpa Sār Sangrah nāmno granth* (Ahmedabad, 1898), 26.

15. In ancient texts, related titles for those skilled in working wood include Rathakara, "chariot maker"; Takshak, "one who fashions"; and Vardhaki, from "cutting or dividing." Contemporary carpenter caste names from different regions include Khati, Badhai, Tarkhan, and Dhiman.

16. Marwar Darbar, *Report on the Census of 1891*, vol. 2, *Castes of Marwar* (Jodhpore,1894), 146.

17. Kailashnath Vyas and Devendrasingh Gahlot, *Rājasthān kī Jātiyon kā Samājik evam Ārthik Jīvan* (Jodhpur: Jagdishsingh Gahlot Sodh Samsthan, 1992), 183–84.

18. Tryna Lyons, *The Artists of Nathadwara: The Practice of Painting in Rajasthan* (Bloomington: Indiana University Press, 2004), 249–50. For more on these artists and their connection to Vishwakarma, see Renaldo Maduro, *Artistic Creativity in a Brahmin Painter Community*, Research Monograph 14 (Berkeley: University of California Center for South and Southeast Asia Studies, 1976).

19. When I came to college in New York, I found that, while names like Smith, Wright, Mason, and Carpenter were familiar, "Contractor" drew a blank. I regularly found myself repeating, slowly enunciating, and even spelling it out. By the time I reached graduate school, I understood that most Indian surnames are arbitrary colonial-era choices and let go of "Contractor," leaving "Narayan"—my middle name and Pa's first name—in its stead.

20. For a summary of this term's range of meanings, see R. Tripathi, "Sūtradhara," in *Kalātattvakośa: A Lexicon of Fundamental Concepts of the Indian Arts*, ed. Bettina Baumer, 2:321–32 (New Delhi: IGNCA and Motilal Banarsidas, 2003). For a historical overview, see R. C. Misra, *Śilpa in Indian Tradition: Concept and Instrumentalities* (Shimla: Indian Institute of Advanced Study; New Delhi: Aryan Books International, 2009), esp. 87–97.

Chapter 2

1. After Hyderabad was merged into newly independent India in 1948, the State of Hyderabad existed until 1956, when states were reorganized on the basis of language—so this book would date to the early 1950s.

NOTES TO PAGES 33–38   257

2. Micaela Soar, "The Tīrtha at Ellora," in *Ellora Caves: Sculpture and Architecture*, ed. R. Parimoo, D. Kannal, and S. Panikkar (Pune: Aprant, 2018), 62–79; Yaaminey Mubayi, *Water and Historical Settlements: The Making of a Cultural Landscape* (New York: Routledge, 2023), e-book, pp. 59–82, DOI: 10.4324/9781003315148-3.

3. Geri Malandra, *Unfolding a Maṇḍala: The Buddhist Cave Temples at Ellora* (Albany: State University of New York Press, 1993).

4. Walter Smith, "Architectural and Mythic Space at Ellora," *Oriental Art Magazine* 42, no. 2 (1996): 13–21.

5. M. K. Dhavalikar, *Ellora* (New Delhi: Oxford University Press, 2003), 7; there are also several other derivations for this temple's name. On the possibility that the deity from Cave 16 was moved to this temple, see James Burgess, *Report on the Antiquities in the Bidar and Aurangabad Districts*, Archaeological Survey of Western India, vol. 3 (London: W. H. Allen and Co., 1878), 82–84. Mubayi, however, argues that the presence of an existing sacred Shiva temple and pond may have inspired the making of the earliest caves. See Mubayi, *Water and Historical Settlements*, 69.

6. Professor Pathy writes that this practice was ended when the Nizam took control, which would have been 1724. He links the association of Caves 1–4 with Dheds and Cave 5 with Mahars—castes then considered untouchable—to this periodic residence of villagers. See T. V. Pathy, *Ajanta, Ellora and Aurangabad Caves: An Appreciation* (Aurangabad: Jai Hind Printing Press, 1978), 47–48.

7. See Pushkar Sohoni, "Continuities in the Sacred Landscape: Ellora, Khuldabad and the Temple of Ghrishneshwara: A Single Social Historical Complex," in *Studies in Medieval Deccan History (14th–17th Century): Dr. M. A. Nayeem Festschrift*, ed. Syed Ayub Ali (Warangal: Deccan Historical Society, 2015), 156–68.

8. See Mahesh Sharma, "Narratives of a Place Named Ellora: Myths, Culture and Politics," *Indian Economic and Social History Review* 58, no. 1 (2021): 73–111.

9. In a similar evocation of a workspace, the cave's name has also been translated as "Carpenter's Shop" in R. S. Gupte and B. D. Mahajan, *Ajanta, Ellora and Aurangabad Caves* (Bombay: D. B. Taraporevala Sons and Co., 1962), 167.

10. Even more astonishing, the excavated temple recreates earlier temples in South India, namely the Virupaksha temple at Pattadakal built up (not excavated) from stone by the architect Sarvasiddhi, which in turn was modeled on the Rajasimhesvara temple at Kanchipuram. See Calambur Sivaramamurti, *The Art of India* (New York: Harry N. Abrams, 1977), 220, 222–23.

11. In Marathi this runs, "chinchechyā pānāvari deul bāndhile / ādhi kalas mag pāyāre." See P. V. Ranade, "Echoes of Ellora in Early Marathi Literature," in *Ellora Caves: Sculpture and Architecture*, ed. R. Parimoo, D. Kannal, and S. Panikkar (Pune: Aprant, 2018), 83. Thanks to Jayant Bapat for help with an alternate translation and for pointing out that this is also the opening of a Marathi *abhang* composition attributed to the sixteenth-century poet-saint Eknath, who once lived on the Sulibhanjan hill facing the Ellora caves from the west.

12. "Account of Tamba Patra Plates Dug up at Baroda in Goojrat with Facsimile and Translation," *Journal of the Asiatic Society of Bengal* 8 (1839): 292–303.

13. R. G. Bhandarkar, "The Rāshṭrākūṭa King Krishṇarājā I and Élāpura," *Indian Antiquary* 12 (1883): 228–30, 228. His son, D. R. Bhandarkar, established the connection with the Kailash temple in "Epigraphic Notes and Queries VIII: The Kailāsa Temple at Elūrā," *Indian Antiquary* 40 (1911): 237–38. Also see a more recent translation in R. N. Misra, "Perceptions of South Asia's Visual Past: Tradition and the Artist," in

Perceptions of South Asia's Visual Past, ed. Catherine B. Asher and Thomas R. Metcalf (New Delhi: American Institute of Indian Studies, 1994), 102.

14. In addition to David Shulman, Devadatta Kali and McComas Taylor offered valuable help.

15. Stella Kramrisch, *The Art of India: Traditions of Indian Sculpture Painting and Architecture* (London: Phaidon, 1954), 14. Kramrisch implicitly draws on Ananda K. Coomaraswamy's formulation of Vishwakarma, articulated most famously in *The Indian Craftsman* (London: Probsthain and Company, 1909).

16. Pathy, *Ajanta, Ellora and Aurangabad Caves*, 57.

17. The Gujarati is "Jindagi saphaltā mā pustako mahatvanām chhe."

Chapter 3

1. In *My Family and Other Saints*, I called my parents "Maw" and "Paw." Here I've spelled their names without the *w*, as "Pa" did in his letters.

2. Geri Malandra, *Unfolding a Maṇḍala: The Buddhist Cave Temples at Ellora* (Albany: State University of New York Press, 1993), 3.

3. See Mhaimbata, *Śrīcakradhara līla caritra*, ed. V. B. Kolate. (Mumbai: Maharashtra Rajya Sahitya Samskriti Mandal, 1982), esp. 124–32 for the sections on Ellora. I await a forthcoming translation: Mhaimbhat, *God at Play*, vol. 1, ed. and trans. Anne Feldhaus, Murti Classical Library of India 36 (Cambridge, MA: Harvard University Press, 2024). For a summary of Chakradhar Swami's biography, see Christian Novetzke, *The Quotidian Revolution: Vernacularization, Religion and the Premodern Public Sphere in India* (New York: Columbia University Press, 2016), 107–14.

4. P. V. Ranade, "Echoes of Ellora in Early Marathi Literature," in *Ellora Caves: Sculpture and Architecture*, ed. R. Parimoo, D. Kannal, and S. Panikkar (Pune: Aprant, 2018), 86.

5. Ranade, "Echoes of Ellora," 86.

6. In the old Marathi of the *Līlācaritra* (*Pūrvārdha* 186), the Shadow Person (*chhāyāpurukhu*) deposits his shadow (*chhāyā*); the notes mention that one edition substitutes the word *pratibimba* for *chhāyā*; in addition to shadow, this can mean a mirrored reflection, or a represented counterpart. See Mhaimbata, *Śrīcakradhara līla caritra*, 130.

7. Ramachandra Cintaman Dhere, *Śodha-śilpa* (Puṇe: Viśvakarmā Sāhityālaya, 1977), 12–16; R. N. Misra, *Śilpa in Indian Tradition: Concepts and Instrumentalities* (Shimla: Indian Institute of Advanced Study; New Delhi: Aryan Books International, 2009), esp. 66–71.

8. Vasudev Vishnu Mirashi, *Inscriptions of the Kalachuri-Chedi Era*, Corpus Inscriptionum Indicarum, vol. 4 (Ootacamund: Government Epigraphist for India, 1955), 555–57.

9. Ranade, "Echoes of Ellora," 88–90; Dhere, *Śodha-shilpa*, 53–54.

10. Dhere, *Śodha-śilpa*, 53.

11. Dhere, *Śodha-śilpa*, 54.

12. Ranade, "Echoes of Ellora," 83; also P. V. Ranade, *Ellora Paintings* (Aurangabad: Parimal Prakashan, 1980), 83.

13. See Ann Feldhaus, "Pilgrimage and Remembrance: Biography and Geography in the Mahanubhav Tradition," in *Connected Places: Region, Pilgrimage and Geographical Imagination in India* (New York: Palgrave, 2003), 185–210.

NOTES TO PAGES 53–61   259

14. Shree Devdatt Ashram Jadhavvadi, *Elāpur Sthān Darśan* (Verul Leni: Shreed-evdatt Mahanubhav Ashram, n.d.), 30–33. The booklet's introduction reveals that in some eras of Mahanubhav history, Ellora was considered off-limits as a dangerous space of Tantric practices. The rituals to be performed in each cave had been known to only a few devotees until the 1960s, when one monk contacted a local guide to the Mahanubhav sites who'd lost his livelihood with the arrival of formally certified guides and was instead selling fruit in the village. The monk then traveled between monasteries to gather other remembered knowledge from elders to compose this booklet.

15. Shree Devdatt Ashram, *Elāpur Sthān Darshan*, 43.

Chapter 4

1. John Seely, *The Wonders of Elora; or, The Narrative of a Journey to the Temples or Dwellings Excavated out of a Mountain of Granite at Elora*, 2nd ed. (London: Geo B. Whitaker, 1825), 336. Seely was told that from the Ellora side, a tunnel to the fort opened from a cave far to the north (267). This appears to be Cave 31, amid the Jain caves.

2. Carl Ernst, *Eternal Garden: Mysticism, History, and Politics at a South Asian Sufi Center* (Albany: State University of New York Press, 1992), 194, 196.

3. R. Sengupta, "Repairs to the Ellora Caves," *Ancient India* 17 (1961): 46–67.

4. Carl W. Ernst, "Admiring the Works of the Ancients: The Ellora Temples as Viewed by Indo-Muslim Authors," in *Beyond Turk and Hindu: Rethinking Religious Identities in Islamicate South Asia*, ed. David Gilmartin and Bruce B. Lawrence (Gainseville: University Press of Florida, 2002), 102.

5. Ernst, "Admiring the Works," 104.

6. Jean de Thevenot, *Indian Travels of Thevenot and Careri*, ed. Surendra Nath Sen (Delhi: National Archives of India National Records series, 1949), 106.

7. Thevenot, *Indian Travels*, 106.

8. Thevenot, *Indian Travels*, 104.

9. Thevenot, *Indian Travels*, 107.

10. Ernst, "Admiring the Works," 111; also see *Ma'sir I Alamgir*, trans. Jadunath Sarkar, 145.

11. Ernst, "Admiring the Works," 109; M. K. Dhavalikar, *Ellora* (New Delhi: Oxford University Press, 2003), 7.

12. A. H. Anquetil-Duperron, *Zend-Avesta ouvrage de Zoroastre*, vol. 1, pt. 1 (Paris: Tilliard, 1771), ccxxxiv. My thanks to Alina Borsa for translating these passages. Since the Buddha had been assimilated into Hindu mythology as the ninth incarnation of Vishnu, and stupas had originally been designed to serve as reliquaries for the Buddha's remains, there's a certain logic to describing the stupa as Vishnu's tomb.

13. Anquetil-Duperron, *Zend-Avesta*, cclix.

14. Govind Sakharam Sardesai, *Poona's Affairs, 1786–1797, Malet's Embassy* (Bombay: Government Central Press, 1936), 357.

15. Charles Malet, "To Sir John Shore, Bart. President of the Asiatic Society," *Asiatick Researches; or, Transactions of the Society* 6 (1801): 386.

16. Malet, "To Sir John Shore," 385; see also Seely, *Wonders*, 333–34.

17. Charles Malet, "Descriptions of the Caves or Excavations on the Mountain, about a mile to the Eastward of the town of Ellora," *Asiatick Researches; or, Transactions of the Society* 6 (1801): 421.

260 NOTES TO PAGES 61–65

18. Malet, "Descriptions of the Caves," 390, 421.

19. Malet, "Descriptions of the Caves," 421.

20. Malet, "Descriptions of the Caves," 422.

21. Malet, "To Sir John Shore," 382.

22. We are very grateful to Holly Shaffer, who first introduced us to this image and who identifies the date of Tambat's drawing as 1793. See her marvelous *Grafted Arts: The Marathas and the British in Western India, 1760–1820* (New Haven, CT: Yale University Press, 2022), 95. Uday Kulkarni suggests that the drawing dates back to Tambat's trip in 1791. See his *James Wales: Artist and Antiquarian* (Pune: Mula Mutha Publishers, 2019), 159, 26. Tambat also drew the cave exterior.

23. Malet, "To Sir John Shore," 383.

24. Kulkarni, *James Wales*, 143.

25. Kulkarni, *James Wales*, 139. For a fuller account of the group's time in Ellora, see 142–65.

26. Kulkarni, *James Wales*, 217.

27. Wales's drawings from Ellora were also used by the engraver Thomas Daniell to make two dozen popular aquatints titled "Hindoo Excavations in the Mountain of Ellora," including an interior of Cave 10 that was wider than all the other drawings, added more detail to the entablature, and brought in a couple beside the Murti. The lion's head had disappeared.

28. Seely, *Wonders*, 143. Seely was employed in the Bombay Native Infantry, a military unit associated with the East India Company, and one wonders how his colleagues reacted.

29. Seely, *Wonders*, 344. Another traveler, who visited two months later, in December 1810, similarly described the region as depopulated, with roaming bands of Bhils. James Mackintosh, *Memoirs of the Life of Sir James Mackintosh* (London: Edward Moxon, 1835), 2:73.

30. Seely, *Wonders*, 153–55. This agreement stipulated that holy men of all orders who lived and cooked within the temple and front portico be moved out; that devotees only enter the inner sanctum at set hours and by a certain path; that Seely and his group have access to water from one spring; and that they not slaughter animals, cook meat, or smoke within the precinct but only at some distance.

31. Seely, *Wonders*, 212; for an entertaining description of this ensemble, see 264–65.

32. Seely, *Wonders*, 345.

33. Seely, *Wonders*, 210.

34. Seely, *Wonders*, 145–47; a version of the same story reappears in Mrs. John B. Speid, *Our Last Years in India* (London: Smith, Elder, 1862), 178.

35. Seely, *Wonders*, 145, 211.

36. Seely, *Wonders*, 212. Sykes, who visited soon after, suggests that the identification of Vajrapani with Shiva was because of "the thin rod twisted round his arm, which universally distinguishes Sew [Shiva] and his followers." W. H. Sykes, "An Account of the Caves of Ellora," *Transactions of the Literary Society of Bombay* 30 (1823): 302.

37. Seely, *Wonders*, 211–12.

38. Seely, *Wonders*, 212.

39. Seely, *Wonders*, 212.

40. Seely, *Wonders*, 213.

41. Seely, *Wonders*, 346.

42. Seely, *Wonders*, 208–9.

NOTES TO PAGES 65–90   261

43. Seely, *Wonders*, 346.

44. Seely, *Wonders*, 346. Curiously, this mention of creative power and unlimited space closely echoes Malet's reflections. Could Seely have confused his sources? Was Malet echoing what he too had been told?

45. Seely, *Wonders*, 220.

Chapter 5

1. Tryna Lyons, researching the genealogical records of painters in Rajasthan, was also suspected of trying to set herself up as a genealogist. See her chapter "Family Matters" and similar claims to origins at Ellora, in Lyons, *The Artists of Nathadwara: The Practice of Painting in Rajasthan* (Bloomington: Indiana University Press, 2004), 247–92.

2. Bachubhai B. Vadgama, *Śri Virāṭ Viśvakarmā Mahāpurāṇ* (Rajkot: Vishwakarma Charitable Trust, 2013), 408, with an expansion of the barley story, 354–57.

3. Mul Raj is thought to have died around 995 CE, as his grandson's great-grandson, Siddhraj, ascended the throne in 1092 CE. When Colonel James Tod visited the Rudra Mal ruins in 1822, he reported on two inscriptions stating that Mul Raj started the temple in 942 CE and that Siddhraj completed it in 1146 CE. James Tod, *Travels in Western India* (1839; Delhi: Oriental Publishers, 1971), 142.

4. Thanks to Hardik Siddhpura, who forwarded this scan on January 1, 2022. This version names Gangadhar's father as Ram Sutar.

5. This history is recounted in a booklet Bhai gave us that especially honors a Dahisaria relative very devoted to the guru Swami Narayan. See Vinodbhai D. Gajjar, *Śrījīnā Ekāntik Bhakt Bhujnā Śrī Sundarjī Sutār* (Bhuj: Rachna Enterprise, 2010).

6. Alka Patel, "Architectural Histories Entwined: The Rudra-Mahalaya/Congregational Mosque of Siddhpur, Gujarat," *Journal of the Society of Architectural Historians* 63 (2004): 144–63.

7. Tod, *Travels in Western India*, 142.

8. James Burgess visited in 1869. See James Burgess and Henry Cousens, *The Architectural Antiquities of Northern Gujarat*, Archaeological Survey of Western India, vol. 9 (London: Bernard Quaritch, 1903), 62.

Chapter 6

1. Acharya Lakshmishankar Pranshankar, "Prastāvanā" [introduction], in *Śri Viśvakarmā Dharmapatrikā* (Mumbai: Nirnaysagar Press, 1901), 7.

2. Pranshankar, "Prastāvanā," 7–8.

3. Pranshankar, "Prastāvanā," 8.

4. The word he uses for "revival" is *punaruddhār*. Pranshankar, "Prastāvanā," 7.

5. *Gazetteer of the Bombay Presidency*, vol. 5, *Cutch, Palanpur and Mahikantha* (Bombay: Government Central Press, 1880), 71.

6. James Burgess, *The Rock Temples of Elurā or Verul* (Bombay: Education Society's Press, 1877), 3.

7. Pranshankar, "Prastāvanā," 8.

8. Pranshankar, "Prastāvanā," 9–10.

9. For example, Gangaram V. Panchal, *Śrī Viśvakarmā Prabhunī Mahākathā* (Mumbai: Shree Vishwakarma Dharm Prachar Samiti, 1978). Here, when goddess Lakshmi

asks her husband Vishnu about his forms, he replies, "I take on the form of Vishwakarma to make this universe and innumerable worlds."

10. L. F. Rushbrooke-Williams, *The Black Hills: Kutch in History and Legend* (London: Weidenfeld and Nicolson, 1958),152.

11. Pranshankar, "Prastāvanā," 10–11.

12. Pranshankar, *Śri Viśvakarmā Dharmapatrikā*, 1.

13. Pranshankar, *Śri Viśvakarmā Dharmapatrikā*. The Acharya quotes Keshavji on 11.

14. This much-used concept is from M. N. Srinivas, and especially his classic article "A Note on Sanskritization and Westernization," *Far Eastern Quarterly* 15 (1956): 481–96.

15. This slogan is often included in South Indian representations of the five-headed Vishwakarma. See Jan Brouwer, *The Makers of the World: Caste, Craft and Mind of South Indian Artisans* (Delhi: Oxford University Press, 1995), 45.

16. Pranshankar, *Śri Viśvakarmā Dharmapatrikā*, 66–67.

17. Pranshankar, *Śri Viśvakarmā Dharmapatrikā*, 119. This is a variation on the classic Hindu formulation of a debt to gods, sages, and ancestors, paid off by studying sacred texts, performing sacrifices, and having sons; sometimes extended to include a debt to all humans repaid through goodness. See P. V. Kane, *History of Dharmaśāstra: Ancient and Mediæval Religious and Civil Law in India* (Poona: Bhandarkar Oriental Research Institute, 1953), vol. 5, pt. 2, 1826. My thanks to Ann Gold for this reference.

18. The Kutch monarch actually gets a very long title that ends with GCIE, indicating that he had received the order of the British empire.

Chapter 7

1. "Sutār Komni Jāgriti," *Pārsi Sansār ane Lok Sevak*, 24, no. 18 (March 2, 1932): 14.

2. *Shree Viśvakarmā kulbhūśan* literally means "ornament of the family of Vishwakarma."

3. Victor Turner, *The Ritual Process: Structure and Anti-Structure* (Chicago: Aldine, 1969).

4. "An Indiscreet Youth," *Times of India*, January 15, 1916, 13.

5. See S. M. Natesa Sastri, *Hindu Feasts, Fasts and Ceremonies* (1903; New Delhi: Educational Publishing House, 1988), 15–17; P. V. Kane, *History of Dharmaśāstra: Ancient and Mediæval Religious and Civil Law in India* (Poona: Bhandarkar Oriental Research Institute, 1953), 4:351, 448.

6. Micaela Soar, "The Tīrtha at Ellora," in *Ellora Caves: Sculpture and Architecture*, ed. R. Parimoo, D. Kannal, and S. Panikkar (Pune: Aprant, 2018), 63.

7. R. E. Enthoven and A. M. T. Jackson, *Folklore Notes*, vol. 1, *Gujarat* (Bombay: British India Press, 1914). The following quotations are all drawn from pages 93–94.

Chapter 8

1. Mandana was a brilliant architect, thought to be originally from the Gujarat area. In addition to overseeing construction and sculpting projects for his royal patron Rana Kumbha, he composed eight building treatises in Sanskrit, with this one translated into Gujarati: *Śilpinu Vāstuśastra temāthī agh Vāstusār nām granth* (Ahmedabad: Maganlal Karamchand, 1878).

NOTES TO PAGES 111–118 263

2. Thanks to Tryna Lyons for this insight about the doorway.

3. We thank Claudia Hyles for pointing out that such colored glass globes can be seen on the ceiling of the royal residence at Mehrangarh fort in Rajasthan.

4. "Gajjar" derives from *gajdhar*, holder of the footrule, the head of a work team. K. B. Gajjar was the father of the famous chemist T. K. Gajjar, who worked with the Maharaja of Baroda to set up a training school in crafts, Kala Bhavan, and to reissue older books like the Rajvallabh. See Sutradhar Mandana, *Rājvallabh athvā Śilpaśāstra*, translated into Gujarati by Narayanbharati Lakshmanbharati Gosain et. al. (Badodara: Veerakshetra Mudralaya, 1891).

5. Kalyanadasa Bhanabhai Gajjar, *Viśvakarmājnāna: Śilpa Sār Sangrah nāmno granth* (Ahmedabad, 1898), 24.

6. Gajjar, *Viśvakarmājnāna*, 26. This evocation of Vishwakarma addressing an assembly of Sutradhars recasts the scene from the Buddha's first preaching at Sarnath while also evoking the layout of many of Ellora's later Jain caves in which a Jina is depicted teaching an assembled group of devotees. See Lisa Owen, *Carving Devotion in the Jain Caves at Ellora* (Leiden: Brill, 2012).

7. This entire section on geology and excavation is indebted to Ken's research. He has allowed me to draw on his notes and adapt his insights from a draft essay: Kenneth George, "Sutradhars and Stone Carpenters."

8. Vidya Dehejia and Peter Rockwell, *The Unfinished: Stone Carvers at Work on the Indian Subcontinent* (New Delhi: Roli Books, 2016), 118.

9. Vidya Dehejia, *Early Buddhist Rock Temples: A Chronological Study* (London: Thames and Hudson, 1972).

10. The most detailed geological studies of Ellora, conducted by the Geological Survey of India, can be found in Manohar Sinha, ed., *Geoscientific Studies for the Conservation of Ellora Caves* (New Delhi: Archaeological Survey of India, 2011).

11. In *The Unfinished*, Dehejia and Rockwell offer details on several caves left unfinished at various stages; also see Geri Malandra, *Unfolding a Maṇḍala: The Buddhist Cave Temples at Ellora* (Albany: State University of New York Press, 1993), 123–26 and fig. 17.

12. Owen, *Carving Devotion*, 195–97.

13. See various contributions in the revised edition of R. Parimoo, D. Kannal, and S. Panikkar, eds., *Ellora Caves: Sculpture and Architecture* (Pune: Aprant, 2018); see also Deepak Kannal, *Ellora: An Enigma of Sculptural Styles* (New Delhi: Book and Books, 1996).

14. For resonances to other sites in Cave 10, see Malandra, *Unfolding a Maṇḍala*, 55–58.

15. Dehejia and Rockwell, *Unfinished*, 146–47.

16. Gregory Schopen, *Buddhist Nuns, Monks, and Other Worldly Matters: Recent Papers on Monastic Buddhism in India* (Honolulu: University of Hawai'i Press, 2014), 258.

17. Schopen, *Buddhist Nuns*, 251–52; 258–63.

18. Shadakshari Settar, *Early Buddhist Artisans and Their Architectural Vocabulary* (Manipal: Manipal Universal Press, 2020), 71–72; Dehejia, *Early Buddhist Rock Temples*, 136.

19. Settar, *Early Buddhist Artisans*, 75.

20. E. B. Havell, *The Ancient and Medieval Architecture of India: A Study of Indo-Aryan Civilization* (London: John Murray, 1915), 190.

264 NOTES TO PAGES 139-148

Chapter 10

1. Veena Das, "A Sociological Study of Caste Puranas: A Case Study," *Sociological Bulletin* 17 (1968): 141–64.

2. See Kenneth M. George and Kirin Narayan, "Readers of the 'Lost' Puran: Mythopolitics and Suthar Caste Identity in Gujarat," *Religion* 52 (2022): 576–94.

3. Ramashankar Muktashankar Joshi, *Asal Viśvakarmā Purāṇ* (Ahmedabad: Mahadev Ramchandra Jagusthe Books, 1965).

4. Vallabhram Surajram, *Viśvakarmānī Caritra, Viśvakarmā Purāṇ Viśvakarmānī Kathā*, 2nd ed. (1911; Dakor: Mansukhram Ranchoddas, 1926).

5. The black-and-white frontispiece identifies the two attendants as Vishwadeva and Morudeejh or Bhorudeejh, names that have mystified everyone we've showed this too. We have also seen a colored poster of this image, with the same names, attributed to the Ravi Varma Press.

6. Geri Malandra, *Unfolding a Maṇḍala: The Buddhist Cave Temples at Ellora* (Albany: State University of New York Press, 1993), 56.

7. Robert DeCaroli, *Haunting the Buddha: Indian Popular Religions in the Formation of Buddhism* (New York: Oxford University Press, 2004).

8. Richard Cohen, "Nāga, Yakṣinī, Buddha: Local Deities and Local Buddhism at Ajanta," *History of Religions* 37, no. 4 (1998): 360–400.

9. Joshi, *Asal Viśvakarmā Purāṇ*, 334–41. *Shesh* means remainder, and Shesh Narayan embodies what's left over when a universe has dissolved. In the moments between creations, Lord Vishnu (Narayan) is said to rest atop Shesh Nag, and when the deity "Shesh Narayan" is invoked, this can encompass them both.

10. Natubhai P. Gajjar, *Mhārā Dādā Śrī Viśvakarmā*, 3rd ed. (Rajkot: Ramy Publication, 2014), 78.

11. Micaela Soar, "The Tīrtha at Ellora," in *Ellora Caves: Sculpture and Architecture*, ed. R. Parimoo, D. Kannal, and S. Panikkar (Pune: Aprant, 2018), 65–69. See Wendy Doniger, *Women Androgynes, and Other Mythical Beasts* (Chicago: University of Chicago Press, 1980), 303–6.

12. For more on the history of these names and of Ila stories in the Puranas, see Mahesh Sharma, "Narratives of a Place Named Ellora: Myths, Culture and Politics," *Indian Economic and Social History Review* 58, no. 1 (2021): 73–111.

13. Girishibhai Rasikbhai Bharadiya, *Śrī Viśvakarmā Pujan Kathā* (Jamnagar: Ramya Publications, 2009).

14. D. R. Bhandarkar, "Epigraphic Notes and Queries VIII: The Kailāsa Temple at Elūrā," *Indian Antiquary* 40 (1911): 237–38, 237.

15. Narrain Row and Anunda Row, *Memoir Descriptive of the Ancient Place of Ellola near Dowlatabad Compiled from the Mahatyams of That Ancient Stullam* (British Library OIOC Eur mss. Mackenzie General, XIV, no. 47), 12. According to Vallabhram Surajram, it was because of Vishwakarma's sons' participation in this sacrifice that Sutars were later not recognized as Brahmins. The Sanskrit text of the Shivalaya Mahatmya is being translated by Micaela Soar, and we eagerly await the full translation.

16. Row and Row, *Memoir*, 11–12.

17. See Uday Kulkarni, *James Wales: Artist and Antiquarian* (Pune: Mula Mutha Publishers, 2019), 160.

18. Nonetheless, this was adapted by Thomas Daniell in the famous set of colored lithographs that form part of the art historical record of the caves. Joining three

NOTES TO PAGES 154–170   265

perspectives, Daniell made a long panorama of the caves set into the mountainside. In "The Mountain Ellora: 3rd View," Cave 10 appears on the far left with the Naga Jadi gushing over Cave 5.

Chapter 11

1. George Watt, *Indian Art at Delhi, 1903, being the official catalogue of the Delhi Exhibition, 1902–1903* (London: John Murray, 1904), 124–25. In this example, the nine planets would include Rahu and Ketu (nodes of the moon), and the lunar month is divided into two halves, alternately culminating in a full moon or a new moon.

2. D. N. Shukla, *Vāstu-Śāstra*, vol. 1, *Hindu Science of Architecture* (Lucknow: VāstuVānmaya-Prakāsana Śālā, 1958; reprint, New Delhi: Munshiram Manoharlal, 1993).

3. This chapter is titled "The *Ālech* Knowledge," but the closest words we could find were *ālekh*, referring to a mental delineation/design, and *āloch*, or "without eyes," indicating the inner imagining of a thing.

4. Vallabhram Surajram, *Viśvakarmāni Caritra, Viśvakarmā Purāṇ, Viśvakarmāni Kathā* (1909; Dakor: Mansukhram Ranchoddas, 1926), chap. 18, 303–13.

5. R. N. Misra, *Śilpa in Indian Tradition: Concepts and Instrumentalities* (Shimla: Indian Institute of Advanced Study; New Delhi: Aryan Books International, 2009), 5, cites this from the *Baudhayana Dharmasutra*; "nityam śuddhāḥ kāruhastaḥ."

6. Mirza cannot definitively recall if this was Cave 10, but it is hard to imagine it is any other cave. Email from Saeed Mirza, June 5, 2019. See Saeed Mirza, *Memory in the Age of Amnesia* (Delhi: Context, 2018); https://scroll.in/article/880502/saeed -mirza-interprets-the-political-history-of-india-and-the-world-through-personal -stories.

Chapter 12

1. Interestingly, Tambat's drawing includes this "cord," but it is absent in the early nineteenth-century published representations, perhaps indicating that Tambat was aware of how oral traditions highlighted this iconographic feature.

2. Vallabhram Surajram, *Viśvakarmāni Caritra, Viśvakarmā Purāṇ, Viśvakarmāni Kathā* (1909; Dakor: Mansukhram Ranchoddas, 1926), 350–52.

3. Charles Malet, "Descriptions of the Caves or Excavations on the Mountain, about a mile to the Eastward of the town of Ellora," *Asiatick Researches; or, Transactions of the Society* 6 (1801): 421.

4. *Viswacurma Donee Talla*, in Narrain Row and Anunda Row, *Memoir Descriptive of the Ancient Place of Ellola near Dowlatabad Compiled from the Mahatyams of That Ancient Stullam* (British Library OIOC Eur mss. Mackenzie General, XIV, no. 47), 7, for what is usually called Don Tal (11) in contrast to Teen Tal (12).

5. See Geri Malandra, *Unfolding a Maṇḍala: The Buddhist Cave Temples at Ellora* (Albany: State University of New York Press, 1993), 25, 125–26.

6. W. H. Sykes, "An Account of the Caves of Ellora," *Transactions of the Literary Society of Bombay* 30 (1823): 265–323, 301; also see Syed Hossain Bilgrami and C. Willmott, *Historical and Descriptive Sketch of His Highness the Nizam's Dominions* (Bombay: Times of India Steam Press, 1884), 2:457.

7. Brahmanand Deshpande, "Verul Yethīl Yādavkālīn Sthambhlekh," in *Śodhamudrā Khaṇḍ* 5 *wā* (Aurangabad: Kailash Publications, 2010), 35–36.

8. James Burgess, *The Rock Temples of Elurā or Verul* (Bombay: Education Society's Press, 1877), 2, 25.

9. James Fergusson and James Burgess, *The Cave Temples of India* (London: W. H. Allen and Co., 1880; New Delhi: Oriental Books Reprint Corporation, 1969), 379–81.

10. In a different context, researching Theravada Buddhist crafting traditions of Northern Thailand, Anthony Lovenheim Irwin discovered stories of injured fingers that illustrate an intimate connection between Buddha images and the craftspeople whose hands make them. See Irwin, "The Buddha's Busted Finger: Craft, Touch, and Cosmology in Theravada Buddhism," *Journal of the American Academy of Religion* 90, no. 1 (2022): 52–85.

11. R. S. Wauchope, *Buddhist Cave Temples of India* (Calcutta: Edinburgh Press; London: Luzac and Co., 1935), 94.

12. Alice Boner, S. R. Sarma, and B. Baumer, *Vāstusūtra Upaniṣad: The Essence of Form in Sacred Art* (Delhi: Motilal Banarsidas, 1982), 62.

13. Meera Mukherjee, *In Search of Viswakarma* (Calcutta: self-published, 1994), 7.

14. Row and Row, *Memoir*, 27; Kalyanadasa Bhanabhai Gajjar, *Viśvakarmājñāna: Śilpa Sār Sangrah nāmno granth* (Ahmedabad, 1898), 25; John Seely, *The Wonders of Elora; or, The Narrative of a Journey to the Temples or Dwellings Excavated out of a Mountain of Granite at Elora*, 2nd ed. (London: Geo B. Whitaker, 1825), 212.

15. For example, Krishna extending a night for an amorous encounter. See Kirin Narayan, *Everyday Creativity: Singing Goddesses in the Himalayan Foothills* (Chicago: University of Chicago Press, 2016), 138–40.

16. For example, the deities in the Jagannath temple, said to be incomplete because an old carpenter sent by Vishwakarma was interrupted. See Roland Hardenberg, *The Renewal of Jagannath's Body: Ritual and Society in Orissa* (New Delhi: Manak, 2011), 434–37.

17. See Kirin Narayan, "Narrating Creative Process," *Narrative Culture* 1 (2014): 109–24.

18. Bachubhai Vadgama, *Suryadev Rāndaldevīnā Dev Lagna* (Rajkot: self-published, 2010), 111. While other booklets assert that Vishwakarma also first manifested at Ellora, Bachubhai identifies his birthplace as "Prabhas" in Saurashtra, distinguishing this from the workplace at Ellora.

19. Vadgama, *Suryadev Rāndaldevīno Dev Lagna*, 117–18; the number six emerges from the five mind-born sons plus Vastu, his adopted son.

20. P. V. Kane, *History of Dharmaśāstra: Ancient and Mediæval Religious and Civil Law in India* (Poona: Bhandarkar Oriental Research Institute, 1953), 4:351. Micaela Soar associates the gender-shifting Ila and a figure named Pururavas, who is said to visit the moon on *amāvāsya/amās* and take Soma nectar from the moon to offer ancestors; Soar, "The Tīrtha at Ellora," in *Ellora Caves: Sculpture and Architecture*, ed. R. Parimoo, D. Kannal, and S. Panikkar (Pune: Aprant, 2018), 89.

21. *Śrī Viśvakarmā Purāṇ Māhiti tathā Vrat* (Ahmedabad, 2007), 7. The booklet even attempts to calculate the millions of years that had passed since Vishwakarma's birth.

22. Girishbhai Rasikbhai Bharadiya, *Śrī Viśvakarmā Pujan Kathā* (Jamnagar: Ramya Publications, 2009), 5.

23. Bachubhai Vadgama, *Śri Virāṭ Viśvakarmāni Kathā* (Rajkot: self-published, 2008) 123–27; also retold in Bachubhai Vadgama, *Śri Virāṭ Viśvakarmā Mahāpurāṇ* (Rajkot: Shree Vishwakarma Charitable Trust, 2013), 354–57.

NOTES TO PAGES 177–187   267

24. Robert E. Buswell Jr. and Donald S. Lopez Jr., *The Princeton Dictionary of Buddhism* (Princeton, NJ: Princeton University Press, 2013), 943–44.

25. My thanks to Randall Law for this possible identification (email, April 23, 2022). Also see his excellent "Appendix: Geologic Observations and Analysis of Rock-cut and Constructed Stone Temples in South India," in Vidya Dehejia and Peter Rockwell, *The Unfinished: Stone Carvers at Work on the Indian Subcontinent* (New Delhi: Roli Books, 2016), 250–62.

Chapter 13

1. Goverdhanarama Devram, *Viśvakarmā padmālā ane Nirdoś Vāstu* (Ahmedabad: Diamond Jubilee Printing Press, 1913), 4. These caste groups are identified as Sutar, Kadiya, Sompura, and Luhar. Sutars in Mumbai, Karachi, and Ahmedabad had supported the book's publication.

2. Devram, *Viśvakarmā padmālā*, 5.

3. *Panchāmrit* is a mixture of milk, sugar, ghee, honey, and yogurt often used to scrub an image that will then be washed down with water.

4. Devram, *Viśvakarmā padmālā*, 5.

5. Devram, *Viśvakarmā padmālā*. 15.

6. R. N. Misra, *Śilpa in Indian Tradition: Concepts and Instrumentalities* (Shimla: Indian Institute of Advanced Study; New Delhi: Aryan Books International, 2009), 185–206.

7. A. H. Anquetil-Duperron, *Zend-Avesta ouvrage de Zoroastre*, vol. 1, pt. 1 (Paris: Tilliard, 1771), ccxxxiv. He describes the Murti as Vishnu, most likely because this was the identification offered by the Brahmins who were showing him around.

8. John Muir, *Notes of a Trip to Kedarnath and other parts of the snowy range of the Himalayas in the autumn of 1853* (Edinburgh: T. Constable, 1855), 56. Muir thought that the Buddha had been transformed into a Surya.

9. A. H. Longhurst, *Conservation Notes on Ancient Monuments*, in *Progress Report of the ASI Western Circle for the year ending 31 March 1911* (Government of Bombay General Department, 1911), 26.

10. R. S. Wauchope, *Buddhist Cave Temples of India* (Calcutta: Edinburgh Press; London: Luzac and Co., 1935), 95.

11. Walter Crane, *Indian Impressions, with Some Notes on Ceylon* (London: Methuen and Co., 1907), 43.

12. This transaction is beautifully explained in the classic book by Diana Eck, *Darśan: Seeing the Divine Image in India* (Chambersburg: Anima Books, 1981).

13. Images we found include those by Henry Cousens (1870s, British Library), Alfred Plate (1890s, Metropolitan Museum of Art), and Raja Deen Dayal (1895, British Library).

14. M. S. Singh, Vinodh Kumar, and Sujata A. Waghmare, "Characterization of 6–11th Century A.D. Decorative Lime Plasters of Rock Cut Caves of Ellora," *Construction and Building Materials* 98 (2015): 156–70; also see Geri Malandra, *Unfolding a Maṇḍala: The Buddhist Cave Temples at Ellora* (Albany: State University of New York Press, 1993), 58.

15. P. V. Ranade, *Ellora Paintings* (Aurangabad: Parimal Prakashan, 1980).

16. See Narrain Row and Anunda Row, *Memoir Descriptive of the Ancient Place of Ellola near Dowlatabad Compiled from the Mahatyams of That Ancient Stullam* (British Library OIOC Eur mss. Mackenzie General, XIV, no. 47), 35; W. H. Sykes,

"An Account of the Caves of Ellora," *Transactions of the Literary Society of Bombay* 30 (1823): 303; John Seely, *The Wonders of Elora; or, The Narrative of a Journey to the Temples or Dwellings Excavated out of a Mountain of Granite at Elora*, 2nd ed. (London: Geo B. Whitaker, 1825), 218–19, 223.

17. Sykes, "Account of the Caves," 297.

18. James Fergusson and James Burgess, *The Cave Temples of India* (London: W. H. Allen and Co., 1880; New Delhi: Oriental Books Reprint Corporation, 1969), 384.

19. Syed Hossain Bilgrami and C. Willmott, *Historical and Descriptive Sketch of His Highness the Nizam's Dominions* (Bombay: Times of India Steam Press, 1884), 2:456–57.

20. Bilgrami and Willmott, *Nizam's Dominions*, 448.

21. James Burgess, *The Rock Temples of Elurā or Verul* (Bombay: Education Society's Press, 1877), 3.

22. Longhurst, *Conservation Notes*, 26–27.

23. *Report of the Committee Appointed by the Government of Hyderabad State under their Order No. 594, Dated 1-8-58*, part II, *Preservation and Maintenance of the Cave-Temples of Ellora*, 14.

24. Plates 196 and 197 by Eliot Elisofon, in vol. 2 of Heinrich Zimmer, *The Art of Indian Asia: Its Mythology and Transformations*, ed. Joseph Campbell, Bollingen Series 39 (Princeton, NJ: Princeton University Press, 1955). Finding the rights proved too complicated to allow reproduction here.

25. A 1961 report describes how, over time, water seeping within the mountain caused damage within the caves and how the local rock, "weathers by exfoliation, shell by shell, with hard fresh rock forming the core . . . and with each erosion of the decomposed product an undecomposed or superficially decomposed layer of the rock is laid bare." R. Sengupta, "Repairs to the Ellora Caves," *Ancient India* 17 (1961): 47.

26. Sengupta, "Repairs," 54.

27. With thanks to Walter Spink, who introduced us to Saili Palande-Datar, who gave us this article: Brahmanand Deshpande, "Verul Yethīl Yādavkālīn Sthambhlekh," in *Śodhamudrā Khaṇḍ 5 wā* (Aurangabad: Kailash Publications, 2010).

28. This is a Buddhist *dharani*, or profession of the faith, neatly inscribed in Pali along a upstairs northern wall: "All things proceed from cause; this cause has been declared by Tathagata (Buddha); all things will cease to exist; that is, that which is declared by the great sramana (Buddha)." See M. K. Dhavalikar, *Ellora* (New Delhi: Oxford University Press, 2003), 22.

29. We don't quite follow how Deshpande calculates his reading of 1121 to be 1036 CE, as a Samvat date would usually be calculated as around fifty-seven years ahead of a CE date, making this 1064 CE. Since the inscription emphasizes a Samvat date, and Shaka dates fall seventy-eight years behind the Gregorian calendar, I wonder if this pillar also provoked confusion for the authors surveying the Nizam's dominions who mentioned an inscription with the date Shaka 1228, or 1306 CE.

30. See R. Nath, "On the Theory of Indo-Muslim Architecture," in *Shastric Traditions in Indian Arts*, vol. 1, ed. A. Dallapiccola (Stuttgart: Steiner, 1989), 197–201. Jaya or Jay, the son to whom this building manual is addressed, is one of the four sons connected with Shilpa Shastras; the others are May, Aparajit, and Siddharth.

31. R. S. McGregor, ed., *The Oxford Hindi-English Dictionary* (Oxford; Delhi: Oxford University Press, 1993), 164 (*kan*). Many thanks to Dnyaneshwari Kamath for her insights.

NOTES TO PAGES 195–203   269

Chapter 14

1. Ahilyabai's husband, of the Holkar royal family, had been killed fighting along-side the Mughal army, and the Ellora area was granted as compensation to the Holkars in 1754. When Ahilyabai's father-in-law and son also died, she became queen in 1765. Ahilyabai was an astonishingly energetic patron for the building and renovation of temples, ponds, wells, and pilgrim guesthouses within her realm and all across India. For overviews of the Kund, see George Michell and Sugandha Johar, "The Maratha Complex at Ellora," *South Asian Studies* 28 (2012): 69–88; James Burgess, *Report on the Antiquities in the Bidar and Aurangabad Districts*, Archaeological Survey of Western India Reports, vol. 3 (London: W. H. Allen and Co., 1878), 82–84. Also see Yaaminey Mubayi, "Ellora-Khuldabad-Daulatabad: Water and Sacred Spaces," in *Water Design: Environment and Histories*, ed. Jutta Jain Neubauer (Mumbai: Marg Publications, 2016), 129–41; Yaaminey Mubayi, *Water and Historical Settlements: The Making of a Cultural Landscape* (New York: Routledge, 2023), e-book, pp. 59–82, DOI: 10.4324/9781003315148-3. The Kund is also described by John Seely in *The Wonders of Elora; or, The Narrative of a Journey to the Temples or Dwellings Excavated out of a Mountain of Granite at Elora*, 2nd ed. (London: Geo B. Whitaker, 1825), 123–24, with mentions of Ahilyabai's patronage, 152, 345.

2. Goverdhanarama Devram, *Viśvakarmā padmālā ane Nirdoś Vāstu* (Ahmedabad: Diamond Jubilee Printing Press, 1913), 10.

3. Devram, *Viśvakarmā padmālā*, 10.

4. Ramashankar Muktashankar Joshi, *Asal Viśvakarmā Purāṇ* (Ahmedabad: Mahadev Ramchandra Jagusthe Books, 1965), 115–16. The Surya Kund carries hot water, and the adjacent Chandra Kund is cold. In local mythology, their namesakes are said to be the brothers Sun and Moon, companionably doing penance together on the Sulibhanjan hill to the southwest of the caves. See Mubayi, "Ellora-Khuldabad-Daulatabad," 133.

5. David G. Mandelbaum, *Indian Society*, vol. 2, *Change and Continuity* (Berkeley: University of California Press, 1973), 458.

6. Mandelbaum, *Indian Society*, 459.

7. For more on this history see Jan Brouwer, *The Makers of the World: Caste, Craft and Mind of South Indian Artisans* (Delhi: Oxford University Press, 1995), 40–49; Vijaya Ramaswamy, "Vishwakarma Craftsmen in Early Medieval Peninsular India," *Journal of the Economic and Social History of the Orient* 47 (2004): 548–82; G. Sudarshan Reddy, "The Caste System, the Colonial Judiciary, and the Struggle for Ritual Status in 19th-Century Andhra," *Proceedings of the Indian History Congress* 58 (1997): 677–85.

8. Satish Saberwal, *Mobile Men: Limits to Social Change in Urban Punjab* (New Delhi: Vikas, 1976), 110.

9. Vallabhram Surajram, *Viśvakarmāni Caritra, Viśvakarmā Purāṇ, Viśvakarmāni Kathā* (1909; Dakor: Mansukhram Ranchoddas, 1926), 196–202.

10. Narayan Ravaji Kshirasagar and Balshastri Ravaji Kshirsagar, *Viśvabrahmakulotsāha or History of Vishvabrahmins*, revised and expanded ed. (Poona: Kalika Prasad Press, 1921); the earlier edition is Narayana Ravaji Kshirasagar, *Viśvabrahmakulotsahā*, 3rd ed. (Poona: Kalika Prasad Press, 1906).

11. Bachubhai Vadgama, *Śrī Virāṭ Viśvakarmāni Kathā* (Rajkot: self-published, 2008), 49.

12. Gopalji Vagji Sharma, *Viśvakarmā ane tenā Vaṃśejo* (Anjar: Shree Gopalji Vagji Sharma, 1957).

13. Bachubhai Vadgama, *Suryadev Rāndaldevīno Dev Lagna* (Rajkot: self-published, 2010), 113.

14. Joshi, *Asal Viśvakarmā Purāṇ*, 251–88.

15. Characterized as "Maya Danav," architect of the underworld, Maya is the proponent of southern forms of architecture, paralleling Vishwakarma in northern building texts. See Bruno Dagens, trans., *Mayamata: An Indian Treatise on Housing Architecture and Iconography* (New Delhi: Sitaram Bhartia Institute of Scientific Research, 1985).

16. Narrain Row and Anunda Row, *Memoir Descriptive of the Ancient Place of Ellola near Dowlatabad Compiled from the Mahatyams of that Ancient Stullam* (British Library OIOC Eur mss. Mackenzie General, XIV, no. 47), 1–2.

17. Charles Malet, "To Sir John Shore, Bart. President of the Asiatic Society," *Asiatick Researches; or, Transactions of the Society* 6 (1801): 385.

18. Seely, *Wonders*, 336.

19. Babubhai Durlabhram Mevada, *Śri Viśvakarmā Parichay* (Ahmedabad, 2016), 32.

20. Jayantibhai Shastri, *Śri Viśvakarmā Purāṇa* (Surendranagar: Sarjanhar Sahitya Seva Kendra, 2017), 93.

Chapter 15

1. See Kirin Narayan, "Who Is Vishwakarma's Daughter?" in *In Search of Vishwakarma*, ed. Vijaya Ramaswamy (Delhi: Primus Books, 2019), 95–113. For the scriptural versions, see Wendy Doniger, "Saraṇyū/Saṃjñā: the Sun and the Shadow," in *Devi: Goddesses of India*, ed. John S. Hawley and Donna M. Wulff (Berkeley: University of California Press, 1996), 137–53; Doniger, *Splitting the Difference: Gender and Myth in Ancient Greece and India* (Chicago: University of Chicago Press, 1999).

2. For example, the goddesses Gayatri, Kali, and Kamakshi in the south; Saraswati in Rajasthan; and Monosha Devi in Bengal.

3. Atul Tripathi, *Solar Deities in Gujarat: Art, Architecture and Contemporary Traditions* (Delhi: Pratibha Prakashan, 2015), 9–10, 145–50.

4. For more on these female deities and their locations in the context of Vajrayana, see Ramesh Shankar Gupte, *The Iconography of the Buddhist Sculptures (Caves) of Ellora* (Aurangabad: Marathwada University, 1964), 97–113; Geri Malandra, *Unfolding a Maṇḍala: The Buddhist Cave Temples at Ellora* (Albany: State University of New York Press, 1993), 58–59, 92–99.

5. I have already retold a story of Vishwakarma's penance at Ellora being derailed by the dancing nymph sent by Indra; that story resulted in a marriage too, though she was not a goddess.

6. Sir Monier Monier-Williams et al., *A Sanskrit-English Dictionary* (1899; Delhi: Motilal Banarsidas, 1990), 303.

7. See Durga Saptashati 5:13, translated in Devadatta Kali, *In Praise of the Goddess: The Devīmāhātmya and Its Meaning* (Berwick, ME: Nicolas Hays, 2003), 101.

8. Acharya Lakshmishankar Pranshankar, *Śri Viśvakarmā Dharmapatrikā* (Mumbai: Nirnaysagar Press, 1901), 140.

9. Harji Lakhoo Desharia, *Śrī Viśvakarmā Sadbodhmālā* (Karachi: Manohar Press, 1921), 15. She is also mentioned in a verse of the song offering instructions for worship

in Goverdhanarama Devram, *Viśvakarmā Padmālā ane Nirdoś Vāstu* (Ahmedabad: Diamond Jubilee Printing Press, 1913), 5.

10. Desharia, *Śrī Viśvakarmā Sadbodhmālā*, 30–31.

11. See Amita Sinha, "Cultural Landcape of Pavagadh: The Abode of Mother Goddess Kalika," *Journal of Cultural Geography* 23 (2006): 89–103.

12. The book of Vishwabrahmin history that Pa gave me carried an invocation to Kali as the goddess of tools, specifically addressing Shirasanghi or Sirsangi Kali, the goddess of Karnataka Vishwakarmas, whose temple is near Belgaum. See Jan Brouwer, *The Makers of the World: Caste, Craft and Mind of South Indian Artisans* (Delhi: Oxford University Press, 1995), 412–23.

13. M. N. Deshpande, "Veruḷ Leṇī," *Marāṭhwāḍā*, Divāli issue, 68 (1958): 46.

14. Interestingly, this form echoes the goddess Bhrkuti, who appears in the Buddhist caves with the matted locks, absence of ornaments, and waterpot of a female ascetic. See Malandra, *Unfolding a Maṇḍala*, 92–96.

15. Narrain Row and Anunda Row, *Memoir Descriptive of the Ancient Place of Ellola near Dowlatabad Compiled from the Mahatyams of That Ancient Stullam* (British Library OIOC Eur mss. Mackenzie General, XIV, no. 47), 9, 24; also see W. H. Sykes's passing mention in "An Account of the Caves of Ellora," *Transactions of the Literary Society of Bombay* 30 (1823): 274.

16. Row and Row, *Memoir*, 9–11.

17. For more on the cosmological significance of this game, along with Carmel Bergson's lovely photographs from Ellora, see David Shulman and Don Handelman, *God Inside Out: Siva's Game of Dice* (New York: Oxford University Press, 1997). In most versions, though, Parvati wins. Also see Micaela Soar, "The Tīrtha at Ellora," in *Ellora Caves: Sculpture and Architecture*, ed. R. Parimoo, D. Kannal, and S. Panikkar (Pune: Aprant, 2018), 69–70.

18. Row and Row, *Memoir*, 4.

19. In the 1911 Surajram Purana, Vastu, Vishwakarma's first adopted child and Deity of Place, witnesses miraculous happenings when a Brahmin redeemed by Vishwakarma at the Vishwa Kund gives an adopted daughter away in marriage; Vastu asks for a sister so his own family can also hold a marriage. In the 1965 Joshi Purana, the request to Vishwakarma for a daughter comes from a mongoose, who hopes to turn fully to gold after being splashed by water from the hands of a father who has just performed the meritorious deed of gifting a daughter.

20. Joshi, *Asal Viśvakarmā Purāṇ*, 131–35.

21. R. N. Misra, *Śilpa in Indian Tradition: Concepts and Instrumentalities* (Shimla: Indian Institute of Advanced Study; New Delhi: Aryan Books International, 2009), 153–55.

Chapter 16

1. Geri Malandra, *Unfolding a Maṇḍala: The Buddhist Cave Temples at Ellora* (Albany: State University of New York Press, 1993), 59.

2. Himanshu Prabha Ray, "From Multi-religious Sites to Mono-religious Monuments in South Asia: The Colonial Legacy of Heritage Management," in *Routledge Handbook of Heritage in Asia*, ed. Patrick Daly and Tim Winter (New York: Routledge, 2012), 69–84.

272   NOTES TO PAGES 228–237

3. Bachubhai Vadgama, *Śrī Virāṭ Viśvakarmā Mahāpurāṇ* (Rajkot: Vishwakarma Charitable Trust, 2013), 13.

Hands inside Hands

1. Vallabhram Surajram, *Viśvakarmāni Caritra, Viśvakarmā Purāṇ, Viśvakarmāni Kathā* (1909; Dakor: Mansukhram Ranchoddas, 1926), 313.

Bibliography

Materials in Gujarati, Hindi, Marathi, and Sanskrit

Bharadiya, Girishbhai Rasikbhai. *Śrī Viśvakarmā Pujan Kathā*. Jamnagar: Ramya Publications, 2009.

Desharia, Harji Lakhoo. *Śrī Viśvakarmā Sadbodhmālā*. Karachi: Kutch Mandli, 1921.

Deshpande, Brahmanand. "Verul Yethīl Yādavkālīn Sthambhlekh." In *Śodhamudrā Khaṇḍ 5 wā*, 34–37. Aurangabad: Kailash Publications, 2010.

Deshpande, M. N. "Veruḷ Leṇī." *Marāṭhwāḍā*, Divāli issue, 68 (1958): 1–50.

Devram, Goverdhanarama. *Viśvakarmā padmālā ane Nirdoś Vāstu*. Ahmedabad: Diamond Jubilee Printing Press, 1913.

Dhere, Ramachandra Cintaman. *Śodha-śilpa*. Puṇe: Viśvakarmā Sāhityālaya, 1977.

Gajjar, Kalyanadasa Bhanabhai. *Viśvakarmājñāna: Śilpa Sār Sangrah nāmno granth*. Ahmedabad: n.p., 1898.

Gajjar, Natubhai P. *Mhārā Dādā Śrī Viśvakarmā*. 3rd ed. Rajkot: Ramy blication, 2014.

Gajjar, Vinodbhai D. *Śrījīnā Ekāntik Bhakt Bhujnā Śrī Sundarjī Sutār*. Bhuj: Rachna Enterprise, 2010.

Joshi, Ramashankar Muktashankar. *Asal Viśvakarmā Purāṇ*. Ahmedabad: Mahadev Ramchandra Jagusthe Books, 1965.

Kshirasagar, Narayan Ravaji. *Viśvabrahmakulotsāha*. 3rd ed. Poona: Kalika Prasad Press, 1906.

Kshirasagar, Narayan Ravaji, and Balshastri Ravaji Kshirsagar. *Viśvabrahmaku-lotsāha or History of Vishvabrahmins*. Revised and expanded ed. Poona: Kalika Prasad Press, 1921.

Mandana, Sutradhar. *Rājvallabh athvā Śilpaśāstra*. Translated into Gujarati by Narayanbharati Lakshmanbharati Gosain et. al. Badodara: Veerakshetra Mudralaya, 1891.

———. *Śilpīnu Vāstuśāstra temāthī agh Vāstusār nām granth*. Translated into Gujarati by Maganlal Karamchand. Ahmedabad: Maganlal Karamchand, 1878.

Mevada, Babubhai Durlabhram. *Śrī Viśvakarmā Parichay*. Ahmedabad, 2016.

Mhaimbata. *Śrīcakradhara līḷa caritra*. Edited by V. B. Kolate. Mumbai: Maharashtra Rajya Sahitya Sanskruti Mandal, 1982.

Monier-Williams, Sir Monier, et al. *A Sanskrit-English Dictionary*. 1899; Delhi: Motilal Banarsidas, 1990.

Panchal, Gangaram V. *Śrī Viśvakarmā Prabhunī Mahākathā*. Mumbai: Shree Visvakarma Dharm Prachar Samiti, 1978.

Pranshankar, Acharya Lakshmishankar. *Śrī Viśvakarmā Dharmapatrikā*. Mumbai: printed by Sutar Keshavji Khimji Bhagat, Nirnaysagar Press, 1901.

Sharma, Gopalji Vagji, comp. and ed. *Viśvakarmā ane tenā Vaṃśejo*. Anjar: Shree Gopalji Vagji Sharma, 1957.

Shastri, Jayantibhai. *Śrī Viśvakarmā Purāṇ*. Surendranagar: Sarjanhar Sahitya Seva Kendra, 2017.

Shree Devdatt Ashram Jadhavvadi. *Elāpur Sthān Darśan*. Verul Leni: Shreedevdatt Mahanubhav Ashram, n.d.

Śrī Viśvakarmā Purān Māhiti tathā Vrat. Ahmedabad, 2007.

Surajram, Vallabhram. *Viśvakarmānī Ćaritra, Viśvakarmā Purāṇ, Viśvakarmānī Kathā*. 2nd ed. 1909; Dakor: Mansukhram Ranchoddas, 1926.

"Sutār Komnī Jāgriti." *Pārsi Sansār ane Lok Sevak*, 24, no. 18 (2 March 1932): 14–15.

Vadgama, Bachubhai. *Śrī Virāṭ Viśvakarmānī Kathā*. Rajkot:0, 2008.

———. *Śrī Virāṭ Viśvakarmā Mahāpurāṇ*. Rajkot: Shree Vishwakarma Charitable Trust, 2013.

———. *Suryadev Rāndaldevīnā Dev Lagna*. Rajkot: self-published, 2010.

Vyas, Kailashnath, and Devendrasingh Gahlot. *Rājasthān kī Jātiyon kā Samājik evam Ārthik Jīvan*. Jodhpur: Jagdishsingh Gahlot Sodh Samsthan, 1992.

Materials in English and French

"Account of Tamba Patra Plates Dug Up at Baroda in Goojrat with Facsimile and Translation." *Journal of the Asiatic Society of Bengal* 8 (1839): 292–303.

Anquetil-Duperron, Abraham Hyacinthe. *Zend-Avesta ouvrage de Zoroastre*. Vol. 1, pt. 1. Paris: Tilliard, 1771.

Bhandarkar, D. R. "Epigraphic Notes and Queries VIII: The Kailāsa Temple at Elūrā." *Indian Antiquary* 40 (1911): 237–38.

Bhandarkar, R. G. "The Rāshṭrākūṭa King Krishṇarājā I and Élāpura." *Indian Antiquary* 12 (1883): 228–30.

Bilgrami, Syed Hossain, and C. Willmott. *Historical and Descriptive Sketch of His Highness the Nizam's Dominions*. Vol. 2. Bombay: Times of India Steam Press, 1884.

Boner, Alice, S. R. Sarma, and B. Baumer. *Vāstusūtra Upaniṣad: The Essence of Form in Sacred Art*. Delhi: Motilal Banarsidas, 1982.

Brouwer, Jan. *The Makers of the World: Caste, Craft and Mind of South Indian Artisans*. Delhi: Oxford University Press, 1995.

Burgess, James. *Report on the Antiquities in the Bidar and Aurangabad Districts*. Archaeological Survey of Western India, vol. 3. London: W. H. Allen and Co., 1878.

———. *Report on the Elura Cave Temples and the Brahmanical and Jaina Caves in Western India*. London: Trubner and Company, 1883.

———. *The Rock Temples of Elurā or Verul*. Bombay: Education Society's Press, 1877.

Burgess, James, and Henry Cousens. *The Architectural Antiquities of Northern Gujarat*. Archaeological Survey of Western India, vol. 9. London: Bernard Quaritch, 1903.

BIBLIOGRAPHY 275

Buswell, Robert E., Jr., and Donald S. Lopez Jr., eds. *The Princeton Dictionary of Buddhism*. Princeton, NJ: Princeton University Press, 2013.

Cohen, Richard. "Nāga, Yakṣiṇī, Buddha: Local Deities and Local Buddhism at Ajanta." *History of Religions* 37, no. 4 (1998): 360–400.

Coomaraswamy, Ananda K. *The Indian Craftsman*. London: Probsthain and Company, 1909.

Crane, Walter. *Indian Impressions, with Some Notes on Ceylon*. London: Methuen and Co., 1907.

Dagens, Bruno, trans., *Mayamata: An Indian Treatise on Housing Architecture and Iconography*. New Delhi: Sitaram Bhartia Institute of Scientific Research, 1985.

Das, Veena. "A Sociological Study of Caste Puranas: A Case Study." *Sociological Bulletin* 17 (1968): 141–64.

DeCaroli, Robert. *Haunting the Buddha: Indian Popular Religions in the Formation of Buddhism*. New York: Oxford University Press, 2004.

Dehejia, Vidya. *Early Buddhist Rock Temples: A Chronological Study*. London: Thames and Hudson, 1972.

Dehejia, Vidya, and Peter Rockwell. *The Unfinished: Stone Carvers at Work on the Indian Subcontinent*. New Delhi: Roli Books, 2016.

Dhavalikar, M. K. *Ellora*. New Delhi: Oxford University Press, 2003.

Doniger, Wendy. "Saraṇyū/Saṃjñā: The Sun and the Shadow." In *Devi: Goddesses of India*, ed. John S. Hawley and Donna M. Wulff, 137–53. Berkeley: University of California Press, 1996.

———. *Splitting the Difference: Gender and Myth in Ancient Greece and India*. Chicago: University of Chicago Press, 1999.

———. *Women Androgynes, and Other Mythical Beasts*. Chicago: University of Chicago Press, 1980.

Enthoven, R. E. *The Tribes and Castes of Bombay*. Vol. 3. Bombay: Government Central Press, 1920.

Enthoven, R. E., and A. M. T. Jackson. *Folklore Notes*. Vol. 1, *Gujarat*. Bombay: British India Press, 1914.

Ernst, Carl. "Admiring the Works of the Ancients: The Ellora Temples as Viewed by Indo-Muslim Authors." In *Beyond Turk and Hindu: Rethinking Religious Identities in Islamicate South Asia*, edited by David Gilmartin and Bruce B. Lawrence, 88–120. Gainesville: University Press of Florida, 2002.

———. *Eternal Garden: Mysticism, History, and Politics at a South Asian Sufi Center*. Albany: State University of New York Press, 1992.

Feldhaus, Ann. "Pilgrimage and Remembrance: Biography and Geography in the Mahanubhav Tradition." In *Connected Places: Region, Pilgrimage and Geographical Imagination in India*, 185–210. New York: Palgrave, 2003.

Fergusson, James, and James Burgess. *The Cave Temples of India*. London: W. H. Allen and Co., 1880; New Delhi: Oriental Books Reprint Corporation, 1969.

Gazetteer of the Bombay Presidency. Vol. 5, *Cutch, Pālanpur and Mahi Kāntha*. Bombay: Government Central Press, 1880.

George, Kenneth M. "Sutradhars and Stone Carpenters." Manuscript, n.d.

George, Kenneth M., and Kirin Narayan. "Readers of the 'Lost' Puran: Mythopolitics and Suthar Caste Identity in Gujarat." *Religion* 52 (2022): 576–94.

———. "Technophany and Its Publics: Artisans, Technicians and the Rise of Vishwakarma Worship in India." *Journal of Asian Studies* 81, no. 1 (2022): 1–19.

Gupte, Ramesh Shankar. *The Iconography of the Buddhist Sculptures (Caves) of Ellora*. Aurangabad: Marathwada University, 1964.

Gupte, Ramesh Shankar, and B. D. Mahajan. *Ajanta, Ellora and Aurangabad Caves*. Bombay: D. B. Taraporevala Sons and Co., 1962.

Hardenberg, Roland. *The Renewal of Jagannath's Body: Ritual and Society in Orissa*. New Delhi: Manak, 2011.

Havell, E. B. *The Ancient and Medieval Architecture of India: A Study of Indo-Aryan Civilization*. London: John Murray, 1915.

Irwin, Anthony Lovenheim. "The Buddha's Busted Finger: Craft, Touch, and Cosmology in Theravada Buddhism." *Journal of the American Academy of Religion* 90, no. 1 (2022): 52–85.

Jamison, Stephanie, and Joel P. Brereton. *The Rigveda: The Earliest Religious Poetry of India*. New York: Oxford University Press, 2014.

Kali, Devadatta. *In Praise of the Goddess: The Devīmāhātmya and Its Meaning*. Berwick, ME: Nicolas Hays, 2003.

Kane, P. V. *History of Dharmaśāstra: Ancient and Mediæval Religious and Civil Law in India*. Poona: Bhandarkar Oriental Research Institute, 1953.

Kannal, Deepak. *Ellora: An Enigma of Sculptural Styles*. New Delhi: Books & Books, 1996.

Kramrisch, Stella. *The Art of India: Traditions of Indian Sculpture Painting and Architecture*. London: Phaidon, 1954.

Kulkarni, Uday. *James Wales: Artist and Antiquarian in the Time of Peshwa Sawai Madhavrao. An Illustrated Chronicle based on Original Documents*. Pune: Mula Mutha Publishers, 2019.

Law, Randall. "Appendix: Geologic Observations and Analysis of Rock-cut and Constructed Stone Temples in South India." In Vidya Dehejia and Peter Rockwell, *The Unfinished: Stone Carvers at Work on the Indian Subcontinent*, 250–62. New Delhi: Roli Books, 2016.

Longhurst, A. H. *Conservation Notes on Ancient Monuments*. In *Progress Report of the ASI Western Circle for the year ending 31 March 1911*. Government of Bombay General Department, 1911.

Lyons, Tryna. *The Artists of Nathadwara: The Practice of Painting in Rajasthan*. Bloomington: Indiana University Press; Ahmedabad: Mapin, 2004.

Mackintosh, James. *Memoirs of the Life of Sir James Mackintosh*. Vol 2. London: Edward Moxon, 1835.

Maduro, Renaldo. *Artistic Creativity in a Brahmin Painter Community*. Research Monograph 14. Berkeley: University of California Center for South and Southeast Asia Studies, 1976.

Malandra, Geri H. *Unfolding a Maṇḍala: The Buddhist Cave Temples at Ellora*. Albany: State University of New York Press, 1993.

Malet, Charles. "Descriptions of the Caves or Excavations on the Mountain, about a mile to the Eastward of the town of Ellora." *Asiatick Researches; or, Transactions of the Society* 6 (1801): 389–424.

———. "To Sir John Shore, Bart. President of the Asiatic Society." *Asiatick Researches; or, Transactions of the Society* 6 (1801): 382–87.

Mandelbaum, David G. *Indian Society*. Vol. 2, *Change and Continuity*. Berkeley: University of California Press, 1973.

Marwar Darbar. *Report on the Census of 1891.* Vol. 2, *Castes of Marwar.* Jodhpore, 1894.

McGregor, R. S., ed. *The Oxford Hindi-English Dictionary.* Oxford; Delhi: Oxford University Press, 1993.

Mhaimbhat. *God at Play,* vol. 1. Edited and translated by Anne Feldhaus. Murti Classical Library of India 36. Cambridge, MA: Harvard University Press, 2024.

Michell, George, and Sugandha Johar. "The Maratha Complex at Ellora." *South Asian Studies* 28, no. 1 (2012): 69–88.

Mirashi, Vasudev Vishnu. *Inscriptions of the Kalachuri-Chedi Era.* Corpus Inscriptionum Indicarum, 4:555–57. Ootacamund: Government Epigraphist for India, 1955.

Mirza, Saeed. *Memory in the Age of Amnesia.* Delhi: Context, 2018.

Misra, R. N. "Perceptions of South Asia's Visual Past: Tradition and the Artist." In *Perceptions of South Asia's Visual Past,* edited by Catherine B. Asher and Thomas R Metcalf, 97–109. New Delhi: American Institute of Indian Studies, 1994.

———. *Śilpa in Indian Tradition: Concepts and Instrumentalities.* Shimla: Indian Institute of Advanced Study; New Delhi: Aryan Books International, 2009.

Mubayi, Yaaminey. "Ellora-Khuldabad-Daulatabad: Water and Sacred Spaces." In *Water Design: Environment and Histories,* edited by Jutta Jain Neubauer, 129–41. Mumbai: Marg Publications, 2016.

———. *Water and Historical Settlements: The Making of a Cultural Landscape.* New York: Routledge, 2023. E-book.

Muir, John. *Notes of a Trip to Kedarnath and other parts of the snowy range of the Himalayas in the autumn of 1853. With some account of a journey by way of Ajunte, Ellora and Carlee in 1854.* Edinburgh: T. Constable, 1855.

Mukherjee, Meera. *In Search of Viswakarma.* Calcutta: self-published, 1994.

Narayan, Kirin. *Everyday Creativity: Singing Goddesses in the Himalayan Foothills.* Chicago: University of Chicago Press, 2016.

———. *Mondays on the Dark Night of the Moon: Himalayan Foothill Folktales.* New York: Oxford University Press, 1996.

———. "Narrating Creative Process." *Narrative Culture* 1 (2014): 109–24.

———. "Who Is Vishwakarma's Daughter?" In *In Search of Vishwakarma,* edited by Vijaya Ramaswamy, 95–113. Delhi: Primus Books, 2019.

Narayan, Kirin, and Kenneth M. George. "Tools and World-Making in the Worship of Vishwakarma." *South Asian History and Culture* 8, no. 4 (2017): 478–92.

———. "Vishwakarma: Hindu God of Technology." In *Technology and Religion in Historical and Contemporary South Asia,* edited by Knut Jacobsen and Kristina Myrvold, 8–24. New York: Routledge, 2018.

Nath, R. "On the Theory of Indo-Muslim Architecture." In *Shastric Traditions in Indian Arts,* vol. 1, edited by A. Dallapiccola, 187–201. Stuttgart: Steiner, 1989.

Novetzke, Christian. *The Quotidian Revolution: Vernacularization, Religion and the Premodern Public Sphere in India.* New York: Columbia University Press, 2016.

Owen, Lisa. *Carving Devotion in the Jain Caves at Ellora.* Leiden: Brill, 2012.

Parimoo, Ratan, Deepak Kannal, and Shivaji Panikkar, eds. *Ellora Caves: Sculpture and Architecture.* Rev. ed. Pune: Aprant, 2018.

Patel, Alka. "Architectural Histories Entwined: The Rudra-Mahalaya/Congregational Mosque of Siddhpur, Gujarat." *Journal of the Society of Architectural Historians* 63 (2004): 144–63.

278 BIBLIOGRAPHY

Pathy, T. V. *Ajanta, Ellora and Aurangabad Caves: An Appreciation*. Aurangabad: Jai Hind Printing Press, 1978.

Ramaswamy, Vijaya. "Vishwakarma Craftsmen in Early Medieval Peninsular India." *Journal of the Economic and Social History of the Orient* 47, no. 4 (2004): 548–82.

———, ed. *In Search of Vishwakarma*. Delhi: Primus Books, 2019.

Ranade, P. V. "Echoes of Ellora in Early Marathi literature." In *Ellora Caves: Sculpture and Architecture*, edited by R. Parimoo, D. Kannal, and S. Panikkar, 83–91. Pune: Aprant, 2018.

———. *Ellora Paintings*. Aurangabad: Parimal Prakashan, 1980.

Ray, Himanshu Prabha. "From Multi-religious sites to Mono-religious Monuments in South Asia: The Colonial Legacy of Heritage Management." In *Routledge Handbook of Heritage in Asia*, edited by Patrick Daly and Tim Winter, 69–84. New York: Routledge, 2012.

Reddy, G. Sudarshan. "The Caste System, the Colonial Judiciary, and the Struggle for Ritual Status in 19th-Century Andhra." *Proceedings of the Indian History Congress* 58 (1997): 677–85.

Report of the Committee Appointed by the Government of Hyderabad State under their Order No. 594, Dated 1-8-58. Part II, Preservation and Maintenance of the Cave-Temples of Ellora.

Row, Narrain, and Anunda Row. *Memoir Descriptive of the Ancient Place of Ellola near Dowlatabad Compiled from the Mahatyams of That Ancient Stullam & an Inspection of the Several Ancient Monuments Existing There by Narrain Row and Anunda Row in 1806*. Translated from the Marattas by Sooba Row Bramin, October 1808. British Library OIOC Eur mss. Mackenzie General, XIV, no. 47.

Saberwal, Satish. *Mobile Men: Limits to Social Change in Urban Punjab*. New Delhi: Vikas, 1976.

Sardesai, Govind Sakharam. *Poona's Affairs, 1786–1797, Malet's Embassy*. Bombay: Government Central Press, 1936.

Sastri, S. M. Natesa. *Hindu Feasts, Fasts and Ceremonies*. 1903; New Delhi: Educational Publishing House, 1988.

Schopen, Gregory. *Buddhist Nuns, Monks, and Other Worldly Matters: Recent Papers on Monastic Buddhism in India*. Honolulu: University of Hawai'i Press, 2014.

Seely, J. B. *The Wonders of Elora; or, The Narrative of a Journey to the Temples or Dwellings Excavated out of a Mountain of Granite at Elora*. 2nd ed. London: Geo B. Whitaker, 1825.

Sengupta, R. "Repairs to the Ellora Caves." *Ancient India* 17 (1961): 46–67.

Settar, Shadakshari. *Early Buddhist Artisans and Their Architectural Vocabulary*. Manipal: Manipal Universal Press, 2020.

Shaffer, Holly. *Grafted Arts: The Marathas and the British in Western India, 1760–1820*. New Haven, CT: Yale University Press, 2022.

Sharma, Mahesh. "Narratives of a Place Named Ellora: Myths, Culture and Politics." *Indian Economic and Social History Review* 58, no. 1 (2021): 73–111.

Shukla, D. N. *Vāstu-Śāstra*. Vol. 1, *Hindu Science of Architecture*. Lucknow: Vāstu Vānmaya-Prakāsana Śālā, 1958; reprint, New Delhi: Munshiram Manoharlal, 1993.

Shulman, David, and Don Handelman. *God Inside Out: Siva's Game of Dice*. New York: Oxford University Press, 1997.

Singh, M. S., Vinodh Kumar, and Sujata A. Waghmare. "Characterization of 6–11th Century A.D. Decorative Lime Plasters of Rock Cut Caves of Ellora." *Construction and Building Materials* 98 (2015): 156–70.

Sinha, Amita. "Cultural Landcape of Pavagadh: The Abode of Mother Goddess Kalika." *Journal of Cultural Geography* 23 (2006): 89–103.

Sinha, Manohar, ed. *Geoscientific Studies for the Conservation of Ellora Caves.* New Delhi: Archaeological Survey of India, 2011.

Sivaramamurti, Calambur. *The Art of India.* New York: Harry N. Abrams, 1977.

Smith, Walter. "Architectural and Mythic Space at Ellora." *Oriental Art Magazine* 42, no. 2 (1996): 13–21.

Soar, Micaela. "The Tīrtha at Ellora." In *Ellora Caves: Sculpture and Architecture,* edited by R. Parimoo, D. Kannal, and S. Panikkar, 62–79. Pune: Aprant, 2018.

Sohoni, Pushkar. "Continuities in the Sacred Landscape: Ellora, Khuldabad and the Temple of Ghrishneshwara: A Single Social Historical Complex." In *Studies in Medieval Deccan History (14th–17th Century): Dr. M. A. Nayeem Festschrift,* edited by Syed Ayub Ali, 156–68. Warangal: Deccan Historical Society, 2015.

Srinivas, M. N. "A Note on Sanskritization and Westernization." *Far Eastern Quarterly* 15, no. 4 (1956): 481–96.

Sykes, W. H. "An Account of the Caves of Ellora." *Transactions of the Literary Society of Bombay* 30 (1823): 265–323.

Thevenot, Jean de. *Indian Travels of Thevenot and Careri: Being the Third Part of the Travels of Jean de Thevenot into the Levant and the Third Part of a Voyage Round the World by Dr. John Francis Gemelli Careri,* edited by Surendra Nath Sen. Delhi: National Archives of India National Records series, 1949.

Tod, James. *Travels in Western India.* 1839; Delhi: Oriental Publishers, 1971.

Tripathi, Atul. *Solar Deities in Gujarat: Art, Architecture and Contemporary Traditions.* Delhi: Pratibha Prakashan, 2015.

Tripathi, Radhavallabh. "Sūtradhara." In *Kalātattvakośa: A Lexicon of Fundamental Concepts of the Indian Arts,* vol. 2 (rev. ed.), edited by Bettina Baumer, 321–32. New Delhi: IGNCA and Motilal Banarsidas, 2003.

Turner, Victor. *The Ritual Process: Structure and Anti-Structure.* Chicago: Aldine, 1969.

Vogel, Jean Philippe. *The Goose in Indian Literature and Art.* Leiden: Brill, 1962.

Watt, George. *Indian Art at Delhi, 1903, being the official catalogue of the Delhi Exhibition, 1902–1903.* London: John Murray, 1904.

Wauchope, R. S. *Buddhist Cave Temples of India.* Calcutta: Edinburgh Press; London: Luzac and Co., 1935.

Zimmer, Heinrich. *The Art of Indian Asia: Its Mythology and Transformations.* Edited by Joseph Campbell. 2 vols. Bollingen Series 39. Princeton, NJ: Princeton University Press, 1955.

Index

Page numbers in italics refer to illustrations.

amās (*amāvāsya*, the new moon): as
day to rest and worship tools, 3,
173; evoked in Cave 10 floorplan,
173, 175–77; as observance for
ancestors, 173–75, 246, 266n20; and
Vishwakarma,105, 173–77, 246
Anquetil-Duperron, Abraham
Hyacinthe, 59–60, 267n7
avesini, 117

Ba, ix, 9, 25, 44, 69, 94, 100–105, 123–25,
125, 239–42
Baroda copper plates, 37–39
Barot (also *Bhat*; caste genealogist):
consultations with Dahisaria clan,
69, 71–73, 73; stories about Rudra
Mal, 76, 80–81; stories about
Vishwakarma, 74, 174
Basire, James, 62–63
Bhai, ix, 27–32, 29, 33, 36, 39–42, 138–41,
192, 238–39, 243, 245–47; memories
of Ellora, 109–11, 113–15; and story
of Rudra Mal, 75–81; theories about
Cave 10, 30, 36, 118–19
Bhandarkar, R. G., 37
Burgess, James, 13, 81, 88, 175–76, 261n8
(chap. 5)

carpenter. See *Suthar*
caste genealogist. See *Barot*
caves, spiritual significance, 9

Cave 5, 215
Cave 10: as Buddhist *chaitya*, 5, 30,
81, 116, 175, 188, 226, 244; exterior
architecture, 30, 31; hereditary
carpenters' association with, 1, 13, 35,
88, 163, 171, 181–84, 187; as hut, 13, 30–
31, 35–36; interior architecture, 6, 11,
21–22, 22, 30, 35, 44, 50–52, 51, 55–56,
63, 64–65, 113, 118, 142, 143, 171, 172–
73, 175–77, 176, 184, 212, 244
Cave 10 Murti: central seated figure as
Buddha or Vishwakarma, 5–6, 6, 8,
21–22, 61, 114,164–65, 166, 167–71, 177,
179, 183, 185, 186, 188–89, 224, 227, 228,
230, 244; Padmapani, 52, 56, 224–25,
225. See also robe edge
Cave 11 (Don Tal), 56, 169–70, 172
Cave 12 (Teen Tal, Rājavihāra), 46, 54–
55, 169–70, 187
Cave 14 (Rāvaṇ ki Khāi), 56, 189
Cave 16 (Kailash), 34, 36–39, 37, 47,
50, 113, 123, 171, 217. See also Baroda
copper plates
Cave 25, 215
Cave 26, 215
Cave 28, 34, 215
Chakradhar Swami, 46–47, 50, 52–56,
169, 258n3. See also Mahanubhav sect
Chamunda Mata, 80, 209–10, 210, 214
Chandra Kund, 146, 197, 216, 269n4
Contractor, Didi. See Ma

Cousens, Henry, 179, 184
Crane, Walter, 184

Dada. *See* Ramji
Dahisaria clan: history, 80–81; hot-headed clan women, 130; members, vi, ix–x, 27, 87, 128, 130, 213
Datta Das, encounter with, 52–53, 55–56
Daulatabad, 57–58, 60, 169, 188
Deen Dayal, Lala, 184–86
Deshpande, Brahmanand, 190–92
Devram, Goverdhanram, 181, 196–97
dharmachakra mudra, 6; in Cave 10 as injured finger, 61, 165, 167, 170; in Cave 10 sculpture, 6, 11, 22, 45, 51, 63, 65, 84, 143, 166, 179, 185, 186; in Vishwakarma iconography, 85, 95, 111, 112, 113, 121, 140, 141, 143, 164. *See also* injured finger

Elisofon, Eliot, 189
Ellora: alternate names for, 35, 147–48, 257n8; geology of, 4, 115–16, 177, 263n10; historical accounts by visitors, 47–48, 57–66; *tīrtha* at, 33, 101, 195, 205, 217
Ernst, Carl, 58

Fergusson, James, and James Burgess, 187

Gajjar, K. B., 113
Ganpat, Purshottam, 175–76
gender shifting, 147, 218
goddesses: and Vishwakarma, 203, 204, 209–10, 214; worshipped at Ellora, 34, 212, 215. *See also* Chamunda Mata; Jogeshwari cave shrine; Kriti; Randal Ma

Ila, 60, 77, 142–48, 159, 205, 216–17, 228, 264n12
injured finger (Vishwakarma's), 61, 165–72, 190; and Cave 11, 169–70; as self-inflicted wound, 167–69. *See also dharmachakra mūdra*
Irwin, Anthony Lovenheim, 266n10

Jayantibhai Gajjar, ix, 149, 151, 157, 160, 223–26; stories about Vishwakarma at Ellora, 152–53, 156–58, 208, 218, 229–30
Jogeshwari cave shrine, 34, 216, 218, 220, 221, 220–22
Joshi, Ramashankar Muktashankar, 200, 204–6

Kailash. *See* Cave 16
Kamlabai Ramji. *See* Ba
Kapil Muni, 54–55
Kapred Kumar Dahisaria. *See* Bhai
Keshavji Khimji, ix, 83, 84, 86–90, 89, 92–94, 96
Khati (Rajasthani carpenter), 22–23, 256n15
Khimji Bhagat, ix, 83, 84, 87, 89, 89; and Bhorara Doors of Khimji temple, 86, 88, 93–96, 93, 95, 99, 131, 138
Kokas, 5–6, 46–50, 56, 244
Kramrisch, Stella, 38, 258n15
Kriti (consort of Vishwakarma), 91, 212–13
Khuldabad, 57, 58, 192, 211, 257n7
kund. See Chandra Kund; Surya Kund; Vishwa Kund

Longhurst, A. H., 188

Ma, ix, 43–44, 98–99, 102, 235–37, 236, 244–45, 247
Mackenzie, Colin, 169, 205
Mahanubhav sect, 51, 52–56, 62, 259n14
Mahendra Bapu (Mahendrabhai Mistri), 211, 229
Malandra, Geri H., 263n11, 263n14, 270n4, 271n14
Malet, Charles, 60–63, 169, 205, 261n4
Mistri, 23

naga (serpent being), 142–48; as sculpted figure in Cave 10, 142, 143. *See also* Ila
Naga Jadi (Naga Jeree), 52, 148, 265n18
Narayan Ramji Contractor (Dahisaria). *See* Pa
navakami, 117

INDEX 283

Pa (Narayan Ramji Contractor), ix, 2, 23, 24, 27–28, 70, 83–84, 98–99, 201, 230–32, 237, 240, 241, 243; and Ellora, 1–2, 43–46, 71, 195; letters from, 13–16, 19, 24–26, 69–72, 74, 97–98, 101, 105, 128–29, 258n1

Pathy, T. V., 39

pilgrimage, benefits of, 9, 75, 86, 88, 92, 163, 181–83, 196–97

Plâté, Alfred, 186

Popatlal Dasadia, ix, 35–36, 118, 127, 131

Prakash Mistry, x, 126–28, 131–33, 132, 135–38, 136, 149–55, 192, 232

Pushti Marg, 87, 141

Ramji (Ramji Seth, Ramji Mistri, Ramji Keshavji), x, 14, 23, 39, 67, 71, 83, 84, 88, 97–105, 124, 126, 198, 235, 238–44; and Vishwakarma worship, 16–17, 94, 99, 244

Ranade, P. V., 46

Randal Ma (daughter of Vishwakarma), 14–15, 26, 210, 217–19, 270n1, 271n19; community worship of, 149–51, 210–11, 233; as consort of Surya (Sun), 149, 215, 217–19; at Ellora, 34, 209, 212, 214–22; in Jogeshwari cave, 216, 220–22; replicates self as Chhaya, 219–20; shrine at Dadva, 15

robe edge (on seated murti in Cave 10): as cord, 2, 171; as stream of blood, 171, 184; detail, 166

Row, Narrain and Anunda, 205, 216–17

sacred thread: ceremony at Vishwa Kund, 1, 23, 65, 86, 88, 146, 195–206, 244; as Sutradhar's cord, 74; on Vishwakarma, 18, 84, 140, 140, 204. See also Suthar: claims to Brahminhood

Seely, John, 57, 63–66, 206, 259n1, 260n28, 260n30, 261n44, 269n1

serpents. See naga

Shukla, D. N., 156

skeuomorph, 30

Soar, Micaela, 146–47

Surajram, Vallabhram, version of Vishwakarma Purana, 141–46, 157, 160, 168, 200, 226, 271n19

Surya Kund, 146, 197, 216, 269n4

Suthar (also Sutar; Gujarati carpenter): claims to Brahminhood, 74, 91, 199, 201, 206, 244; as corruption of Sutradhar,18; as descendants of Vishwakarma, 1–3, 19, 22–23, 87, 160; fields of work, 27, 154; four groups of, 19; Kutchi Gujar Suthar, 19, 83–95; publications circulated among, 29, 74–75, 83–87, 113, 201–2, 213; title given by Vishwakarma to his sons, 159, 162; work at Rudra Mal, 76–80

sūtra: as code, principle, or formula, 18–19, 22, 126, 153–54, 156, 171; as cord, 18–19, 22, 74, 126, 141, 153–54, 165; "Eight Sutras" diagram, 155–56; as sacred thread of Brahminhood, 74; as tool, 18, 155, 155–56

Sutradhar, 16, 18, 22, 25–26, 117, 165; author as sutradhar, 26, 243; curing the king, 77; as derivation for Suthar (Sutar), 18; honoring Vishwakarma, 111–13, 112; made from Vishwakarma's body, 113; pilgrims to Cave 10, 111–13, 187, 190–93, 197, 244; pillar inscription in Cave 10 by, 190, 191; as sculpted figures in Cave 10, 65, 113, 171; Vishwakarma depicted as sutradhar, 140–41, 140, 183, 196. See also Suthar

Swami Narayan, 40, 41, 87, 99, 104, 141,239, 261n5

Sykes, William H., 170, 187, 260n36

Tambat, Gangaram Chintaman, 61; drawing by, 11, 62–63, 184, 186, 260n22, 265n1

teaching pose. See dharmachakra mūdra

Thevenot, Jean de, 58–59, 192

tīrtha, at Ellora, 33, 101, 195, 205, 217

tools: belonging to hereditary artisans, 153; brought on artisans' pilgrimage to Cave 10, 162–63; chisel and danger of injury, 171; for excavating caves, 115; and livelihood, 14; as sutra, 155–56, 155; treated with reverence, 162; worshipped on amāvāsya, 3, 173; of writing, 14; yantra and tantra as terms for machines and technologies, 91. See Vishwakarma and tools

284 INDEX

Vadgama, Bachubhai, 74–75, 139, 167–68, 172, 174, 204, 229, 266n18
Velganga (Ila Ganga, Yella Ganga), 34, 147–48, 211, 215–17, 220, 220
Vhalabhai Gajjar, 118, 227–29, 232
Via-Via, 127
Vishwabrahmins (artisans as Brahmins), 65, 88, 141, 198, 200–203, 206, 269n7, 271n12
Vishwakarma, 18–22; and *amās* (*amāvāsya*), 105, 173–77, 246; as Buddha, 60–61, 74, 119, 167–72, 190; in Buddhist pantheon and Jataka tales, 21, 117; and caste mobility movements, 87–88, 91–92, 139, 188–200; epithets for, 19–20; and goddesses, 210, 212–14; as source of divine inspiration for artisans and workers, 38–39, 119, 131–32, 153, 160
Vishwakarma, iconography of: as caste "grandfather", 7, 7, 16–18, 17, 19, 132–34, 133, 210, 210; in Cave 10, 6, 11, 84, 85, 111–13, 112, 121, 139–41, 140; in form of Padmapani at Cave 10, 224–25, 225; in Shiva-like form, 201–4, 202, 203
Vishwakarma, stories about: arrives at Ellora because of Ila, 141–48; does penance at Ellora, 74, 174–75; gives sons right to wear sacred thread, 200–201; gives sons tools after taking away their mantra power, 152–53; hosts Randal Ma's wedding to Surya (Sun) at Ellora, 218, 2019; instructs sons about conduct, 91–92; instructs sons as Artisan Guru, 113; lessens Surya's excessive heat, 219; makes caves at Ellora, 60–61, 64–65, 113, 169–70, 217; makes Rudra Mal at Ellora, 75; makes three Kunds near

Ellora, 195–97; manifests as Kokas, 48–50; manifests as Murti in Cave 10, 167–72, 190; manifests in Shiva-form for Vishwaavasu, 204–6; marries goddess Kriti, 212–14
Vishwakarma and tools: emblematic tools in iconography, 6, 7, 18, 21, 133, 161; opening of third (inner) eye of Vishwakarma when worker grasps a tool, 131, 160; rainbow as footrule, 16; tools brought on pilgrimage at Cave 10, 162–63; Vishwakarma takes away mantras from sons and gives them tools, 36, 152–53, 156, 158–64. See also *sūtra*
Vishwakarma Puranas, 18, 100, 121, 137–47, 198, 200, 217–18, 228–29, 232, 237; by Goverdhanram Devram, 181, 196–97; by Ramashankar Muktashankar Joshi, 200, 204–6; by Vallabrahm Surajram, 139–41, 157–60, 200–201, 226; by Bachubhai Vadgama, 75, 139, 167–69
Vishwa Kund, 195, 196, 197–208, 269n1; as abbreviation for Vishwakarma Kund, 195; connection to Shiva, 195, 203, 205, 207; for healing and pilgrimage, 205–6; other names for, 195, 205, 207; and right to wear sacred Brahminical thread, 1, 195, 198, 206, 244; songs about, 181, 196; as step in Suthar pilgrimage to Ellora, 182–83, 232; and story of King Ila, 205–6; and story of Vishwaavasu, 204–5; Vishwakarma makes, 146, 196–97; Vishwakarma's footprint at, 208

Wales, James, 62, 148
Watt, George, 15